TIM CLISSOLD has worked in China for sixteen years and travelled there extensively. After graduating in Physics from Cambridge University and working in London, Australia and Hong Kong, he developed a fascination with China. He spent two years studying Mandarin Chinese before co-founding a private equity group that invested in China.

Mr. China

Tim Clissold

ROBINSON
London

Constable & Robinson Ltd
3 The Lanchesters
162 Fulham Palace Road
London W6 9ER
www.constablerobinson.com

First published in the UK by Robinson,
an imprint of Constable & Robinson Ltd 2004

A copy of the British Library Cataloguing in Publication data
is available from the British Library

ISBN 1-84119-788-2

Printed and bound in the EU

1 3 5 7 9 10 8 6 4 2

For
Christian, Honor, Max and Sam

A Chinese Chop

'The events that I describe in this book actually happened; but this is the story of an adventure, rather than an exposé, so I have changed the names of some of the companies and people who appear.'

*Everything under heaven is in utter chaos;
the situation is excellent.*

天
下
大
亂
形
勢
大
好

Chairman Mao

Contents

Mr. China

通

The idea of China has always exerted a pull on the adventurous type. There is a kind of entrepreneurial Westerner who just can't resist it: red flags, a billion bicycles and the largest untapped market on earth. What more could they want? After the first few visits, they start to feel more in tune and experience the first stirrings of a fatal ambition: the secret hope of becoming the 'Mr China' of their time, the *zhongguo tong* or 'Old China Hand' with the inside track in the Middle Kingdom. In the end, they all want to be Mr China. They want to be like Marco Polo roaming China as the emissary of the Kublai Khan. Or the first pioneering mill owners lolling about in the opium dens in Shanghai, dreaming of the fortune to be made if every Chinese would add an inch to his shirttails. Kissenger must have felt like Mr China as he schemed against Russia with Zhou Enlai; Edgar Snow may have been the same as he stood on the Gateway of Heavenly Peace with Chairman Mao. And of the countless businessmen who come to China with high hopes of the 'billion three market', how many long to become the ultimate China Hand, the only outsider, the first and only *laowai* to crack China? But in the end, it's an illusion.

One

同是天涯沦落人, 相逢何必曾相识?

We are Wanderers at the Ends of the Earth;
But to Meet Each Other Here,
Why Must We Have Met Before?

Bai Ju Yi: Pi Pa Xing
Tang Dynasty
AD 650–905

For anyone whose mood is affected by the weather, Hong Kong in October is heaven. There's a month of perfect blue skies with a bite in the air and a sharpness in the light that accentuates the dense green on the Peak against the brilliant blue of the harbour. So with my spirits buoyed up in the sunshine, I cut through the Botanical Gardens on my way towards Admiralty. A colleague in Shanghai had set up my meeting and I had no particular expectations. There was still plenty of time so I stopped to admire the orchids for a while.

I took the lifts to the eighteenth floor and waited. There was silence apart from the slightest breath of the air-conditioning. The deep red thick-pile carpet absorbed all

1

traces of footsteps. Terracotta figurines stood in carefully backlit alcoves; there were lacquer vases with twigs of twisted hawthorn and one or two high-backed Chinese antique sandalwood chairs. The faintest scent of pollen drifted across from the huge white lilies in the tall glass vase on the table. And the silence. As I waited on the black leather couch, I couldn't help feeling that it was like so many other offices in these tall glass towers where nothing ever seemed to happen. Maybe I was about to meet another wealthy US business executive using the boom in Hong Kong as a cover for an early retirement away from the wife back home. Or maybe not. There was more style to this place than the average.

I was shown into an office behind a frosted glass wall. There were matching leather sofas, a full-length map of China on the wall and a spectacular view of the harbour. Behind the vast black polished desk there were shelves lined with 'tombstones', those little perspex blocks that investment bankers keep as trophies for their deals, with miniature copies of the public announcement of the latest buyout or merger inside. A framed copy of the front page of the *New York Times* hung on the wall. It reported comments about the Black Monday crash from prominent players on Wall Street. There were two photographs on the front page: one was of Rockefeller, the other was of Pat.

'How y'doing?'

An enormous figure strode into the room, squeezed my hand and gestured towards the low table near the windows. Tanned and relaxed, he looked like he was in his mid-forties. Difficult to tell: he was fit, I thought, that was for sure, powerfully built, a real bruiser in fact; the only clue to his age came from the slightest frost at the temples. After the small talk and the exchange of name cards, he leaned back in the chair, threw his arm over the back, and, with one foot on the edge of the glass coffee table, started out on his story.

'Let me give you a bit of background and go through what I'm doing out here,' he said.

The story that unfolded over the next hour instantly seized my attention. The son of a steelworker from Pittsburgh, Pat had been on Wall Street for twenty years. His athletic appearance must have come from his passion for American football in earlier years and his conversation was still laced with references to the sport that I couldn't always follow. He told me that he had majored in American history at Yale and, after graduating in the early 1970s, he joined one of the top investment houses on Wall Street. 'All the smart guys go into investment banking,' he said, 'that's where all the money is.' After a few years, he went to study for his MBA at Harvard Business School and graduated with high distinction.

When he went back to Wall Street, he joined one of the mid-tier investment banks that looked as if it was on the way up. He said that joining a mid-tier bank had helped him learn the ropes and stand on his own two feet. 'At the top-tier banks, you'd just be part of a machine and rely on the brand-name rather than your wits to win the deal.' It seemed as though it had been a smart move; the more conservative establishment banks might have been tough going for someone with his background. He worked on M&A at the bank.

'Mergers and acquisitions,' he said, 'taking smart ideas to the CEO, persuading him to buy up another business and then raising the capital to do it.'

He was good at it and ended up running the whole investment banking division. In his first year as head of investment banking, revenues doubled and, by the end of

3

the great bull run of the 1980s, Pat had a seat on the Board and had collected his millions on the way up. 'Yeah,' he said with a huge laugh, 'I had the Jag, an apartment on Park and houses up-state, just like all the other buffoons on Wall Street.'

By that time, the bank was poised for further growth but didn't have the money to compete with the real Wall Street heavy hitters: it needed a big capital infusion to take it to the next level. Pat had led the protracted and complex negotiations with a big Japanese investment house to recapitalize the business. He eventually signed the deal that brought nearly three hundred million into the bank to fund the next level of growth. He was a hero. But by then he'd climbed to the top of the ladder and he was looking for something new.

'You know, Wall Street goes in phases,' he continued. 'It's a question of getting there first and being ahead of the curve; creating the leader in whatever's gonna be the next big story. Just like Millken did with junk bonds.'

'Junk bonds? How?' I asked.

'Well, basically he realized before anyone else did that if you took low-quality paper – you know, debt securities of mid-sized companies and so on – and you securitized it at a fat discount, you could end up creating a whole new market.'

'Right,' I said, smiling but not having a clue what he was talking about.

'The same happened in the LBO business. You see, KKR were first movers for LBOs and once they got a hold on the market, no one else really got a look in.'

'KKR?'

'Yeah.' A quick glance my way. 'Dominated the LBO market in the mid-eighties.' He looked curiously at me again. 'LBO, yeah?'

LBO. LBO. 'Leveraged buyout,' I said triumphantly.

'Right!' A second sixty-decibel laugh exploded in my ear. They were infectious, those laughs, I thought. This could turn out to be fun.

He told me that while he was at the investment bank he had raised a lot of money for one of America's big media moguls. John Kleaver had come to him when he needed money to build up his company, MediaStationOne, by buying up radio stations all over the country. 'The scheme was so successful,' said Pat, 'that a few years later, when Kleaver sold out, he was worth about three billion.'

'Three billion?'

'Yeah, so I set up an LBO firm with Kleaver. He provided the capital but I ran it. Still, we were a bit late in the cycle,' he continued. 'The LBO business was getting competitive. We did a couple of deals but it didn't look like it'd work out long term so I started figurin' out where the next big movement of capital would be. The smart people figure out where the money flow will be and get there first. It's a question of riding the next wave and that's why I'm in Asia.'

I pieced together the next bit of the story from an article I found in the *Asian Wall Street Journal* a few weeks later. It seemed that Pat had teamed up with an ex-colleague from the bank who ran the risk arbitrage department. Bill was one of Wall Street's best arbitrageurs or take-over stock traders. The rumour was that he quit the bank after a row when they only paid him an annual bonus of twelve million dollars. Bill was convinced that the Asian economies were on the way up and decided that Hong Kong would be one of the best places to make money over the next decade. He convinced Pat to join him and the two of them had made several trips out to Asia to 'kick the tyres'. They had toured

Japan, Korea, Indonesia and the Malaysian peninsula. It seemed as if Asia was on the way up and that it would need huge amounts of capital to build the roads and the power stations and the car plants to modernize the economy and develop new markets. Billions of dollars, maybe; and the only place that could provide that kind of money was Wall Street.

They came out on three trips and met with bankers and big business leaders all over the region. Pat said that he was amazed how receptive people had been. 'It was just like we'd walk in off the street and people would see us. No one would do that back home unless they were pretty desperate for capital.'

All this had convinced him of two things. First, that there was an enormous need for money but no one was really in the market for providing it; second, that the real action was going to take place in China.

Everywhere Pat went, people were talking about China; whether they were enthusing about the opportunities for new markets or were nervously looking over their shoulder and fretting about the new entrepreneurs with their factories and cheap labour up the coast, they were talking about China. So Pat had taken a few trips up to Shanghai and Guangzhou – and he had liked what he saw.

'It's amazing what's going on up there – it's really buzzing. The timing's just right because they've started off but there's no way for them to get capital up there. And it's not like India. India is dominated by a few powerful families, it's a real clique and they've already got money. Just like Japan and Korea. Why are any of these guys ever gonna give you a place at the poker table unless it's just to take your money? China's different. I reckon there's a way in for an outsider. The economy grew up on the lines of a planned economy so government officials control it rather than big families like in India. I just figure that if these officials have a chance to get capital to grow their businesses, they're gonna grab the opportunity.'

I agreed.

'So, anyway,' he continued, 'what's your story?'

Two

千里之行始于足下

A Journey of a Thousand Li
Begins From Under One's Feet

Lao Zi: The Tao and Its Virtue
c. sixth century BC

Five years earlier, I'd arrived as a blank sheet of paper.

As I flew to Hong Kong from London for the first time, I had no idea where it was. I didn't care. Flying in from on high in the late afternoon, I gazed down on a scattering of islands that looked like pebbles thrown carelessly into the South China Sea. I could pick out a rocky peak half hidden by heat haze and surrounded by a belt of glass spikes. Ten minutes later, after a momentary shudder through the dense patches of cloud lower down, the plane took the last-minute hairpin to the right. As we bounced to a halt on the tarmac, the smell was in the cabin before the doors opened. Damp heat.

I still remember vividly the taxi ride from the airport to the seedy hotel in Wanchai. Night had fallen and neon characters of every size and description leered at me through the taxi window. It was a new world. The streets were teeming. Nobody slept.

Over the coming weeks, new sensations seeped into me. The smells, the dress, the food, the sounds, the written word. Wherever I looked, the Chinese were bargaining, unloading from boats, hammering in tiny factories. I couldn't believe that such a concentration of human life could exist in a state of perpetual motion. The pace of life was so relentless that I became swept up by its momentum. I soon felt like a part of some vast machine.

As the days passed, I quickly grew to like the place and started to take in more of the surroundings. I often went up to the little path near the summit of Hong Kong Island that winds around the Peak from the tram station. After about half a mile in the shade of the India-rubber trees with their roots trailing out of the branches down to the ground, round a bend the leaves suddenly clear and the path opens out on to the sky from the cliff face. On first sight, the view over the harbour to the mountains on the other side quite catches your breath, it is so dramatic: a vast modern city with glass towers and spikes set in a huge natural amphitheatre with the ocean as its floor. I stared out over the harbour, breathing in the atmosphere as the city churned below, counting the scores of ocean ships in the port and the planes queuing up to land at Kai Tak from the west. I could see a tiny trail of smoke from the green and white funnels of the Star Ferry as it inched its way across the harbour. A distant roar rose up to the skies from far below: the sound of a thousand engines, the clatter of trams, the hammering of piledrivers, the occasional shout from a worker perched high on the bamboo scaffolding around the next half-built glass tower.

From any direction, the geography of Hong Kong draws the eye towards the mainland. The island seems to wrap itself around the tip of the peninsula opposite like a giant horseshoe, so that from any point the view focuses on the row of nine hills behind the mist on the other side. Whenever I went over to Tsim Sha Tsui, I took the Star Ferry and sat on the polished wooden seats with the spray on my face, taking in the smell of oil and the sound of the ropes creaking as they strained against the vast iron stubs anchoring the ferry to the quayside. As I sat there on the ferry, gazing ahead through the heat haze, I found myself wondering about China, wondering what it was like behind those nine hills beyond Kowloon on the other side.

Hong Kong had never really seemed English to me. Sure, there were the bars in Lan Kwai Fong where, if it weren't for the heat, I might pretend that I was in Fulham. There might be the odd judge hurrying along in his wig and red coat-tails near the High Court and plenty of pinstriped bankers in Central, but that was only on the surface. Scratch below that and everything that mattered was Chinese.

The papers were full of stories about some huge power struggle up in Beijing but I couldn't figure out exactly what had been going on. The names were all so similar (and back to front) that I could never quite see who had done what and to whom. There were photographs of a dour-looking man with thick glasses, an unconvincing smile and collars that were slightly too big who seemed to be the Prime Minister. But the country was ruled by an eighty-year-old recluse who did little but play card games; that and control the Army. I found an old guidebook in a second-hand bookshop in Hollywood Road and, as I thumbed through the disintegrating pages, I was amazed at the size of China: vast areas of uninhabited frozen wastelands in the west, huge deserts further north and then an incredible crush along the coast. The faded sepia pictures of pavilions and sweeping tiled roofs in the Forbidden City caught my imagination and I wanted to see them for myself. I knew that parts of China had been open to foreigners from the early 1980s and when I met the odd person who had been there I questioned them eagerly. Some seemed lost for words, almost annoyed by the place: 'Don't go there, it's absolute chaos.' Others seemed puzzled in an amused sort of way: 'Of course, it was all very interesting, but the people were a bit odd. They always pretended that they didn't have train tickets when you knew that they did, or that the restaurant was full when you could see that it was empty.' But for some it was in their blood. They seemed possessed. And when they couldn't explain exactly why, it fed my curiosity.

Slowly, an idea developed in my head: why not head back for England overland through China and take the Trans-Mongolian railway through Moscow on the way? So I started reading up about China and found that the pass over the mountains from northern Pakistan had been opened. I heard that it was possible to follow the Silk Road along the northern edges of the deserts in north-western China. There was also a southern route but no one knew whether it was open. I tried to learn the odd phrase of Chinese, for emergencies, but the words came out in a way that just drew blank stares. Still, I persisted and, the following spring, I set off for China.

I went in through the Karakoram Mountains, where Afghanistan, Pakistan and China meet. The mountains there are capped with thick glaciers and in places the road almost disappears. At last it descends towards the deserts in north-western China. Heading east towards Beijing, I followed a string of oasis towns on the edge of the desert. After ten days in a bus, aching and bruised, I reached the railhead

11

and boarded a train for central China. Three months later and a stone and a half lighter, I slipped through the Wall and crossed the grasslands to Moscow.

As I sat on the train through Russia and watched the endless pine forests recede towards the east, I couldn't assemble all the things that I had seen into any coherent form in my mind: the street urchin who pushed a knife through his wrist for a few coppers, the blind people's massage parlour, the pickled human heads in an underground city, peasant villages and huge polluted cities, the crush of people in the stations. But I had a sense of something so vast and so old, so chaotic and so utterly foreign, that it took me right out of myself.

I knew that I had barely scratched the surface, but I could see that hundreds of millions of ordinary Chinese were on the march for a better life. It was like Hong Kong but on a cosmic scale. I felt energized; there was such a sense of purpose in among the chaos. An age-old culture had somehow taken a wrong turn, but I could feel the determination to catch up.

And there was something else, something funny about China that told me not to take it all too seriously. I had just caught the tail end of the planned economy, where Beijing still tried to manipulate the minutiae of China's vast economy. On the macro scale it was madness; how could the bureaucrats in Beijing coordinate the annual production of a billion pairs of trousers, or two billion pairs of socks across a country several times the size of Continental Europe? Even on the streets I often found that common sense seemed swamped by some vast nonsensical central plan. It completely inverted the normal relationships where the customer was king. Here the planners provided everything and the customer, it seemed, was supposed to be grateful. Huge arguments arose over the simplest of trans-actions. At times, for example, it might take half an hour to persuade a receptionist to let me stay in a hotel. She'd say that it was full and that there were no rooms available. At first I was puzzled and went away wondering where all the guests were. But I figured out that under the planned economy, it made no difference whether a hotel was full or empty and if there were guests there would be more work to do. Since everything was owned by the State no one cared; in fact, no one higher up even knew what was going on. So the receptionist would simply announce that they were full and wave people away so that she could go back to her newspaper.

The trick was to come back with objections until they finally agreed to let you in. It was the same in shops, at bus stations, in restaurants or when hiring bicycles. Sometimes I had to persuade a shop assistant to sell me something that I could see behind the counter; she'd say it had already been sold or that it was broken or that it was the last one and had to be kept for display. I'd go into a restaurant and they'd tell me that there was no rice or I'd go to a bar and they'd pretend to be out of beer. I even found a restaurant in Xi'an that closed for lunch. But after a while, I learnt to probe and question, cajole and persuade – and never to give in! So I barged into kitchens in restaurants to find something to eat and went upstairs in hotels in search of an empty room; I grabbed whatever I needed from behind shop counters and searched sheds for bicycles to hire. Even going to buy vegetables was a challenge but I sensed a rapport with the people I met; it was almost as if they enjoyed the game of wits and they often gave me a laugh or a smile once they finally gave in. I never felt any malice from them; it was more like a bad habit that no one seemed able to kick.

There were many other habits that could push a new-comer into either loving or hating China: the extreme curiosity towards foreigners in the 1980s, for example, or the dogged adherence to incomprehensible rules. When the attendant on a railway carriage woke you up in the middle of the night for the third time to clean under your feet with a filthy black mop, just because there was a regulation to sweep the floor every two hours, you would, as they say, either laugh or cry. There wasn't much middle ground. On the other hand, ordinary things like hotel notices or restaurant menus were full of bizarre rules and mistranslations. There were signs everywhere that said 'Beware of Smoking' and 'Stop Spitting!' The regulations in the Shanghai Peace Hotel included restrictions on 'bring-ing poisonous or radioactive substances into the hotel' or 'letting off fireworks in the room', as if such matters were perfectly normal occurrences. Also banned was 'fighting, gambling, drug taking, whoring or making of great noise', and there was a rule that no guest was (sic) 'allowed to up anyone in their room for the night'. Another hotel had a brochure which described its wonderful gardens and said that they hoped that 'all our guests will be depressed by the flowers'; the Chinese version meant 'impressed.' Restaurant menus were similar; I found an upmarket restaurant in Guangzhou which served 'camel's hump in wonderful taste', 'double boiled deer's tail in water duck soup' and 'roasted sausages in osmanthus flowers'. Another one down the road, which was slightly more modest and obviously trying to attract foreigners, had its menu in English offering 'lunch on meat with egg' and 'scramfled egg with lunch on meat', but it rather lost track with the 'squid beard' and 'fried field snail in bear sauce'. I thought it must have meant 'beer' sauce, so I looked up the Chinese characters, but they seemed to mean something to do with 'bell peppers' so I was none the wiser.

Over and above the chaos on the streets, the mistranslations and endearing absurdity, there were huge changes under way that brought to mind the old aphorism attributed to Napoleon: 'Let China sleep, for when she wakes up she will shake the world.' True, China was starting from a low base but the vast majority of the changes was positive. The UN reported that in the 1980s alone over a hundred and twenty-five million people had been lifted out of absolute poverty. I became convinced that the country was on the way up as the shackles of the Communist system fell away. There was a sense of optimism everywhere, a feeling that things would continue to get better.

So, by the time that I left China after that first solo journey of three months back in 1988, I knew that I had found something that completely absorbed me. I felt that it might change my life; and it did. In retrospect, sixteen years on, I can recognize something common in many people new to China. I had become almost intentionally dazzled. I had set off wanting China to be something special and therefore it was. It was a kind of wilful infatuation.

Three

不入虎穴焉得虎子

*If You Won't Go into the Tiger's Lair,
How Can You Catch the Cubs?*

*Han Dynasty Proverb, 202 BC–AD 220:
'Nothing ventured nothing gained.'*

When I got back to London, my head was still in China. I found myself straining to catch the odd Chinese character out of the corner of my eye from the top of a bus, or absent-mindedly wandering towards Chinatown to rummage in the bookshops and enjoy the familiar smells. I had found something new and exciting but in London little had changed. Two more years up the ladder, many of my colleagues were climbing a structure without ever pausing to wonder whether it ought to be climbed. I couldn't re-engage. I couldn't take it seriously when, on the other side of the globe, an epic struggle was under way.

As I sat in an office dreaming of the chaos, the packed railway stations and crowded street markets, I toyed with schemes that might get me back there. Surely with changes on such a scale and at such a pace, there had to be a way

16

back for anyone willing to take a risk? I spent hours every day dreaming about starting a business out there, building pagodas in the sky and scheming. Eventually, I went to see the senior partner of the firm to ask whether he'd send me back. I thought that I might be able to persuade him to set up an office in China to help clients invest, but the interview was a disaster. I had been shown into an office and my heart sank as I saw the figure behind the desk: late-fifties, perfect blue pinstripe, silver hair with not a strand out of place, hands resting palms down on the surface of a huge pine-wood desk in an office overlooking the Thames. There was something unnerving about the desk, that enormous clean expanse of bare wood; an uncluttered desk shows an uncluttered mind, I supposed dejectedly. So the interview went about as badly as it could have done; he clearly thought that I was a lunatic. So I went back to my desk to hide. But after a while I thought, 'Sod it!' I found a Mandarin course and handed in my notice.

About a week after I left my job, I suffered a momentary loss of confidence. The headline on the front page of *The Times* describing the crisis in Tiananmen Square read 'Peking in flames as China slides into Chaos.' My mind flew back to the last few hours I had spent in Beijing a year earlier, just before I got on to the train to Moscow. I had sat for a while on the steps of the huge monument to the People's Heroes in the middle of Tiananmen Square. The old men were flying their kites; beautiful yellow paper kites, with lions' heads and dragons' tails. I watched as they shuffled back and forth across the paving in their soft cloth shoes and the kites swooped and soared around the great stone obelisk. Everything had seemed so calm then, perfectly set into its allotted place. But a year on, after the tanks had rumbled on to the Square, the world had changed.

When I got back to China in the summer of 1990 the monument was all fenced off and surrounded by guards. As I stepped out on to the vast open surface of the square, people were tense, unwilling to engage, wary of contact with the few foreigners who had returned to China. The last rays of the setting sun caught the yellow tiled roofs of the Forbidden City. In the distance, I could see the faint smile of Mao Zedong on the Gateway of Heavenly Peace, the face in the giant portrait silently watchful. A smile just like the Mona Lisa's: serene, humourless and utterly ambiguous – just right for a tyrant.

The atmosphere in the university where I had enrolled in a Mandarin course was just the same. People were cautious. It was no time to take risks or to stick out from the crowd, so it took several months before I was able to make Chinese friends.

I lived in the university for nearly two years. At times, I was the only white boy among a thousand Chinese. Foreign students were kept apart in a separate building. There was a campaign against 'spiritual pollution' but after a while Chinese students sought me out. Their natural curiosity soon got the better of the vague regulations designed to separate us. It was still a novelty for them to talk English to a foreigner rather than reading it from a book. When the first few students found that I was receptive, many more followed.

My time at the university was my first brush with the real China, the China from which you cannot escape. At first it was intimidating. For a start, I wasn't used to the constant intrusion. There was never a second of privacy, never a moment of silence, a moment for repose, or an opportunity to gather one's thoughts. I was bombarded with noise: at six o'clock the campus speakers blared out marching tunes for compulsory early morning exercises; at ten-thirty they announced lights out. I often came back to my room to find a line of students waiting. There was no escape from the endless, grinding requests for English lessons. I could see why there was no Chinese translation for 'privacy' in my dictionary; the concept didn't exist.

I wasn't used to all the restrictions imposed by the authorities and matters were made worse by the vagueness of the regulations. I was jumpy because I never really figured out what I could or could not do. Once my brother came to visit me in Beijing and slept on the floor in my room. The next morning the Dormitory Chief, in his blue overalls and thick glasses, arrived stony-faced at the door. He had been tipped off by one of the girls who delivered the hot-water thermoses that I had a guest in my room. He was furious because I hadn't asked permission. I apologized and said that it had never occurred to me that I needed to ask; we weren't doing anything harmful. But he wasn't to be put off and it developed into an unpleasant row. My brother had to leave and find somewhere else to stay. A few days later I went back to the dormitory office; I wanted to avoid any more exhausting scenes like the last, so I called through the little hatch to the Dormitory Chief and politely asked for a copy of the rules. He said that I couldn't have them so I asked, 'Why not?

'Those rules are internal and not to be told to the outside.'

'What does that mean? If I don't know what the rules are, how can I obey them?'

'Our regulations are very clear.'

'Oh, I'm sorry, but that's not my point,' I replied. 'If I don't know what rules you have, I can't follow them.' After a few more rounds, I gave up. I never did get a copy. I discovered years later that this 'internal rule' concept was

19

applied across the board in China, even to things like income tax. It's hardly surprising that China's tax system is so inefficient when no one knows what they're meant to be paying. At the university, the only thing I ever knew for sure was that it was lights out at ten-thirty with all the doors locked. If you were caught with a girl after hours, you'd be thrown out of the country.

Vast amounts of time seemed to be taken up by the most mundane tasks. I stood in endless queues at the university canteen, where they served only cabbage and rice for months on end in enamel bowls shoved through a hatch in a brick wall. I waited an hour and a half for a shower. But as the months rolled on, I settled into a semblance of routine.

The Beijing autumn is very short and after a few weeks of golden leaves and vermilion sunsets, winter howls in from Mongolia. My room, which faced north, was a stark concrete box on the second floor of a brick dormitory building. It came with an iron bedstead, a forty-watt bulb hanging on a wire from the ceiling – and not much else. In winter, the freezing wind blew straight through the metal-framed windows until I sealed them up with tape. The cold was bad enough, but the cruellest part of the winter was the dryness. Wood cracked, earth dried to powder and skin creased and aged in the desiccating cold. Every morning, as I scraped a thin layer of ice off the inside of my window, I tried to keep warm with a small electrical stove. Stoves were banned and the authorities soon found me out. They monitored the electricity on each floor. There was a search but I refused to hand the heater over. Then one day the electrical wire, which was far too thin for the current, burst into flames, leaving a large black hole in my bedcovers. After a huge row, my stove was confiscated and I took to wearing several layers of clothes.

Cleanliness suffered in the winter. The only hot water came in a green plastic thermos left outside the door each morning, and it was difficult to keep clean. For months on end, I felt grubby, as if I were on a camping holiday. Clothes became grimy because there was only a stone sink and a bucket for washing. I used to wash my jeans there, but in winter the water was so cold that the bones in my hands ached unbearably. Wringing out clothes was agony. Afterwards, when I hung them out to dry, they froze solid in minutes. I often carried them back inside clutched under my arm with the legs sticking straight out in front like a cardboard cut-out.

When I eventually ventured into the Chinese students' domitories, I felt a lot less sorry for myself. I had never seen anything like it. Seven students crammed into a tiny room in bunk beds, with inadequate lighting, wire cages over the windows and not much in the way of heat or sanitation; and that for the best scholars in China. The rooms were arranged off a central corridor and the students threw rubbish out of their rooms on to the floor for collection later on. The walls were blackened to waist height and hadn't been painted for years. The girls' dormitories were even worse because they cooked on makeshift electrical stoves perched on top of piles of bricks in the corridors so that the floors were covered in scraps of food, pools of dirty water and discarded tins. At the end of the corridor, where the toilets were, great piles of used sanitary towels had been tipped out of the wire baskets in each cubicle and swept out over the floor into the corridor outside. The concrete floor was cracked with potholes, so it was impossible to clean up properly.

Although the dull winter months in Beijing could be dispiriting at times, the planned economy still provided some light relief. Beijingers have a tradition of eating cabbage in the winter. It resists the cold and doesn't get damaged by the frost so, in earlier years when food was less plentiful, the Government organized cabbage to be brought into Beijing and distributed free to the people. Each year, from early November, long convoys of trucks, queued up on the outskirts of the city, waiting until nightfall to rumble in with their vast loads of cabbage into the city. Thousands and thousands of tonnes of the vegetable were brought in and piled up at the main intersections in the city. Teams of elderly women guarded it by night and handed it out during the day. The whole process took about a month and the huge mounds on the street corners became a familiar sight. However, in the run-up to that first winter in Beijing, the government set the price too high and the peasants in the surrounding countryside grew nothing but cabbage. The result was a massive glut. The piles of cabbage grew and grew until they were ten feet high and hundreds of yards long. After a month, cabbage leaves were everywhere: on the pavements, on the roads, inside buildings, stacked up on window ledges. The leaves soon mashed down into a thick, slippery green slime on the ground. Bicycles collided, cars bumped gracefully into each other and people spent half their time picking themselves up off the floor and scraping cabbage sludge off their trousers. It got so bad that the Mayor of Beijing went on the radio and made a speech during which he said that it was everyone's 'patriotic duty' to eat cabbage. Although all the political sloganeering over the years had dulled the Beijingers' senses, the Mayor's remark provoked howls of derision and, to this day, long-leafed cabbages are still known in northern China as 'Patriotic Cabbage'.

As winter changed to spring, there was an almost tangible

relaxation as the ripples from Tiananmen receded together with the cold. Even the political campaigns on campus became half-hearted. I heard that there were still compulsory Marxism lessons on Tuesdays, but the students generally sat around reading novels. The teachers were bored senseless, just like the students, so they made no attempt to impose discipline. Gradually, the flavour of life changed. As the spring came round, the cherry trees blossomed and the regimen as well as the weather seemed to thaw out.

Between the lighter moments provided by the planned economy and the restaurant menus, living in China was much harder than I had expected. All the same, I felt that I was peeling back the layers to find out what was at the core. I made slow but steady progress with the language and after a year or so I could enjoy a simple conversation with a stranger. Although I knew that life in China could be tough, I felt I was slowly mastering it, but from time to time I came across small incidents where I felt a hardness that I had never known at home and which would set me back a few weeks. I remember once seeing an old man, dazed on a sidewalk, who'd been knocked off his bicycle and concussed. He was sitting unattended in the broken pieces of a pot of pickled vegetable roots that he had been carrying, surrounded by pedestrians all arguing about whose fault it was. Occasions like that would shake me. Another time I met a leper sitting on the pavement not far from Tiananmen Square. His skin was terribly sore, red and messy, and his hands were all distorted. I went to get a carton of milk and fitted a straw into it for him. I passed by the same place about half an hour later and found some people in uniform questioning him sharply, wanting to know where he had found the milk. A truck arrived. They threw him in the back like a sack of potatoes. I screamed at them, but it was as if I wasn't there. I was an embarrassment. As they drove off, he looked at me out of the back of the truck and smiled Mao Zedong's smile, serene but expressionless. I'll never know quite what it meant but I was starting to sense a sort of protective detachment that some Chinese people needed in order to survive.

At the same time, of course, there were many kindnesses, small acts of charity that meant so much to me as I struggled in unfamiliar surroundings. They showed the human side of China.

These experiences made me feel as if the rigidity of the regime in China magnified each side of human nature: the good and the bad; the pettiness and the generosity. But what would it make out of me? I felt under stress dealing with such a foreign environment, and if the pressure really built, which way would I turn?

After a year at the university I was rapidly running out of cash. I had been studying full time and had quickly got through everything I'd saved in Hong Kong so I found a job writing up books in my shaky Mandarin in an office down the road. I used to get there on my bike each day, about half an hour if the wind was with me.

A sandstorm blasted through Beijing one day in April 1992 and caught me on my way to work. The dust storms in northern China in the late spring are often so dense that at times they blot out the sun and the light fades into dusky sepia colours. It took me an hour straining against the wind before I got to the office and when I arrived I was filthy. After I'd rubbed the grit out of my eyes, I found on my desk a letter from England. A friend had sent me a copy of a job advertisement from the *Financial Times* in London. 'Mandarin Speaker Needed by Large Financial Services Company.' It looked interesting. They needed someone to help them advise investors how to get into China. My mind's eye instantly flew back to the short interview in London and that awful un-cluttered desk. I could have written that job spec three years earlier when I'd gone to see Old Roy back in London.

I cobbled together a CV and sent it off. When I called the number later in the week, the voice at the other end of the line was chuckling. 'You won't believe who it is,' I heard him say through the crackles from London. 'It's your old firm. Andersen!'

'What?' I said as it slowly sank in.

'Yeah, it's Arthur Andersen!'

'Yes!' I shouted punching the air. The interview was a walkover and, two years after I left them in London, I went back to rejoin the firm in Hong Kong that summer.

During my time in Beijing, I had started to figure out that China was ruled by complex and ceaselessly shifting alliances within a group of very old men, known as the 'Eight Immortals'. I never made any serious attempt to understand how it all worked, but at the centre of these fluid coalitions was a man called Deng Xiaoping.

Deng had been a senior member of the Red Army prior to Liberation and for years afterwards he was a key figure at the top levels of power. His reputation was that of an able, pragmatic politician who was more interested in getting the job done than in worrying about political dogma. After the People's Republic was founded in 1949, he rose through the ranks and ended up as the Number Two to China's President Liu Shaoqi. But in 1966 both Liu and Deng fell from power during the Cultural Revolution.

Mao and Liu were old political rivals, and Liu had gained the upper hand when the Great Leap Forward, Mao's mad dash for economic growth, ended in famine. Liu tried to put China on to a path of stable growth based more on sound economics than politics. But it didn't last long; Mao hit back in 1966 when he launched the Great Proletarian Cultural Revolution by encouraging young men and women to break all forms of social convention by attacking 'bad elements' in society and waging 'perpetual revolution'.

The country rapidly descended into chaos. Schools and universities stopped functioning when the more radical students became Red Guards. They started to attack anyone suspected of being Mao's political opponent, labelling them 'Rightists' or 'Capitalist Roaders' and parading them through the streets in dunces' caps. Factories ceased production as the Red Guards formed 'Mao Zedong Thought Propaganda Teams' and demanded that the workers spend hours a day in study sessions. Rival factions of Red Guards set up speakers in the streets that blared out propaganda until the early hours, and festooned walls and gateways with posters criticizing each other. Mao personally pasted a 'big character poster' on to the doors of the Great Hall of the People calling for the masses to 'bombard the headquarters', and held a series of massive rallies, one of which was nearly a million people strong, in Tiananmen Square.

With Mao's implicit support, the Red Guards began to target senior figures in the Government, ransacking their homes and arresting family members. Social order collapsed completely. No one attended to the normal functioning of the State; everything revolved around politics. Government ministries stopped functioning because officials were too frightened to go to work, and large crowds of Red Guards besieged foreign embassies. A huge notice was erected on the front of Beijing station that summed up the nonsensical politicization of the times: 'Better a socialist train that's late than a capitalist train on time.'

Liu Shaoqi, China's President and Mao's principal rival, and Deng, as Liu's Number Two, rapidly became targets. There is a photograph of Liu standing in the Central Government compound, Zhongnanhai, being denounced by a large crowd of thugs wearing Red Guard uniforms. One can almost smell the fear coming out of the picture. Liu died a year later on the floor of a jail in Kaifeng.

But while many around him perished, Deng survived. From 1967 to 1974, stripped of all power, it seems that he spent most of his time working in a tractor factory in Jiangsu. His son 'fell' out of an upstairs window in Beijing University where he had been studying physics and has been paralysed from the waist down ever since. After Mao died in 1976, there was a protracted power struggle before Deng emerged triumphant three years later. Paradoxically, he succeeded by resigning. It forced his opponents to resign as well, whilst he continued to manipulate real power from behind the scenes. One of his first steps was to start to rehabilitate many of the people who were unjustly attacked during the Cultural Revolution and insist on the trial of the Gang of Four, the chief protagonists of the chaos, led by Jiang Qing, Mao's third wife. There was a televised trial lasting several weeks where Madame Mao repeatedly shouted down the judges and refused to recognize their right to try her. She claimed that she was acting on Mao's orders and that the court had no authority to question him: 'I was Mao's dog,' she said. 'What he said "bite", I bit.' She was sentenced to death 'suspended for two years to see if she would behave' and spent the next twelve years in jail, making cloth dolls, until she committed suicide in 1991.

Deng was incredibly tough. It seemed as if he was made

of an indestructible material, a kind of political tungsten carbide, and, by the time he emerged as China's paramount leader, he was well into his mid-seventies.

After Tiananmen Square, the Chinese economy had crashed and businesses everywhere faced very difficult times. Most were starved of cash as the Government tried to rein in State lending. Whilst Deng was no liberal, he was a pragmatist and realized years before his Russian counterparts that if the Chinese Communist Party was to survive, it had to deliver the economic goods. Tiananmen Square had shown that he would not shrink from using force, but he knew that in the longer term power grew from rising living standards rather than from the barrel of a gun. Immediately after the crisis, the Government had slammed the brakes on the economy, but by mid-1991 Deng had had enough of the austerity and wanted to get back on track. Even though he had won the battle for the top place in the Chinese hierarchy, Deng could not just set policy as he pleased, and when he tried to recharge the economy he faced serious opposition from the conservatives.

The battle raged on behind the walls of the Party compounds throughout the months towards Chinese New Year in 1992. After months of infighting, Deng had had enough and he decided to seize the initiative. At the age of eighty-eight, he gave China one last shove towards further reform by grabbing centre stage from his opponents. Just as Mao had done at the start of the Cultural Revolution when he travelled to Wuhan and swam across the Yangtse, Deng achieved a huge shift in policy by a seemingly insignificant event: he went on holiday and planted a tree.

On what is now written into Communist Party folklore as

Deng's 'Southern Tour', he arrived at Shenzhen Station in the southern seaside town next to Hong Kong with his family and went sightseeing. At a theme park the next day, he planted a tree for the cameramen and repeated his old slogan, 'To get rich is glorious.' Proceeding regally up the coast, he toured factories and visited the huge new development zone in Shanghai. Behind the scenes, the struggle intensified and Deng held meetings at Cadre Training Schools and Party Committees all along the coast. He talked directly to local officials about the need to 'guard against the left', and pushed his agenda for greater reform.

Back in Beijing, his octogenarian opponents watched these antics in horror; they knew that Deng had deliberately bypassed all the normal Party structures and had reached out directly to local officials. They also quickly realized that they were fighting a losing battle; the rank and file liked what Deng had to say and the tide was against them. Although it was several weeks before anyone dared to publish the story of Deng's trip in the Chinese press, the news that he wanted more reform and further 'opening up' of the economy eventually broke and by April the country was in a state of great excitement. I remember several meetings of my Chinese work colleagues when they went off to study the latest bulletins. China appeared to be on the move again.

Deng's speeches that spring galvanized the whole country into action and officials everywhere set up investment zones and held trade fairs to attract foreign investors. By the end of the year, the news that China's growth rates were on the rise had filtered through to the world outside. The New York bankers started arriving in Hong Kong in their pinstripes and tasselled loafers, intent on setting up offices as a launching pad into China. Specialist investment companies appeared overnight in Hong Kong, all fighting for press coverage. Barton Biggs, one of Wall Street's most influential money allocators, arrived in town and told the newspapers, 'After six days in China, I'm tuned in, overfed and maximum bullish.' In the next few days, as his words flashed across the wires in America, two billion dollars sloshed into Hong Kong's stock market and share prices went through the roof. Investors started to gather huge amounts of capital to put to work on the mainland and, by the time I went back to Andersen that summer, there were millions of dollars sitting in 'China Funds' in Hong Kong all trying to find a way into the Middle Kingdom.

My job was to help these investors find projects in China so the first thing I did was call up all my old contacts in Beijing. Over the next few months I shuttled back and forth between Hong Kong and the mainland, visiting Shanghai, Wuhan, Chongqing, Tianjin, anywhere I could get a meeting with officials. Given the overall hype, it wasn't difficult to find a receptive audience. At each of these places, I'd go through my pitch, explaining that there were large amounts of money sitting in Hong Kong and that my job was to help invest it in China. Everyone I met seemed keen to get in on the act and promised to introduce me to good businesses needing expansion capital. 'If you give me a few weeks, I'll organize a tour of all our best factories,' they'd say. But as the months went on, and I went back on second or third visits, they just kept talking, talking, talking. It was the same old story without anything actually happening. Endless tales like, 'My cousin runs an aspirin factory in Jilin, and they really want to do a joint venture.' But I could never actually get anyone to do anything. One man out of all those I spoke to was different.

*   *   *

Ai Jian was in his early forties when I met him. He was one of the 'lost generation', the people born just after Liberation who were swept up in the madness of the Cultural Revolution during their teens. The universities and schools had been closed for nearly ten years and, just like millions of others, Ai had been sent to the countryside to work in the fields.

He was born in Jining in the eastern province of Shandong and later moved up to the capital, Beijing. His father, who was well educated, had been assigned to be the Party Secretary of a tank factory up in Harbin so the family had moved on to the north when Ai was a boy. It was a familiar story: a comfortable, even privileged childhood blown apart by the Cultural Revolution. Like almost everyone else of his age, Ai had been seduced by the excitement of those first heady days in the late summer of 1966, and he had joined the Red Guards.

Ai had soon been brought down to reality. After his father was targeted, the family fled back to Beijing to hide with relatives. A group of Red Guards from a rival faction travelled the seven hundred miles back to Beijing to find him and, terrified that the whole family might be arrested, Ai's father gave himself up. The Red Guards dragged him back to Harbin where he endured years of humiliation and physical abuse. Ai told me that on one occasion after the Red Guards had 'struggled' against him for hours, his father had died.

'He was beaten and beaten until he died on the floor.'

I corrected him gently; I knew that his father was still very much alive and well. But he was insistent.

'No, my father actually died on the floor and he only came back when they threw a bucket of freezing water into his face,' he said.

It couldn't have been literally true but it was a telling metaphor and I let it ride. The pity of the Cultural Revolution was that Mao had calculated so deliberately, so callously when he set up young people to humiliate and destroy their elders. In a society where face was everything, the fear and humiliation had literally killed thousands and thousands of older people, many of whom took their own lives. The shame was so total that for many children, their parents had 'died' whether or not they happened to remain on earth.

By the late 1960s the Cultural Revolution had created such chaos across the country that even Mao feared that he might lose control. His main political rivals had been destroyed so he attempted to rein in the Red Guards. He did this by sending them to work in the countryside to 'learn from the peasants.' All forms of intellectual learning were regarded as useless. Only politics mattered and Mao had hijacked politics to regain control. The campaign to move people to the countryside quickly grew and, in the early 1970s, millions of young people were reallocated from the towns to the countryside. Ai was one of those millions; he was sent to Jiangxian County in a remote part of Shanxi Province, a few hundred miles to the west of Beijing.

I had been to Shanxi the year before. It lies in the northern part of central China on the banks of the Yellow River where, five thousand years ago, there were the first stirrings of the Chinese civilization. The yellow-grey loess soil there, which gives river its name, is like powder and is difficult to farm. The whole dusty landscape is pitted with deep ravines caused by rainwater washing away the light soil over the centuries. I knew that some of the counties in Shanxi were amongst the poorest in China and that many people still lived in caves.

For four years Ai rose with the sun and slept as it set, the daylight hours spent in the fields.

'The peasants there were very kind,' he said. 'But they had nothing. Nothing! They knew nothing, they had nothing, they did nothing except work in the fields.'

There was no machinery, no electricity, at times not enough food. Nothing but the prospect of another day's hard labour in the fields. But at least Ai was removed from the political campaigns and the incessant din of the slogans from the loudspeakers in the city. In Shanxi, free from the constant fear that he might become the next target, there was at least a semblance of peace.

He recalled the one luxury of those years; sometimes on rainy days, if things were particularly good, he would sit inside on the *kang* with his workmates. A *kang* is a big raised platform used as a bed for the whole family and made out of beaten earth with a primitive wood-burning stove built in. They would sit listening to the falling rain and enjoying the occasional cigarette rolled out of newspaper.

Once a tractor came to the village, Ai remembered. 'Some peasants from over the hill had walked ten miles to come and gawp at it,' he said, 'and it was all decked up in ribbons and red rosettes. Afterwards there had been a celebration with speeches about how grateful we should be to Chairman Mao for giving us a tractor.' But the following day the tractor went to the next valley and the peasants walked back over the hill with their shovels.

After Mao died, life slowly returned to normal. Ai was accepted at an engineering university in Xi'an where he met his future wife. On graduating, he found a good job in Beijing.

'The problem was,' he went on, 'that at that time in China you had to have a *hu kou*.' The *hu kou* was a rigid system of residence permits that made it impossible for ordinary people to move around the country without the little red chops, or Chinese seals of approval, from the Public Security Bureau. Ai's wife had not been able to obtain a *hu kou* for Beijing so she had to stay in Xi'an. Even in the first few years of marriage, they were only allowed to see each other twice a year, at the Chinese Spring Festival and in the summer. It was nearly ten years before she got a *hu kou* for Beijing and for the first seven years after Ai's son was born he only saw him for three weeks a year.

I felt that all these experiences might have hardened and embittered Ai, but, years later, as we sat in a bar in Beijing, the strongest feeling I had from him was his burning ambition for his one son. He had a fierce hope that his son would be spared all the troubles and political turmoil that had blighted his own early life, and that China would be stable so that the next generation would be free to use their time more constructively. Years later, his boy got a place to study in America.

After coming back to Beijing, Ai was assigned to work for the ministry in charge of foreign investment. Never the diplomat, he got into difficulties after the Tiananmen protests. The Party apparatchiks, or 'cadres' as they are known, decided to muzzle him so he had been sidelined to run a business centre in one of Beijing's hotels. It was somewhere that they thought would keep him out of trouble.

I met Ai through a friend. She'd been pestering me to see him for months but our paths never seemed to cross. 'If you want to get anything done round here,' she said, 'you should talk to Ai.' So I eventually called him and fixed a time to meet. Dumped into a backwater by the cadres and pushed away from the action, he was in a restless, searching mood when I found him; and as I described what had been happening in Hong Kong, he quickly latched on to the opportunity.

I knew that Ai was different from my other contacts in China when I came back a few weeks later. Whilst the others just talked and talked and made endless promises, when I met Ai for the second time he reached into his drawer and pulled out a cardboard box full of handwritten letters. He had written twenty-six letters to his colleagues in local governments all over China. He only got three replies, but that was enough to start.

Over the next six months, we travelled all over China in search of investment projects. At the end of each trip, I went back to Hong Kong to talk to investors. It was frustrating work. They never quite knew what they wanted and seemed reluctant to come up to China. We found steel-rolling mills and watch factories, power equipment works and lock makers. Every time we found something that looked promising, I wrote it up and send it to investors in Hong Kong. But they never seemed to bite.

Eventually I managed to persuade some fund managers from a big New York investment house to come up to Shanghai. It was an important visit, so one of my colleagues, Maneksh, flew out from London. He'd been in India and brokered a few deals so I was glad of his company.

The trip was a disaster. These bankers, still slightly jet-lagged from Wall Street, stared with disbelieving wonder at the chaotic traffic, gesticulating policemen and the waves of bicycles. They kept checking their Rolexes, sighing un-naturally loudly and repeatedly looking through their air tickets as we sat sweltering in near-gridlock on Hengshan Road. They had sent me a fax beforehand saying that they were interested in 'real estate and consumer packaged

35

goods' so the first meeting I arranged was with the Land Bureau of the Shanghai Government.

Despite the considerable power that came from controlling land during those times of spiralling property prices, the Land Bureau was in a dilapidated building at the end of the Bund, the sweeping avenue that looks out over the river in Shanghai. It was squeezed in among the grand colonial buildings next to Suzhou Creek. The contrast between the bankers with their highly polished shoes and designer silk ties and the bureau officials could not have been sharper. As we were led down a corridor with enormous old-fashioned frosted-glass lampshades like Olympic torches set into the walls, the bankers noticed a huge gash in the ceiling with lathe and plaster hanging through. In the meeting room, they settled on to a lumpy sofa with their knees tucked up to their chests. Sitting between a pale green plastic thermos flask and a spittoon, they tried not to stare too hard at the torn brown curtains flapping limply in the windows or the suspicious-looking holes in the skirting boards. The meeting started with the Deputy Bureau Chief offering them some melon seeds to chew on and it got worse from there on in. It didn't last long; there was no way they were ever going to get their heads around buying up land in Shanghai.

As they left, muttering under their breath and shaking their heads, they asked what was next.

'Er, the Rubber Bureau,' I said.

'So that's consumer products, right?'

'Kind of,' I said nervously, not knowing quite how to break the news. I spent the next hour sweating quietly in the back of the car, hoping that the traffic would be so bad that we'd have to call the meeting off. Then suddenly, out of the blue, inspiration seized me.

'You know, the one-child policy is quite controversial in

the West, isn't it? But I reckon that the population here is so huge that it'd be kind of irresponsible just to ignore it, don't you think?'

'Uh-huh!'

'You know, in China, even though there's the one-child policy, there are only seven condom factories. Amazing really, isn't it?'

'Uh-huh!'

'Yeah, only seven in the whole of China,' I went on.

'What of it?'

'Well, the whole condom production of China is only eight hundred million a year. There's more than a billion people here, so there's got to be, say, four hundred million blokes out there all needing condoms. But that's about two each a year. Must be a huge demand out there – if only we could figure out a way to get at it!'

'You're not saying–'

'Well, you said you wanted consumer packaged goods!'

'I do not believe we're doing this' they said, all exasperated sighs and rolling eyeballs. 'I do not believe we're doing this!'

But by that time there was little prospect of escape. The traffic was running smoothly and we were miles from the hotel. As the car drove through the gates of the Shanghai Great Unison Condom Factory, Madame Tao, who was in charge of foreign investment at the Rubber Bureau, came panting down the steps and took us to a meeting room with a display case at the back. We stared at the contents. The packaging was primitive: it was poorly printed in slightly garish colours and with a line drawing of a long-nosed couple – who were clearly meant to be Westerners – embracing against a sunset backdrop.

'What the hell's goin' on there?' said one of the pinstripes.

It was a classic example of the Chinese confusion towards Westerners: on the one hand, they were a target in campaigns against spiritual pollution at the university, and on the other they were used on condom packets to conjure up an image of something rather daring that might be secretly admired.

'Terrible, isn't it?' said Maneksh, picking up one of the packets. 'You know, Mrs Tao, you need to redo all this packaging. It's far too dowdy. You need to make it more exciting for the consumer. Back in the UK there's all sorts of stuff available. Different colours and shapes, even flavours – banana, strawberry, whatever takes your fancy. Maybe here it'd be shrimp-and-peanut flavour, or spicy bean curd . . .'

'Er, yes, thanks, Maneksh,' I interjected hurriedly. 'Shall we go and see the workshops?'

The machinery that we found at the top of a rickety staircase leading to the first floor of the warehouse at the back of the factory was a botched-up Heath Robinson affair; it looked like some bizarre homespun contraption cobbled together with bicycle parts and bits of old washing machines. There was a huge sagging rubber belt strapped between two wheels that was pulled slowly through a tub of melted latex. On the belt, set at every conceivable angle, some of which were anatomically simply not possible, were hundreds of glass penises. As the belt drooped into the tub, the latex coated each one with a thin layer. Weighed down by latex and by then at slightly less inspiring angles, they clanked onwards into a small chamber that had what looked like a couple of hairdryers inside blasting away to make the rubber set. At the other side, two colossal women with beefy forearms hauled off the condoms from the legions of approaching penises and threw them in handfuls into a plastic tray on the floor.

There was a rather frosty atmosphere in the car going back to the hotel. The next day we were due to see a pig farm but that was too much. We parted rather stiffly. It was back to the drawing board.

Four

踏破鐵鞋無覓處，得來全不費工夫

*We Tramped and Tramped Until Our Iron Shoes Were Broken
and Then, Without Looking, We Found What We Sought*

*The Water Margin:
Unattributed Ming Dynasty Novel*

After six months of searching in China but still getting
nowhere with the investors in Hong Kong, I felt that we
were spinning our wheels. I was beginning to lose heart.
Then I had the chance introduction to Pat that was to
change the course of my life for the next ten years.

A month or so after our first meeting, I took Pat to meet
Ai Jian in Beijing. We found him in his dim little office,
poring over a confused mass of handwritten papers in the
fading sunlight of a wintry afternoon. He leapt to his feet as
we came in and fussed over some tea for a while. Once he
had settled down and Pat started on his introductions, I saw
that Ai, unusually for him, was in a state of great nervous
tension. His almost anguished concentration on Pat's every
word was so intense that it looked as if something inside
him might suddenly snap at any moment. He had im-

mediately sensed that this was no courtesy visit but a one-off opportunity that might be lost if he didn't grab at it with both hands.

I could understand Ai's desperation; when the ex-Red Guard and forced-peasant-turned-bureaucrat met this Wall Street banker, he already knew that the whole world had tilted in favour of America and its overwhelming financial power. Mao's China had never had enough money but after Deng there wasn't even a clear political creed to cling to, or a hero to worship; just the Great Chase of catching up with the West. Ai had sensed that this might be his one chance to get off the sidelines and out of the dismal backwater that the cadres had thrown him into. So, despite his nerves, the first meeting went well and he was in a state of great excitement after Pat had left.

It was understandable. Pat was in a league of his own. I had come across the odd career banker who had learnt the ropes in Hong Kong, but there was no one else who was remotely as convincing when it came to talking about financing China's growth. Pat would talk about raising the odd hundred million and consolidating whole industries in a manner that most of us might use to comment on the weather. This lack of pretentiousness only made his story more compelling. Years later, when recalling that first meeting, Ai had said, 'I had spent years hoping to find a chance to do something big. Searching and searching – and then, suddenly, it was as if a film star had walked into my life!'

Pat was an enormous personality. His blue eyes, swept-back hair and J.P. Morgan nose gave him a presence that soon dominated any conversation. He was the archetypal Wall Street adventurer, full of the financial bravado of the 1980s when Wall Street pushed deal-size to the limit and reputations were made or lost purely on how far one dared to go. He even came packaged up with the pink silk handkerchiefs and blue pinstripe, an ear-splitting laugh and an insatiable appetite for oysters, champagne and Cuban cigars. Late into the evenings, he would sit around after dinner in clouds of smoke, with wineglasses strewn about the table, bantering and howling with laughter, all the time fiddling with the enormous red rubies on his gold cuff links. He knew how to have a good time, that was for sure, and preferred an audience to a good night's sleep. But it wasn't just a carefully cultivated image; this was the real thing. An American icon: the steelworker's son risen from the bottom rung to the top of the ladder through his wits and force of personality, with plenty of guts and hard work thrown in. By the time that we met him, Pat had become a man with a mission, a pioneer on a single-minded quest to create a machine – a machine for bringing money from Wall Street to Asia. And like me, but for a thousand different reasons, his focus was China.

At first I was puzzled. How had this man summoned the courage to uproot himself from everything he knew? Why had he left the security of the top rung on Wall Street, with all the comforts of a high position, to attempt another and much more hazardous ascent in a totally alien environment? He had certainly aroused my curiosity; and he had my admiration. I could see the drive and determination, the tremendous optimism and thirst for adventure. But it seemed that the trappings of Wall Street had not been enough. I knew that Pat had money; I guessed that what he wanted next was fame.

Pat had told Ai to work the phones. 'I want to see every project you can find,' he said. 'We've got to think big on this one. There are whole industries out there that need a ton of money and we've got to get there first. In a few months, the whole of Wall Street's gonna be crawling all over this place, so I want power stations, toll roads, phone systems, steel, all of that kind of stuff, anything that's big, and I want it now.' With that he got on a plane back to the States, and told us he'd be back in two weeks.

While he was away, Ai called every ministry that he could think of. Although China had started reforming its system of central planning, back in the early 1990s most of the economy was still controlled by the ministries in Beijing. The Government had a much greater role in running industries than was the case in any Western country at that time, so it was the right place for us to start. Ai had such a brass neck that he sat for days in his dingy office, cold-calling government officials all over Beijing, pestering them for meetings. By the time Pat came back, Ai had arranged to see officials everywhere: iron and steel, telecommunications, paper, electronics, chemicals, rubber, building materials, float glass, cement, light industry, power generation, even aircraft maintenance.

Ai managed to dig out a black Mercedes from somewhere to ferry us around the ministries. 'It gives us more face and that matters here,' he said as we left the hotel on the first day wondering what to expect. As the days rolled on, each visit seemed to merge into the next. As we sat in the traffic in the Beijing spring sunshine, moving from one ministry to another, I mused to myself that it was amazing that government departments existed at all for half of these industries. The bureaucratic waste was absurd; a whole ministry just to administer the production of paper and probably a major consumer at the same time. Most of them have since been abolished.

The ministries and the officials we met with all seemed

the same. For days on end, we tramped around Beijing, turning down some leafy side street somewhere in the centre of town through a set of gates with vertical white signs hanging on either side. The columns of Chinese characters showed the work units inside: black characters for Government offices, red for the Party. Then up some concrete steps into an enormous draughty hallway with high ceilings, creaky wooden floors and spittoons outside the doorways. At the end of some fusty corridor with peeling paintwork we'd invariably find a meeting room with rows of brown sofas draped with antimacassars and a table in the middle with a bowl of oranges, each wrapped up in crinkly cellophone. It was the same everywhere we went. Drab colours, the smell of dust and old floor polish, high ceilings, the bowls of fruit, green plastic thermos flasks, wooden-framed windows that didn't fit properly and the same old frosted-glass lampshades in the shape of an Olympic torch, just like the ones in the Land Bureau in Shanghai. And at every meeting the opening line from the officials on the other side was the same: '*Xingku la! Chi dian'r shuiguo*. You must be tired after your journey. Do have some fruit!'

The force of Pat's message to the ministries seemed undulled by Ai's translation; it was well received. He told the officials that investors believed that China was set for record growth and would need unprecedented amounts of capital. The only place that could come up with that kind of money was Wall Street and, with his decades of experience in investment banking and his willingness to come to China, he was the man to get it. Whoever got this money first in China would far outgrow their domestic competitors so we should grab the chance together.

Pat's powerful dynamism, his self-confidence and undeflectable optimism all came across clearly in his manner and gestures and the officials liked what they saw. As he spoke, he seemed to work himself into the story, growing with it, almost as if by the strength of his own feelings he had set about convincing himself as well as those who were listening. He seemed to have a knack of explaining overwhelmingly complex situations by reducing them to a simple set of economic forces. He could explain trends in whole industries in a couple of sentences that seemed so simple that we were all left wondering how we could have missed something so obvious in the first place.

As I sat absorbed in those meetings in the Chinese ministries, I had my first clue of how simple the world might seem, viewed from those towers on Wall Street. From there, everything seemed so straightforward, just another enormous case study like they do at business school. It was the simplicity that made it all so convincing. On Wall Street, everything came down to relative power: eat or be eaten, buy or be bought. And the key to survival was capital. Without capital, businesses die. The winner in the endless struggle for capital was the one who got biggest first, the one who dominated a market or managed to get to the stock market before the others. It all came down to capital; and to get it, you needed to speak the language of Wall Street. At this, Pat was the master. He took the whole of China and reduced it to a couple of growth trends so powerful that they would transform the whole country into an economic superpower within a decade. The officials loved what they heard; Pat thought that investors back home would feel just the same.

We were almost always invited back by the officials for follow-on meetings with their bosses, and we steadily worked our way up the hierarchy. Pat's message was so compelling that it seemed at the time that we hadn't needed the inside connections, the Chinese *guanxi*, that most foreigners thought underpinned Chinese business. In about six weeks, we were meeting with deputy ministers for the industries that we had targeted.

Over the weeks, as we pieced together the story we got from each visit, reassembling our scribbled notes back in Ai's tiny office, an overall picture of China's economy seemed to come slowly into focus. There were some industries, like telecommunications or power generation, that were so basic that it was probably a safe bet that they'd grow quickly. But often, in those areas, the government restricted foreign investment, so we couldn't get in. Then there were other areas that looked much more tricky, like consumer goods where local tastes and brands were almost impossible to understand. How could we ever contribute to a marketing campaign for cans of 'prickly hawthorn juice', for example? Or come up with a best-selling brand name like 'Golden Bean' for upmarket leather handbags? No, consumer goods were clearly too difficult.

But some industries did seem to make more sense, like the automotive industry. With the economy expanding, it seemed like a safe bet that there would be more and more trucks and buses and cars needed to move people and goods around the country. One of the ministries we visited had been spun out of the vast Chinese military complex some years earlier. They were busily converting their factories from the manufacture of military products to civilian use. Many of them were making simple parts for China's big truck-makers. It sounded as though it might be an interesting area so we arranged to take a look.

Over the next three months, we were on the road continuously, visiting almost every part of China. We started in the south-west, in Sichuan, accompanied by two officials from this Ministry. Later we moved on to the central regions of China, Hunan and Hubei, ending up in the frozen oilfields in the extreme north-east near the Russian border by Qiqiha'r.

The first trip started in the south-west in Chongqing, China's largest city. Together with the surrounding counties, Chongqing has a population of nearly thirty million. I could scarcely imagine it: this vast city hidden right in the depths of China, little known outside, with a population bigger than that of many countries. As we came into town from the airport on that first trip, I noticed that, unusually for China, there were few bicycles in the streets. This vast city sits in a steep-sided valley at the confluence of two mighty rivers, the Jialing and the Yangtse. The winding stone-flagged streets there are much too steep for riding. The density of people was staggering: millions and millions swirling in the roadways, passing through from the surrounding countryside, all in faded blue overalls and with piles of baggage, blocking the gates at the station, crammed into buses, milling about on the pavements. Even late at night, around the quayside, at the point where the two rivers meet, wave upon wave of porters in identical blue overalls struggled up the steep-sided hills, carrying heavy loads on the end of bamboo poles, staggering up the stone steps towards the city centre. Early next morning, I noticed that the natural foggy, damp climate in Sichuan combined with the smoke from the hundreds of factories in the hills around the city to create spectacular colours at sunrise. But by mid-morning, the air was almost opaque and the taste of diesel fumes was never out of my mouth.

Hemmed in by the two rivers, until recently Chongqing only had two bridges strung high across the waters. The traffic congestion at these bottlenecks was quite unbelievable. On bad days, it could take three hours to drive a couple of miles across the city; it was much quicker to walk. In the late 1990s a third bridge was built but it collapsed shortly after it was opened, sending forty people down to a watery death. Several officials were arrested and at least one was executed afterwards. It was one of China's recurrent corruption cases, which all seem so drearily familiar; another contractor using sub-standard materials to save money and officials turning a blind eye in return for bribes.

We soon set into a routine that spring, travelling hundreds of miles a day in our small bus, marvelling at the scale of the countryside around us. Sichuan is a vast and fertile province and, towards the west, it rises up into the foothills of Tibet. It was a towering landscape and many of the factories that we visited were tucked away in narrow gullies near the mountain passes, hidden from the densely populated valleys far below. As the bus laboured up the hillsides, I rested my head against the window and stared down over countless steps of rice terracing down to the valley floors. I could see a distant coloured patchwork of fields far below: squares of bright yellow rape set amongst the emerald shades of the first shoots of rice. Higher up, in among the withered trees and the damp mists, there were little groups of houses made from rammed earth and with stooping eves and thatched fences at the front. Groups of scruffy schoolchildren ran out and chased after the bus, shouting as we passed through the tiny villages. Back down in the valleys, the narrow roads and stone bridges were often blocked by great jostling flocks of ducks running towards the streams while all around, visible only in the distance, the peasants toiled in the fields, squelching barefoot in the thick fertile mud.

In the following weeks, we visited about twenty factories in Sichuan alone. It was exhausting work. Every day we rose at six, complained that there was no hot water, went down to a breakfast of fried dough sticks and hot water-buffalo milk and were on our way by seven. Then it was three or four hours on the bus to the next factory where Pat would go through the pitch, with Ai translating. We'd do a quick tour of the factory, interview the management and then pause for lunch. Unfortunately, we were often the first foreigners ever to have visited the factory so it was 'party time' for the locals. Lunches normally involved fifteen or more courses and at least a crate of beer. Then it was back on the bus – with a thick head – for another three hours and the next factory tour. The evenings normally ended at one or two in the morning in the upstairs room of some awful karaoke bar with cracked mirrors and faded Christmas tree decorations sellotaped to the walls. I often had a splitting headache and a sore throat from the clouds of cigarette smoke. And all that with nothing else to look forward to except the alarm at six and no hot water in the next hotel.

Most of the factories that we saw were vast, more like towns than manufacturing plants, with populations of many thousands hidden behind high walls and gateways with their own hospitals, kindergartens, cinemas and shops. The size of these facilities was startling enough, but it was the choice of location that struck me most. The factories were in the most incredibly remote locations, far from the cities, out at the edge of the world, hidden right up in the highest mountain passes. Several times we drove for an entire afternoon up a dirt road through steep-sided ravines to find a vast factory at the head of the valley, churning out red smoke and dirty, foaming water. In one particular place, called Tianxing, the factory with its three thousand five hundred souls was set in a valley so narrow that there was direct sunlight for only a few hours a day. I remember the translator at the factory attaching himself to us with a desperate ardour. He literally ran to the bus as we stepped down. We were the first foreigners ever to come to the factory and he had almost never heard English spoken by a native speaker. With the valley sides so steep and so high, there was no chance even of listening to radio broadcasts so he clung limpet-like to me right through the factory tour.

I found seeing so many people marooned in these artificial encampments up in the hills troubling, even a little frightening. There was something grotesque about them being stranded up in these godforsaken places. It made me feel nervous, jumpy, and almost a little guilty when we left the factory. Why were they there? These heavy industrial plants, with their old buildings, the broken windows and piles of rusting machinery, the chimneys and the heaps of coal next to the boilers were all set in scenes of the most spectacular natural beauty.

During lunch at the third factory – a gearbox plant, I think – I cautiously asked our host how he had ended up in the mountains. The factory director was away so a Mr Che, the chief engineer, had shown us around. He was a real rough diamond, quite unfazed by the sight of these two foreigners in suits and ties walking gingerly between the heaps of raw castings and the rows of ancient machining centres in his battered workshops. After the tour, he took us for lunch and sat at the huge round table in the workers' canteen, a flat cap on his head and an oily measuring gauge sticking from the pocket of his factory jacket. As soon as we sat down, about a dozen different dishes arrived. Sichuan food is my favourite: fiery sauces and pungent flavours, ideally washed down with a couple of crates of the local beer that comes in big green bottles.

After the small talk, during which I asked Mr Che whether he'd been abroad and he said there wasn't any point because the food was so bad, I asked him about the factory's location. I figured I'd probably get a straight answer from him, but at first he wouldn't be drawn. The beer flowed and the atmosphere relaxed slightly, so I had another go. He sighed, took off his cap, placed it on the table and, after a few moments staring into the middle distance, said, 'It won't make any sense to you, of course. You foreigners, you're not clear about our China. I was in Changsha, but our work unit moved to the mountain valleys. Now it all needs to be changed, of course. But back then, it was just Mao's Third Front.'

'Third Front?'

'Don't you know? The third line. The third line of national defence,' he said. 'After Liberation, in the 1950s, Russia was our Big Brother. After so many years of civil war and the fight against the Japanese, Russia helped us set up our New China. They sent us hundreds and hundreds of advisers, and all the designs and materials to build factories all over the country.'

Mr Che sighed and, after pausing for a moment, took another long silent draught of beer.

'But after Stalin died, Mao and those new Soviet leaders, they just couldn't get on. Mao Zedong said Khrushchev wasn't a good communist. All that "revisionism" – no one felt surprised when they rose up in a fight.'

His mood suddenly changed and he grinned, 'You know, I've heard it said that one time, when Khrushchev came to China, Mao forced him into his swimming pool. Mao knew Khrushchev couldn't swim, of course. Made him look a fool and lose face in front of all those officials, floating around in a rubber ring!'

Mr Che went on to explain that the relationship became worse and worse until, one day, Khrushchev lost patience and recalled all the Russian advisers.

'You think about it,' Mr Che said. 'Thousands of 'em, all gone in one day. Bridges and dams and power stations and tractor plants all half-built right across China and the Russians just patted their arses and went off home. All home in a week. The drawings and blueprints all taken with them. We were really at sevens and eights, a whole mass of confusion.'

'Right,' I said, wondering why Chinese always went a step further than English, even with an expression to describe utter chaos.

Mr Che went on and told me that by the mid-1960s Mao thought that things had got so bad that there would be war, so he ordered all the military factories to move out of the towns and the coastal areas and go up into the hills. In the next few years, hundreds of factories were all relocated into the steep-sided valleys in the remote hills out of sight of the bombers.

One of the officials from Beijing joined in. 'Yes, it seemed to make sense in those days. We had such a low base to build from. After Liberation, there was such a strong spirit, it felt like we were all together. So all the factories moved up into the hills. We were all willing to go to help defend the country. But now there are sixteen million people hidden up in these mountain valleys and no one knows what to do.'

'Sixteen million! Is that really true?'

'True. But now, of course, they want to try to move us back,' said Che.

'Move back? Why?'

'Well, now, you see, all that worry of war, it's all in the past. The Central Government spends on construction these days, not on the military. So they came up with a new policy called "change military to civilian". They want us to start making other stuff – you know, motorcycles, tractors, car parts, that kind of thing. They don't have the resources to support so many military factories any more. But it's all the same; in every campaign the slogans are many, but the money is short.'

Mr Che explained that the money from Beijing just dried up and many factories were stranded without orders. 'Some of them – the smart ones, that is – managed to start making civilian products using the machinery they had in the mountains. If you can make parts for a tank, it doesn't take much to change to manufacturing parts for trucks or buses.' So that was what happened.

'Some of them were terrible failures, of course. Funny, really; the ones that were best at getting money from the ministry, they're really in trouble now. They got all that really specialist equipment. We all wanted it then, but now it's useless. All that money gone to waste. The good ones,' he went on, 'the ones that changed, well now, the government wants to move them all back down the valleys. You can't run a factory up here; can't ever get anything done. But the locals, they don't want us to move out. Once we've gone, who's going to buy their vegetables? With the factory gone, they'll not get through the days so easily.'

It seemed as if this second move was causing as much heartbreak as the first. The factory workers had been in the hills for so long that many had married locals. Now there was to be a second break-up that would tear apart families and loved ones once more. I heard later that, despite severe punishments, in some places the peasants were so desperate that they tried to sabotage the move by cutting the electricity lines and telephone cables. I remember once using the phone up in the hills and the line suddenly went dead: not even a click, just total silence.

It wasn't surprising that after a month we were exhausted, bad-tempered and in need of a good workout. More to the point, despite travelling for thousands of miles, bouncing around in the back of a bus, we hadn't found a single factory that made the remotest sense for investment. We had been presented with scenes of complete anarchy at most of them: huge workshops with vats of boiling metal and men wearing cloth shoes pouring it into moulds on the floor; groups of women squatting down on their hunkers, with rusty old files gnawing away on vast heaps of aluminium castings; accountants' offices piled high with shoe-boxes stuffed full of wafer-thin paper covered in indecipherable characters. Even if we spent months getting to the bottom of what was going on, I could see that it would take millions of dollars to restore these rotting warehouses and heaps of broken machinery.

But Pat remained optimistic. The big picture still made sense to him and he was determined to find a way to invest. He was convinced that we were at the start of the next new investment wave and he wasn't going to be put off. This was a unique opportunity and Pat, the perpetual optimist, even managed to turn the remote locations into a positive. 'Just think,' he said, 'if we can get the money, we'll transform these factories. Wages will go up and create demand for a whole range of new products. And we'll be sitting there with a captive market. There's thousands of people stuck up there with nothing to do. We can bring in restaurants, shopping malls, gaming halls, the lot. There'll be a huge demand for entertainment and once the market reaches the right size, we can try for a McDonald's franchise. If we've got twenty factories, that's a huge market already, maybe fifty thousand people right on the doorstep with nowhere to go. So we can set up transportation companies to take them on trips down the valley, and they'll need gas stations, repair shops, maybe even banks. The key's to get exclusive rights before someone else muscles in. We can do that now because they need capital and we can get it. And people are going to want cable TV. We'll be plugged in to the right officials when the licences come up so that we'll be the ones to supply it. Kleaver made a fortune on cable TV in the States. And all this will affect the value of property. If we buy up some of the key sites in the factories now, who knows what they'll be worth when we get the place really humming?'

But the real difficulty with all of those factories was that we never actually felt we knew what was going on. Were they really making motorcycle parts or were they still involved in the old weapons programme? I thought that getting money to help these factories change from military to civilian products was something that was thoroughly worthwhile, and not just in financial terms. But could we be absolutely certain how the money would be used? My nagging doubts were removed on the third or fourth visit to the gearbox factory. The subject of the old weapons programme had come up again at lunch and the managers had been cheerfully evasive.

An hour later, we were standing in the small square outside the office block, just about to get on to the bus. Suddenly there was a colossal explosion from behind a row of sheds at the back of the factory. There was no possiblity of having missed it, but the conversation continued uninterrupted as if nothing had happened. But I had seen the briefest lapse in Mr Che's genial expression. As we drove off on the bus, Ai Jian looked at me and said, 'You know, even Sunzi's *Art of War* says that sometimes the best strategy is just to run away!'

Failure in the hills, however, did nothing to dampen our enthusiasm. Although none of the individual factories we'd seen up in the mountains were viable for investment, the picture of the industry as a whole was encouraging. A consistent story of growth came out of the many discussions we had with the different factory directors. So we persisted and changed our emphasis towards the larger towns; we found that the factories there were more promising. The first real signs that we were on the right track came when Ai arranged a trip to Changchun in the north-east where China's largest truck factory had just started a project to make passenger cars.

First Auto Works had been set up jointly with the Russians in the mid-1950s up in Changchun in the north-east of China. The city grew with the factory and much of the architecture still retains a strong Stalinist influence, particularly the government buildings and the huge solid hotels, with their endless corridors, high ceilings, dusty chandeliers and heavy double doors that open in to enormous, draughty banqueting halls. I had taken a trip up to Changchun when I was at the university in Beijing, but that trip had been in the summer and there had been a gentle breeze in the park at the centre of town. The children splashing about on the boats in the middle of the lake had reminded me of Hyde Park years before. There had been a relaxed feel to the tree-lined streets, almost a holiday mood, with customers at the lively restaurants spilling out on to the pavements. But, when Pat, Ai and I went on that first trip northwards, it was still cold with temperatures twenty below and the familiar icy blast howling in from Mongolia.

A couple of officials met us at the airport. They had been sent by the Changchun Government to escort us around the factories and they went through the itinerary as we drove into town.

The first visit was to First Auto Works, which sits in a suburb some way out from the centre. Just like the factories in the hills, it was vast and spread over several square miles with dormitories, hospitals, kindergartens, even cinemas hiding behind the high walls that encircled the compound. The massive gates, with the guards standing to attention on little white platforms and the familiar vertical signs strung up on either side led onto a broad avenue. Inside the gates, we found a perfect image of the decaying rust-belt factory. On either side of the broad street there were rows of shattered warehouses, along with the familiar sight of smashed windows, heaps of coal, workers in oily blue overalls wandering about on bicycles, and pipework with torn lagging strung up over the roads. The skyline ahead was dominated by a huge square boiler house, with black-ened brickwork. On top, four vast chimneys, covered with fins and wrought-iron ornamentation, periodically dis-gorged vast clouds of black smoke out of iron chimney pots that looked like fantastic spiky crowns at the top.

At that time, the factory only had two products. They had both been designed in Russia in the 1930s and had been transferred into China before Mao had had his fight with Khrushchev. The first was an ancient truck with a bulbous nose, a split windscreen and great round wheel arches. It had been introduced into China shortly after the founding of the People's Republic, so it was called the 'Liberation Truck'. The other was a vast upright limo called the 'Red Flag', which was used to ferry around government officials who sat on lumpy back seats, hidden from public view by thick brown curtains draped in the windows at the back. The trucks were always dark green; the limos were always black.

When we visited the assembly lines in the brick factory buildings we started to have a sense that we might be homing in on something big. In contrast to the factories up in the hills, with their scores of idle workers and offices crammed with people slurping tea out of big jam-jars behind well-thumbed copies of the *People's Daily*, here all was activity. Workers in blue overalls climbed all over the half-finished trucks as they moved along the production line. Engines and gearboxes came down on chains through the ceilings and were bolted onto the chassis. Arc welders flashed as the cabs were attached to the front. At the end of the line, several hundred yards ahead, young girls with blue caps and pigtails drove the fully assembled trucks out of the factory for testing.

But even this was nothing in comparison to the new car plant being built down the road together with the Germans. It was colossal; about a mile long. Although it was only half-built at the time, it was already impressive. The assembly lines were being set up; there were automatic welding machines and electronic sensors everywhere and, at the side, workers tore open huge wooden crates with more equipment shipped in from Germany. They were obviously gearing up to make thousands and thousands of passenger cars; the investment must have been enormous.

That afternoon, we saw several components factories in

the town. They made simple parts – electrical connectors, switches and the like – but the one that caught my interest was a factory that made ignition coils. It was run by a Madame Tan who was only in her late-thirties. She seemed knowledgeable about her business and she had just won the contract to supply ignition coils to the huge factory that we had seen in the morning. With demand about to go through the roof, she was looking for some money for expansion. As we left through the factory gates, I told her that I'd come back for another look.

On the way back, the officials told us that we had been invited to dinner at six by the Mayor of Changchun. That was a good sign: Mayor Huang was the top official in the Municipal Government. With support from him, I felt sure that we'd soon be in business.

We met the Mayor in the hotel that evening. Pat gave a brief description of the day's visits, sitting rather stiffly on the familiar old sofas in a drafty meeting room, and told Mayor Huang that he'd been impressed with the factories that we'd seen. The Mayor was pleased; he was one of the younger generation of leaders promoted after Deng's Southern Tour. He seemed smart and came back with quick comments, speaking with animation about how he hoped to bring foreign investment into Changchun. He had only been in Changchun for six months or so, and the transfer from Yangzhou, at the mouth of the Yangtse in the gentler climate near Shanghai, must have been a shock. Nevertheless, the Mayor seemed to have found his feet quickly. He appeared to be firmly in charge and determined to improve the city.

Mayor Huang was totally different from the plodding cadres we had been more used to in Beijing, and he had long abandoned the traditional Mao jacket for a snappy

Western suit and tie. I liked him. He was alert, interested and supportive of what we were trying to do. He was in his early forties: a shortish man with neat features, thick hair, sparkling eyes and teeth whose whiteness was accentuated by the clean, slightly tanned look of the southern Chinese. As he listened intently to Pat's explanation of the recent excitement about China in the financial markets, I sensed that he was wondering how he could get his hands on his share of the spoils.

Soon it was time for dinner, so we trooped out of the meeting room, through cavernous hallways with thick dusty carpets and followed the Mayor into a private room. There was a huge circular dinner table with a glass turntable in the middle placed at the centre of the room under an enormous chandelier.

'Qing zuo,' said the Mayor, 'Please sit,' as he gestured towards his right.

I looked at the expanse of white tablecloth in front of me, the perfectly aligned plates and the flowers and elaborately carved vegetables on the circular glass stand in the centre. I leaned back in my chair and breathed in slowly. 'This', I thought resignedly, 'promises to be an epic.'

The food eaten in ordinary homes, factory canteens and local restaurants in China is tasty, diverse and healthy. Within reason, you can stuff as much down as you like without getting fat. It bears no resemblance at all to some of the glutinous, oily Chinese food served up in restaurants in Britain. But banquet food is quite another matter. The whole purpose is to impress. Chefs compete to create the most elaborate and obscure dishes. Excess, both in the amount and the nature of the food, is meant to flatter the guests. I thought back to the factories in the hills and hankered after some simple, spicy Sichuan dishes, but unfortunately my first guess had been right: the dinner we had that evening with the Mayor of Changchun was an absolute classic.

It started off, as it always does, with a fight about the seating arrangements. At these events there is a strict hierarchical order to the places at the table and there is always a prolonged argument amongst the middle-ranking Chinese officials about where they should sit, with plenty of jostling and pushing, each person protesting loudly that the others should take the more senior places. Once everyone had settled, during the small talk little glass cups appeared beside each guest's place and were silently filled with *baijiu* by waitresses who moved noiselessly through a concealed door in the panelling.

Baijiu looks like gin but it tastes much stronger. It is distilled from grain and sorghum and there are many famous brands of the drink in China. *Wuliang ye* or 'five-grain liquid' comes from Yibin in Sichuan, and *maotai*, the most famous in China, comes from Guizhou, further south. At the lower end of the market, there is *er guo tou* or 'the top of the second wok', which is distilled in Beijing. A really good bottle of *maotai* can cost the equivalent of several months' salary. *Baijiu* is always taken neat but, thankfully, in small doses. The idea is to knock it back in one go with a cry of '*Gan bei*', 'Dry the cup!' The problem is that drinking *baijiu* at a Chinese banquet is compulsory; it is slightly viscous, has a smell like exhaust fumes mixed with a trace of chocolate and seems both fiery and sickly at the same time. It burns the inside of your mouth and throat and leaves you with a sensation rather than a taste. There is an immediate feeling of heat and tingling that creeps up the back of the neck and radiates out all over the scalp. I already knew that these formal banquets entailed elaborate drinking rituals designed to get the guests hopelessly drunk, so I braced myself for the deluge.

Baijiu loosens tongues almost immediately although I've never met anybody, even at the heights of alcoholic derangement, prepared to admit that they actually liked the taste. After drinking it, most people screw up their faces in an involuntary expression of pain and some even yell out. But there were plenty of people who liked the sensation and the atmosphere that a couple of bottles of *baijiu* produced at a dinner. It created the best parties and the worst hangovers imaginable and the smell seemed to seep out through my pores the following day. A German friend once summed up the experience perfectly. She said, in her perfect *Hochdeutsch*, that when her husband had been out drinking with his Chinese colleagues and had hit the *baijiu*, it was as if she had 'woken up the following morning next to an oily rag that had been soaked in diesel'.

The Mayor was obviously pleased that we had had a good day. He was anxious for foreign investment in Changchun. Although I knew that bringing substantial foreign investment to Changchun would be good for his career, I still felt that he was genuine in his desire to see the city develop and improve the lives of the people there. So the *baijiu* flowed freely and the atmosphere relaxed. Nevertheless, as the waitresses started bringing in the plates, I eyed the food with deep suspicion.

The starters were served cold. First, there was a dish of duck webs in a thick yellow sauce. It turned out to be the strongest mustard that I had ever tasted. It sent a searing pain up the back of my nose and brought tears to my eyes. Next came 'husband and wife' lung slices. Mayor Huang roared with laughter as it was translated and poured some more *baijiu*. He told us that it was a Sichuan speciality:

cow's lung soaked in chilli sauce. The lungs were followed by goose stomachs, a couple of dishes of pickled vegetables, a plate of steamed lotus root and a chicken that looked as if it had been attacked by a madman with a machete: its bones stuck out at all angles. Then onwards to the hot dishes.

It seemed as if the cooks had entered a contest to serve up the strangest parts of animals in the weirdest combinations. The pile of stacked plates grew on the table in front of us: fish lips with celery, monkey-head mushrooms, goats' feet tendons in wheat noodles, ox's forehead, roasted razor-blade fish and finally a tortoise in a casserole. There was one dish that looked like a bowl of ribbon pasta served up plain and without the sauce, but it was crunchy and almost tasteless. It couldn't be pasta, so I asked what it was. 'A Shandong speciality,' said the Mayor. 'Steamed rabbits' ears.'

Halfway through the main dishes, the conversation, by then well-oiled with *baijiu*, was flowing freely. Mayor Huang was telling us about Changchun's ambitions to be China's Hollywood. There were several large film studios in the town and he wanted to set up an international film festival. The Mayor said that obviously they'd never be able to compete with Hollywood.

'Your America is so much more developed than our China,' he said. But Pat replied that, from everything he had seen, it looked like China was catching up fast.

'You see, China's exactly like the States was in the late 1800s,' said Pat.

This remark was greeted with a faint smile from the Mayor and a polite gesture with his chopsticks towards a plate of duck's tongues.

Pat went on. 'Yeah, thanks. Y'see, China's standing right on the verge of a huge expansion, just like the States in the late 1800s. Everything changed in the thirty years from about 1870 to 1900. The same's gonna happen here,' he enthused, 'but this time it'll be bigger 'n' quicker.'

Once this had been translated, it was obvious that the Mayor was warming up. Pat now had his full attention. How could any Chinese official fail to be flattered and excited by this comparison with the world's greatest economic superpower? The idea waxed in his mind. It was clearly time for another toast.

'Y'see, it's like this,' Pat went on. 'America and China are the only two countries in the world that are big enough to support big companies with just their own domestic market.' Another *gan bei*. 'That gives you economies of scale in your own market. No one else can match that. China's the last market on earth that has that potential. A billion-plus people out there working their asses off for a better life. Just like the States a hundred years ago!' With the slightest pause to gauge the reaction, Pat raised his glass and ended with a flourish, 'So, you see, we're really just the same!'

Another round of toasts, howls of laughter and invitations to have more tortoise. By this time, the table seemed to be creaking under the weight of stacked-up plates and the waitress arrived with another clay pot.

'Eels,' said the Mayor.

'Great!' we all replied.

'In the States, y'see, it all started with the railroads. But you know what, in China, it's gonna be auto!' he said, fixing the Mayor with a jubilant stare. 'Trucks, buses, cars, limos, tractors, the lot, millions of 'em – and that, Mr Mayor,' he said, 'is why we are here today.'

I could see, through rapidly thickening clouds of cigarette smoke, that Mayor Huang was starting to enjoy himself. But I was struggling. I had been taken on by two of the officials from the Investment Bureau who were alternately toasting me at every opportunity. I was beginning to feel that familiar queasiness rising up in my stomach, but I was forced into trying another Chinese cigarette whilst Pat worked his magic with the Mayor. Protestations that I didn't smoke were brushed aside as entirely irrelevant and another box of Red Pagoda Mountain, China's best, arrived on the table.

Pat was in the midst of convincing the Mayor that it had been a stroke of destiny that he had ended up in charge of industry in this northern city of Changchun. What might have seemed to the Mayor like an exile to the desolate northern rust belt could now be turned into a chance of glory. His was to be a role at the centre of an economic supernova that was about to be detonated by this Wall Street banker.

'All you have to do is give us a few good factories and we'll light the blue touchpaper. It's gonna be an economic explosion that'll go down in world history!'

It was all getting a little out of hand. Another round of toasts followed, with speeches, general agreement on how much Chinese and Americans all had in common and several more glasses of *baijiu*. Pat ploughed on.

'Back in the 1870s, there were thousands of small-scale businesses all over the States, "Mom 'n' Pop shops". But they couldn't survive. The smart guys built operations on a scale where the smaller ones couldn't compete, and then they just took 'em out.'

'Took them out?'

'Yep, crushed them or bought them up. They built markets right across the country. And the railroads were key to all that. If you couldn't shift goods around the country, you'd never grow a national market.'

'But in our China, the iron roads indeed have limits. With the tall blue-green mountains and the endless yellow plains, our China is vast and rather unsuitable for this new machinery.'

A sideways glance at the translator. 'What? Er, yeah, right,' Pat said recovering quickly. 'But anyway, here it's the *roads* that matter. Everywhere I've been, the government's building highways. Just imagine the thousands of trucks needed to move all this stuff around China. People like Vanderbilt, back in the last century, they just bought up all the small railroad companies in America and joined 'em together. Then you had a national railroad system that no one could rival. We can do that here with auto.'

More toasts.

'The railroads in the States, they needed steel, millions of tons of it. So then they started building huge steel plants. Pittsburgh was the centre of steel for years.'

A toast to Pittsburgh.

'Then Carnegie brought in new technology. By the end of the 1890s, the mills in Pittsburgh could produce a thousand of tons of steel a day with only a handful of workers.'

A toast to a thousand tons a day with only a handful of workers.

At this point there was a minor distraction from the story as a plate of black scorpions arrived. The Mayor explained that you eat them whole with a couple of pieces of shredded radish and popped in a few to show us. I said I thought they were poisonous but he said reassuringly, 'Not if they're cooked properly.'

'But the really interesting thing didn't happen until all these businesses, you know, the railroads and steel mills, got capital. That's where Junius Pierpont Morgan came in. J.P

66

Morgan, the biggest kick-ass financier in history. Morgan figured that if he bought up lots of different companies all in the same industry, forced 'em to work together rather than against each other, then he could take out the competition in the market. That way, one plus one equals three! Yeah! So his idea was to build up something big that dominates a market, and sell it on for more than he paid for each piece! Morgan did that with US Steel. After Carnegie sold out to him, Morgan just bought up all the competition. We can do that here.'

At this point, the soup arrived. Despite the fact that it looked like a bowl of lukewarm pond water with a few weeds floating about, it was good news since it signaled that we were nearing the end of the meal.

'So, Mr Mayor, Changchun's gonna become the Detroit of China. The assemblers are already here and what you need is components. We're gonna buy up factories, pump in a few hundred million and build the biggest components company in China.'

'The biggest components company in China!' The Mayor just loved it. 'Just like J.P. Morgan!'

He raised his glass. 'To the J.P. Morgan of China!'

More toasts, cheers, hoots of laughter and the grand finale arrived.

'Deer's whip!' said the Mayor.

A waitress had brought in a flat white oval dish and placed it centre stage. In the middle, chopped up neatly into sections and then meticulously reassembled, surrounded by carefully arranged pieces of broccoli and carrot and with just the faintest traces of steam rising up from the edges, was unmistakably an enormous penis.

'Deer's dick! Oh, Lord, how horrible!'

The Mayor, smiling broadly, leaned forward, picked up a

67

piece with his chopsticks and placed it on my plate. The tip, so it seemed, was the best part.

I don't quite remember how we got out, but I do remember the freezing air hitting me as we stumbled towards the cars. And I also remember noticing the steady and purposeful stride of the Mayor as he walked over to a waiting group of officials to discuss our itinerary for the next day. It left me with a vague suspicion that whilst our cups had been filled with *baijiu*, his might have contained just the mineral water that I had noticed earlier on the sideboard. But, as the cars drove off, I put my mind more to controlling the waves of nausea welling up in the pit of my stomach.

Five

三個臭皮匠,賽過一個諸葛亮

Three Vile Cobblers Can Beat the Wisest Sage

Rhyming peasant saying: literally, 'Three smelly cobblers (with their wits combined) can beat Zhu Geliang (the Master)'
– quoted famously by Mao Zedong in the 1950s

Over the coming months, after the hangover had cleared, Mayor Huang bent over backwards to help us invest in Changchun. Within the Municipal Government he set up a special office whose only purpose was to facilitate our investments. After the disappointments up in the mountains in Sichuan, the Mayor's enthusiastic support was a welcome change. So we decided to focus on Changchun and than gradually spread out to cover China's major cities: Tianjin, Wuhan, Shanghai and Beijing.

In the 1950s, the central planners had located the main truck factories in China's larger cities and, thirty years later, when the foreign passenger-car companies started to arrive in China, the Government encouraged them to go into partnership with the big truck businesses there. We thought that the component factories in those cities should have a bright future, given the huge new demand on their doorsteps. So we trawled round the government bureaux and investment offices in each of these cities, visited factories and gradually built up a picture of the overall industry. From these first trips, we found leads to other factories in more distant locations across China and patiently expanded the net.

During the late spring and the summer, we visited almost every part of China in our search for good factories. The contrasts between the different landscapes and local customs that we saw and the vast distances that we travelled were all so great that, if it hadn't been for the language, it would have been difficult to believe that they were in the same country. In Zhejiang and Jiangsu, the two provinces either side of the mouth of the Yangtse near Shanghai, we crossed vast areas of dreary flat-lands, where each town looked like the last with their monotonous rows of modern two-storeyed buildings covered in cheap white tiles. The water-table is high in the whole area and there are thousands of interconnected canals and lakes. The hulks of boats loaded with vast piles of sand or gravel passed along the canals in an endless, doleful procession, taking building materials to the next new factory town. Everywhere, the lakes were covered with bits of polystyrene and empty plastic bottles which I thought must have been rubbish dumped into the water. But I soon discovered that they were floats in the oyster beds. Jiangsu is the world's largest producer of freshwater pearls.

Further north, the Shandong peninsula juts out towards Korea between the Bay of Chihli and the Yellow Sea. The coast there becomes more rocky and mountainous. Inland, out from the dusty plains and the orchard groves, China's sacred mountain, Taishan, rises to the smoke-filled temples at its peak. Nearby, in Qufu, the ancient home of Confucius, the family's ancestral graveyard still sits in a woodland surrounded by high walls and filled with ancient knotty pines and grassy burial mounds. The inscriptions on the headstones stretch back seventy-eight generations.

We travelled to the various points of the compass: Guangdong in the south, Jilin in the north and Urumqi in the far west. The scale of the industrial zones, especially around Shenzhen in the south where Deng had planted his tree, were enough to strike fear into any foreign business-man. As we drove through the region, mile upon mile of multi-storey factory buildings flashed past the window, each one churning out clothing and cheap manufactured goods for export throughout the world. In the north, the conditions were at the opposite pole: the forgotten rust-belt cities, with their shattered factories, broken chimneys and vast crowds of people milling around in the streets with a lost look in their eyes.

By the end of the summer, we had visited more than a hundred factories all over China. We'd seen every type of business that I could imagine: huge iron foundries, steel-rolling mills in workshops a mile long, badly lit shacks near Shanghai with row after row of young women assembling tiny electrical motors. One thing was for sure; there were plenty of factories that needed investment and seemed poised for expansion as the foreign passenger-car compa-nies nudged China towards the next century. And more to the point, the factory directors wanted American investors.

Looking back on it, the frenetic pace and the tremendous extent of those travels, as we lurched across China from one grubby hotel to the next, now seem rather fanatical – even manic – unless they are set into the wider context of what was going on in the country as a whole. In the months following Deng's Southern Tour, whole swathes of the Communist Old Guard in Provincial Government offices across China had been swept aside and replaced with younger and more reform-minded cadres. These changes set off a chain of events which led to local officials all over China, especially along the coast, scrambling to set up new 'investment zones' and dispatching trade delegations across the seas in search of foreign partners. The economy expanded rapidly and in the first half of 1992 the Shanghai Stock Exchange rose more than tenfold. News of the paper millionaires in Shanghai who had started with nothing and earned fortunes by speculating on the stock markets spread across China. People all over the country fell into the grip of an investment fever and started buying shares, pushing up prices even further. On one day in August of that year, half a million people queued to buy shares in a newly listed company outside the Stock Exchange in Shenzhen. When the application forms ran out, rumours spread that officials had grabbed all the forms for themselves and their relatives. There was a riot which left cars overturned and windows smashed; it took the police several hours to bring it under control.

In many ways, the reaction inside China was to be expected. People were fed up with the austerity programme; it had lasted for nearly three years after Tiananmen and they wanted change. They immediately grabbed onto Deng's lead and quickly became caught up in the new mood. But the excitement in the domestic economy was nothing in comparison to the delirium sparked off outside China. Chief executives from all over the world stampeded into China in a cavalry charge waving chequebooks under the noses of their smiling but slightly bemused hosts. For a time, it looked as though many of them had abandoned conventional business logic in the search for the mythical 'billion-plus market' while money poured into the country. The investment frenzy soon gained a self-sustaining momentum that probably surprised even Deng, its hoary old instigator.

The real detonation, however, occurred in the financial markets. With the China investment frenzy at its height, in early 1993 an obscure Hong Kong-registered car company with assets on the mainland applied to list on the Stock Exchange. It wanted to raise about eight million dollars, but it received application monies for just under four billion! Encouraged by these wild successes, the Chinese Government authorized nine domestic Chinese companies to list in Hong Kong. The first one was Tsingtao, China's biggest beer company, and the share issue was massively oversubscribed. The Hong Kong stock market was in the ascendant; it went up 35 per cent in the first few months of 1993. Gradually, the news that 'something big' was happening in Hong Kong floated across the Pacific towards America.

In the third quarter of 1993, while we were completing our factory tours in China, the huge American institutional investors started moving into Hong Kong. They wanted to get in on the act and the 'money allocators' were in town, the hugely powerful analysts who advise the markets where to put their dollars. That was when Barton Biggs, one of the most influential voices on Wall Street, had made his famous remark about being 'maximum bullish' after a six-day banquet marathon up in the Middle Kingdom. In the months following his visit, the stock markets soared and investors scrambled over each other to grab whatever investment in China they could get hold of. At the end of the previous year, a small bus company called Jinbei had gone public in New York and raised millions of dollars; it was the first listing of a Chinese company on the New York Stock Exchange, but now investors wanted more. The only way to access more deal-flow was to invest in Hong Kong or, even better, in China itself. So it was in this heady atmosphere towards the end of 1993 that Pat went back to America to raise money.

Throughout the year, Pat had been warming up some Wall Street heavyweights. He said, 'I know it can be difficult to raise money on your own and we need someone with real firepower behind us.' Through some old contacts, Pat had been introduced to IHC, a huge money manager with offices in midtown New York. 'They're one of the best money managers around,' Pat had said. 'If we can get them on our side it'll make the whole process of raising money much easier.' He'd also been talking to one of the biggest New York stockbrokers and, although investing in factories in China hardly came within their normal sphere of business, they seemed interested as well. 'It'd be good to have a big broker behind us,' he said. 'It'll help when we go public in New York.'

IHC, the money manager, routinely raised hundreds of millions of dollars from the big corporate pension funds and other institutional investors in the States. There were also some individuals who invested with them, but you had to be rich; they weren't interested in anyone with less than fifty million. Pat wanted to persuade IHC to take a 'China Fund' to their investors. IHC's name would add credibility and they were always on the lookout for new and intriguing investment ideas for their clients. China was flavour of the month, so Pat was hopeful; if we could attract IHC's interest and get them to raise capital for us, we could then buy up the factories that we had found in China. 'If we can get IHC to take it to their clients, I think we'll raise enough money to keep us busy for a while,' he said.

Pat sparked enough interest for IHC to look at the idea seriously and in August the president of the company, Myron Rubel, had come to China together with Bob Smith from the brokerage firm. They flew to Hong Kong in IHC's jet, grumbling about having to 'go commercial' into China; at that time, the Chinese Government was not too keen on private planes whizzing around in its airspace.

The trip was a strain. I found Rubel a nightmare to deal with. Thin and wiry, with frizzy white hair, he was a hyperactive man who could never sit still. He was about fifty when I met him and he had only just become president of IHC. Managing sixty billion dollars was bound to entail a lot of pressure, but Rubel was the archetypal stress-junkie; an erratic eater, constantly fidgeting around, shaking his legs up and down on the balls of his feet under the table, taking out his diary, looking at it for a split second, putting it away and then taking it out again. He had a concentration span measured in a couple of picoseconds and seemed to have a hundred things all jumbled up in his head at any one time, things that seemed to fall out in no particular order. He'd fire off questions about exchange controls and half-way through the answer suddenly ask for statistics on the auto market that we'd already given him the previous day. He was exhausting company.

Cheerful, red-faced Bob Smith from the brokerage firm could not have been more different. He was far more rounded than Rubel in both personality and physique. He was a jovial man who would talk you to death if the chance arose. His breakfast meetings in America were legendary for lasting well past lunchtime; sometimes whole days were consumed in the process as one meal merged into the next. At first I suspected that his slightly absent-minded manner might have been a ploy to put you off guard; given his high position on Wall Street, it was not wholly convincing. However, after his secretary told me that she once found a bonus cheque for nearly a million bucks in the pocket of a suit jacket that had been hanging on the back of his door for months, I began to have my doubts.

I was only convinced that Smith's eccentric manner was genuine after I saw his office. It was famous throughout the brokerage and I was once taken in for a viewing by one of Smith's analysts who'd previously checked to make sure that Smith himself was out of town. I could hardly get through the double doors. Piled from floor to ceiling, on desks, under chairs, blocking the windows and stuffed into bookcases were thousands and thousands of documents: prospectuses, contracts, offering documents, long form reports and financial statements stacked in great tottering piles right up to the ceiling. A path had been trodden through the middle of these disorganized heaps and towers of paper across to the corner of a desk. The desk itself was piled three or four feet high with binders and magazines, but a small space, about a foot square, had been cleared on the corner where there was a battered plastic telephone next to a collection of bottles containing pills and vitamin tablets, and a pair of knackered old training shoes. Apparently, Smith sometimes locked himself in there for hours on end, bumbling down the phone and rummaging around, looking for his headache tablets. Most of the documents were years old; his secretary told me that some of them dated back to the 1970s but that whenever she tried to clear up he yelled at her. Bob Smith insisted that he knew where everything was but of course he could never find anything; we always made several extra copies for him, knowing that most would end up being tossed into the vortex.

I never really figured out what made Bob Smith tick, but one thing was for sure: his slightly shambling walk and amiable manners were the perfect antidote to Myron Rubel's hyperactive volatility, and he progressed sedately on his tour through China unperturbed by the whirlwind raging around him.

Before their trip, Ai Jian had fixed up meetings for Rubel and Smith with the ministries in Beijing. We had also arranged to take in the best factories in Beijing and Changchun but Rubel didn't want to see them.

'Nah, I've seen enough factories for one lifetime,' he said. 'If the guy wants our money, get him to come and see us.' So Ai Jian called around and the factory directors duly trooped in to see us. Fortunately Mayor Huang was in Beijing anyway, so that avoided the embarrassment of telling him that we weren't coming up to Changchun.

The meetings were stiff and uncomfortable; several were at ministerial level and kept to a set pattern. Although the rules at these types of meeting are less rigid than at a formal dinner, there is still an etiquette to dealing with high-level Chinese officials. When they are introduced to new acquaintances in a formal setting, the Chinese have an elaborate self-deprecating habit of talking themselves down. But the customary expressions of worthlessness from the host are expected to elicit strong protests from the guests who should respond with excessive compliments elaborating on the fame of their host, the lavishness of the surroundings or anything else appropriate that springs to mind. Of course, I knew that the shabby hallways and rusting pipework in the ministries were not exactly what Rubel and Smith were used to in their offices in New York. But my nerves were still frayed when the ministers made the standard opening apologies for the poor surroundings and they just nodded their heads in agreement.

I sat anxiously through the meetings, waiting at each pause for Rubel's next question. There is a strict hierarchy to the seating at meetings in China; the most important participants sit at the centre of the long meeting tables. Given the august company, Ai Jian and I had been consigned towards the opposite extremities, so I couldn't even influence his translation with the odd undercover whisper.

The meetings generally went well; Rubel asked his pointed questions and the Chinese gave their elliptical answers, but generally there seemed to have been some form of a meeting of minds. Towards the end of the trip the atmosphere grew gradually more relaxed and on the last day, just before Rubel and Smith left for the airport, we had lunch with the Mayor of Changchun. We had figured that it might be tempting fate to end up with a *baijiu* dinner. Ai Jian ordered the dishes so the meal was a relatively straight-forward affair, with the only excitement – minor, at that – caused by a plate of sea slugs. Rubel fired off questions from every angle as Smith fumbled with his chopsticks and Pat and I finished the beer until, just before we got up to leave, Rubel asked his last question.

'Well, Mr Mayor, we are very impressed with you but we've heard that officials in China move about a lot. So if you move to another city how do we know that your successor will follow the same policies?'

The answer came without the slightest blink.

'Well, Mr Rubel, *we* are impressed with *you* but we've

heard that executives in America move around a lot. So if you move to another company how do we know that your successor will pursue the same strategy?'

The Mayor had delivered his reply absolutely deadpan and held Rubel's gaze for a moment. Then, just as the tension was mounting, his face, with perfect timing, broke into a broad grin. To his credit Rubel laughed as loudly as the others but it had been a great put-down and probably a close call. I loved the self-confidence, the almost barefaced cheek of the new generation of Chinese officials. Here was a man landed with the responsibility for a deadbeat industrial city in northern China with all its poverty and unemployment and decay, up against a visitor from a distant land who controlled sixty billion dollars. It was pretty obvious who held all the cards but the Mayor never once let the mask slip; I admired his gall in taking them on eye-to-eye. He seemed able to meet them on their own level with the same mixture of brazen self-confidence and bluff. In another life, Mayor Huang would have thrived on Wall Street.

By the time that Rubel and Smith left China, they had seen enough to get them interested. Pat went back to the States late that August and went up to one of Rubel's holiday homes in Vermont together with Smith. They sat on the porch in the late summer sunshine. That night, Pat called me in China and told me, 'We got the deal!'

IHC had agreed to go out and raise a hundred million bucks for the Chinese auto industry.

With IHC behind him, Pat was on a roll. By October the documents were ready and he toured the States. He visited all of IHC's major clients and, after about six weeks, I got one of his regular calls in Beijing. 'So, how's it all going?'

Several minutes into the conversation, he said, 'Well, I've got eighty-five for you.'

'Eighty-five?'

'Yeah, eighty-five million. We got circles on eighty-five million of cash from investors. Should be up to a hundred and fifty by Christmas. You'd better be able to invest it!' And with his characteristic roar of laughter, Pat put the phone down.

Eighty-five million bucks. That seemed like a lot of money. Godammit, it *was* a lot of money! Bucket loads, in fact, especially in China. In those days, raising that kind of capital inside China itself was virtually impossible whereas in the States it had seemed almost routine. Gradually, I began to understand the power of the money machine in America. There, every day, multimillion commitments were made by small groups of people and were based on, maybe, a two-hour meeting and some macro-analysis of countries that they had never visited. It just depended what was in vogue at the time. In the late 1990s, it was dot.com. Back then, it was China.

Pat told me that during his tour of the States in early December, he had travelled up from New York to Stamford together with Rubel to talk to a large pension-fund investor. They went through their pitch and then went back to Manhattan, about an hour away on the train. When they got back to IHC, there was a message from the investor left on Rubel's desk. It read; 'Myron, you and Pat did a great job today. You got your fifteen million, Pam.' That was it! The same investor came up with another ten million a few months later.

Despite these surprises, it was the wealth of individual people in America rather than that of the institutions that really amazed me; I had no idea that such vast fortunes were

80

controlled by families or individuals who had either made or inherited money. During Pat's first money-raising tour, IHC had arranged for him to attend a breakfast meeting with a group of wealthy individuals in Houston. Although the smallest permitted investment was a million dollars, there were seven people at the breakfast all fumbling around with their toast and marmalade, dropping their napkins and shouting for more coffee and 'grits' as Pat gave his presentation. When he had finished, one of them asked two questions. Pat couldn't answer the first as it was about some obscure tax loophole, but the next one was easy.

'How many factories have you personally visited in China?'

Pat launched into a set-piece exposition about how we had visited a hundred factories in a hundred days on our Long March across China. It must have been convincing. A few days later, on the basis of that hour-long breakfast meeting and two questions – one of which hadn't even been answered – the investor signed up to invest five million dollars of his personal money and wired it across a few weeks later.

I found it difficult to pull the people at Pat's 'Breakfast in America' and the workers up in the Chinese hills into the same world-view. It seemed as if the factories, where raising a hundred thousand dollars could take years of effort, were on a different planet. Curiously, that was something that excited me. I found the real prospect of bridging that colossal cultural and financial gap hugely inspiring; we were about to embark on an adventure, that was for sure, but it was one that might bring hope to those forgotten communities that had no way to access the resources that they needed to survive. Here was a unique opportunity, the chance to bring capital into China on a scale that could rejuvenate businesses that employed thousands; and in a scheme where both sides could win.

Things fell into place quickly afterwards. Once the 'high-net-worth-individuals' – as really rich people in America were known – had signed up for their eighty-five million, the big institutional investors moved in. Early in the New Year, it looked as though we would raise two hundred million dollars. But Rubel back in New York was nervous. 'OK, I know you've seen all these factories, but how do we know you'll actually be able to invest all this money? Two hundred is a lot for the first pull.' Eventually, he cut back the commitments and we accepted a hundred and fifty-eight million dollars. Pat didn't like it. He wanted to get as big as possible at the first strike, but he relented and at the end of February the contracts were signed and the first instalment squirted into our bank account. I still couldn't quite believe it. The first money-raising round had exceeded my most optimistic expectations; once the celebrations had died down, we turned our minds seriously to investing it. It looked as if all the hopes were about to change into reality.

With a hundred and fifty million bucks at out disposal, it wasn't difficult to make waves throughout the whole industry. Although we had actually spent many months patiently researching China, building up the big picture and visiting factories across the nation, to the outside world it seemed as if we had suddenly burst onto the headlines from absolutely nowhere. We were all over the press. The *Asian Wall Street Journal* ran a whole page on us. The article, which was entitled 'The Insiders versus the Outsiders', compared our chances with another group of Hong Kong investment managers who had raised ninety million for one of the big Beijing-based industrial groups. We were the 'outsiders' from Wall Street up against the 'insiders' from Hong Kong who claimed to have all the right relationships in the inner chambers up in Beijing. The article was inconclusive but said that the 'outsiders' had a more coherent investment strategy; it might pay off in the long run if 'the outsiders' could navigate their way through the tangled relationships up in China and find the right businesses to buy.

With all that money burning a hole in our pockets, the pressure was on to invest so I was relieved when I managed to persuade an old colleague from England to come out to China and help us figure out what to do. Michael and I had worked together at Arthur Andersen before he left to join a private equity house in London and I knew that he had much more experience with the nuts and bolts of investing than I had. Together, we hired a team of eight bright young Chinese graduates who had studied English or finance at one of China's top universities. They helped us churn through the reams of figures we'd collected and figure out which were the best factories to invest in. I thought that we had the right team in place, but Rubel became more and more nervous as the weeks passed. He wanted to see some action and the telephonic board meetings between China and the States started to become tetchy.

We had agreed to focus on Changchun to start. We had to get something done quickly before Rubel exploded. The Mayor was on our side and the factories up there were smaller than many in the other big cities, so we felt that it was the right place for us to begin. The Director of Mayor Huang's special government office, Mr Jiang, accompanied us to each of the factories and entertained us in the evenings. But the visits were tough going and we made slow progress. The businesses were so confusing: sometimes it was even difficult to figure out exactly what the factory made; trying to understand their markets was verging on the impossible. We seemed to spend hours in freezing offices, squinting at schedules of figures that never quite tied up.

The 'entertainment' in the evenings was also a strain. The Mayor had told Jiang to keep us happy, so there were nightly banquets which, though not quite on the scale of the Mayor's epics, still involved multiple courses overspiced with garlic and washed down with *baijiu*, or beer if we were lucky. The parties afterwards were even worse. Night after night we were invited to dances at the various factories. Even in March, the temperature outside was still well below freezing and the heating in the dance halls never seemed to work. We all wore coats inside and, as we sat huddled on the rows of chairs on the edge of the dance floor, with our frosty breath illuminated by the disco lights, we were dragged out to dance with girls from the factory. Egged on by the doggedly well-meaning but hopelessly unobservant Jiang, the factory girls would come out, one after the other, in endless succession to ask to dance. It seemed to go on for hours, but I never had the heart to refuse. We'd stand swaying to the reverberating sound of the Chinese version of 'Only You' until midnight in a freezing dance hall with flashing Christmas tree lights taped to the walls, clasped in the arms of a female factory worker who was wearing three overcoats. With all the padding, my arms hardly reached round my dance partner's back. Michael said that it felt as if he was 'dancing with a bear that'd washed its hair in garlic.'

Michael and I spent many weeks in Changchun with Madame Tan trying to 'put the numbers in the spreadsheet,' as Pat had rather tactlessly put it to Michael. Pat was still focused on the big picture, impatient with the distracting details of each individual factory but convinced that the strategy would work as a whole.

Madame Tan was the Director of the ignition-coil factory that we had visited on our first trip to Changchun when we'd met the Mayor. She was a jolly round-faced woman in her late thirties. Her ignition-coil factory was perfect for a first investment. The products were simple and Madame Tan thought that she only needed about two million dollars to push the factory into overdrive. She had just landed big orders from the new German passenger-car line down the road, so the market seemed secure. She just needed our money to buy more equipment to meet the new demand. As we waded through the figures and the weeks rolled on, the four huge iron chimneys at First Auto Works, with their spiky crowns on top, became a familiar sight on the horizon.

In those days, foreign investment in China was almost exclusively in the form of a 'joint venture' where both the Chinese and the foreign side had a share in the business going forward. Generally, the foreign partner invested cash while the Chinese partner contributed the assets at the factory. Once the deal was struck, the contracts had to be approved by the Government; without the red 'chops' from the 'relevant department' no foreign investment contract was valid in China. But the regulations were confusing; even Director Jiang seemed vague about the details. It was just like at the university where many of the regulations were 'internal,' but this time it seemed as if the people on the inside didn't really understand the rules either. No one could tell us which documents were needed and which of the municipal committees and commissions had to give their chop before final approval. There was a maze of confusing regulations requiring accountant's certificates, tax registrations and valuation reports before the joint venture could be approved. Many government officials didn't have a clue how even to start working their way through the labyrinth and whenever we asked what to do, each one gave a different answer.

Sometimes Madame Tan could be equally perplexing. She had imported some specialist equipment from Italy the previous year but it was still locked up in a warehouse. When we asked to see it, she was evasive. During one of her many trips out of town, we persuaded one of the other managers to open the warehouse for us. We found that the machines had never been used; they were still in their packing cases. So why did she want more equipment? We had noticed that there was another factory on the same site as Madam Tan's – the Changchun Number Two Wireless Factory – but she seemed extremely anxious to prevent us from meeting anyone from the wireless factory.

At times, Madame Tan would suddenly disappear for a few days without any explanation. At first, I didn't think anything of it; after all, she could have been on a normal business trip. But after one such absence she came to collect us from the hotel in a huge black stretch limousine. It was a Cadillac. I'd never seen one in China before. The crowds of early-morning bicyclists stared at us as we left the hotel. The car, with its enormous length and gleaming black paint-work, slowly wound its way with almost feline stealth around the potholes in the road and the huge clouds of steam that poured out of the manhole covers into the freezing air. But a couple of weeks later the Cadillac had gone; it seemed as if the ignition-coil team had suddenly fallen on hard times since they appeared to have no car at all. At lunchtime, when we went to a restaurant just down the road, we were driven over on an old 'Liberation' truck. We sat there, in our suits and ties, shivering on a battered sofa that had been dumped onto the back of the truck together with some filthy old sacks.

Meanwhile, back in New York, Rubel was becoming increasingly nervous and unpredictable. As we struggled to reach a deal with Madame Tan and find our way through the maze of government regulations, the drum beats from New York got louder and louder. My heart sank when I heard that Rubel had arranged to come to China in May. But that was still two months ahead; we hoped that by then we would have signed the deal with Madame Tan and that it would keep him off our backs.

In April, the deal was struck. It was small; just the right size for us to cut our teeth on. We agreed to invest a million dollars for 60 per cent of the business. Madame Tan would invest the factory's land and buildings, plus the equipment, for her 40 per cent share. And she would continue to run the factory. It seemed like the perfect deal. Rubel was pleased and the tension abated. We were relieved as well; with the first deal out of the way, we could get on with the job of putting the rest of the capital to work.

A few weeks later, Madame Tan called to say that there was a problem. 'Our factory's land, you know. It's not registered in our name so we can't put it in. Does that matter?'

Michael had taken the call. 'Of course it matters!' he said. 'If you don't own it, who does? They'll want to charge rent. Anyway, if you can't put the land in, how are you going to pay for your 40 per cent?'

Madame Tan said that the wireless factory next door

owned the land. When I heard the news, I said, 'That'll be fine. We'll just get Mayor Huang to sort it out. The land's all owned by the State anyway, so it shouldn't be a problem.'

We had several meetings with Director Jiang and his Investment Bureau and, later on, with Mayor Huang. He promised to instruct the Land Bureau to re-register the land. There was a lot at stake for the Municipal Government; if we made that first investment in Changchun, others would surely follow. But the weeks dragged on. There was no news and the tension mounted as Rubel's arrival drew closer. Then, a week before he was due in Beijing, Madame Tan called to tell us that it was all off. A huge dispute was raging over the title to the land. Mayor Huang had thrown his weight behind Madame Tan, but the wireless factory had been lobbying the Changchun Party Committee. There was deadlock. We were confused. How could such a simple matter of a small and not particularly valuable piece of land become so complicated? It was puzzling and the timing was awful. At that stage, all we had to look forward to was Rubel's reaction when he heard the news.

I was not in China when Rubel arrived but I heard that the meetings were horrible. Michael called me afterwards in a state of despair. He had been given the task of presenting the progress of our investment programme to Rubel and his team of simpering assistants. Rubel kept butting in, firing distracting questions at Michael, not really concentrating on the answers and complaining that it was all too complicated. At one point, when Michael was going through the government-approval process for foreign investment, Rubel just wouldn't let go of a particular detail. As Michael struggled to explain a process that many Chinese government officials themselves didn't really understand, Rubel became highly agitated. In practice, local officials often interpreted the vague regulations in ways that suited local conditions, but this didn't stack up with Rubel. He smelt a rat. When Michael, with increasing exasperation, said, 'But Myron, you're just looking at it through a Westerner's eyes,' the long-awaited explosion erupted. 'But I *am* a Westerner,' Rubel yelled, 'I *am* a Westerner. How the hell *else* am I supposed to look at it? I wanna know where every investment project is in the system. I want a list of projects at each stage of the process. You must have that, so show me the list!'

The Chinese staff were by then looking uncomfortably at their shoes. This was definitely not their style.

'Show me the list!' Rubel shouted, bouncing up and down in his chair.

'What?'

'Show me the list!'

'But there isn't a strict sequence to how things get done.'

'Show me the list! Show me the list! Show me the list!'

Apparently, the ranting continued for several minutes until Pat suggested a break. They were all exhausted by the time that Rubel left for Japan the following day.

After Rubel left, we regrouped. The experience up in Changchun had taught us a lesson: the workings of Chinese business, and apparently even parts of the Government, were much more chaotic than had appeared from the outside. In retrospect, events and comments that we had passed over in the hills in Sichuan took on a new significance. I had been puzzled at times by the factory directors' apparent disdain for our two fellow-travellers from Beijing – they were reasonably senior officials from the Ministry on a mission to bring money to the remote valleys, but often their requests for information had been brushed aside. The directors had been openly scornful of the Central Government bureaucracy, those 'old men who squatted in their offices in Beijing'. When I told Ai Jian that I couldn't understand why everyone seemed to ignore the officials from the Ministry, he used an old Chinese adage: 'The hills are high and the Emperor is far away.' It seemed as though the far-flung extremities of the ancient kingdom still paid little attention to the capital.

After these experiences, it was fast becoming obvious that if we were to invest our money safely we would have to take a majority share in each of the businesses. That way we'd be able to retain a reasonable degree of control. Negotiating a majority stake would be difficult; but Pat said that he reckoned that most of the businesses we'd seen were so desperate for capital that they'd agree in the end. He was right. We eventually came up with a formula that we thought would be acceptable to both sides: the original factory directors would remain in charge of the daily operations but, in return for our money, we would always take more than 50 per cent of the shares and a majority on the Board. And Pat would be chairman.

The summer that year in Beijing was unusually hot and wet; every day a cycle seemed to set in with blue skies at dawn and a gradual build-up of heat and humidity during the day that cleared again in the late afternoon with colossal thunderstorms. Often the clouds in the late afternoon were so thick that the city would be plunged into darkness as the rain came down in great black streaks. The rising tension in the weather through each day matched the wider mood as the months rolled on, but eventually it broke at the end of the summer when we closed our first deal.

We finally made our first investment in a factory high up in a steep-sided valley with mountain streams, stone bridges and bamboo groves, tucked up far away in the central province of Anhui. It had been founded in the early 1980s by one of China's new breed of entrepreneurs, a Mr Shi. Originally from the river town of Jiangyin in the flat-lands of Jiangsu, he had ended up in the mountains after the Cultural Revolution and had never gone back. His factory had always been outside the state-owned system so Old Shi had grown it from nothing, relying entirely on his own resources. Fifteen years on the business was making a fortune supplying rubber parts to China's automotive industry.

The negotiations to establish the joint venture were surprisingly straightforward. Somehow Shi seemed to know how to deal with foreigners; he was clear about what he wanted, he wasn't hemmed in by a state-run bureaucracy and he made quick decisions. He was flexible and only dug his heels in on two points: our cash had to come quickly and he was to remain in charge. After a couple of months, we agreed a handshake deal: twelve million dollars for a 60 per cent stake in the business. The accountants and lawyers were dispatched to work out the details.

During this lull in negotiations, I had to go to America for a commitment that I had been dreading. IHC wanted me to address a large group of investors in Los Angeles. My topic was China so it should have been easy. But the speaker immediately after me was Dr Henry Kissinger. The prospect of lecturing in front of hundreds of prominent investors and a man who had personally known Mao and Deng sent me into a paroxysm of nervous tension. As I got up to speak, I scanned the audience anxiously for the famous horn-rimmed glasses reflecting the stage lights. In fact, Kissinger appeared neatly from one side of the stage after I had given my pitch and spoke for forty minutes, without notes, on the balance of global power between almost every significant country. Short and rather stout, he mesmerized his audience and was fallen upon by fawning millionaires once he had finished speaking. Fame, it appeared, was a more highly valued commodity in America than the odd hundred million. But 'The Doctor', of course, had both.

When I arrived back in Hong Kong on the journey back to China, I was in for a shock. I knew that Old Shi, with his factory up in the hills, was a risk-taker, and that he had borrowed heavily from local banks during the boom that had been set off by Old Deng's Southern Tour. But two years on, the government had started to rein in the over-heating economy and Shi was under pressure from his bankers. While I was away, he suddenly arrived in Beijing and presented Pat with a draft investment contract.

Pat had called me as I arrived in Hong Kong a couple of days after Shi's visit.

'Yeah,' he said, 'Shi came up to Beijing with this draft contract, so I signed it.'

'What?'

'Yeah, I signed it.'

A pause.

'You know that the lawyers haven't signed off on the wording yet?'

'Yeah, I know.'

'And the accountants are still checking the numbers?'

'Well, you know that the contract isn't valid until it gets chopped by the Government. It'll take ages before Shi gets the approval.'

'And the Board papers.' I continued cautiously. 'You know, Rubel's never even heard of the deal.'

'Look, I'm fed up with all the bleating from New York.

What are we supposed to do with all that cash? Just leave it in the bank account? I don't think so! So, stop worrying, it'll take Shi months to get the approval. Anyway, how was I supposed to refuse?'

'Well, you could have said "No",' I suggested.

'Well, you know me,' Pat said. 'If I was a girl, I'd always be pregnant!'

Pat received Shi's jubilant call before the end of the week. After he'd met with Pat in Beijing, Shi had flown directly to Hefei, the provincial capital in Anhui, clutching his precious contract, and had procured the government's red chop the same day.

'The documents are all approved,' said Shi. 'When can I get the cash?'

The telephonic board meeting linking New York with China that night resulted in a display of pyrotechnics that would have impressed even the Chinese. Storms of protest burst from the speakerphone in front of us. The other directors had never heard of the deal and Pat had sent the contract over to New York with a rather disingenuous attached note saying: 'Here is the conditional contract that I signed in Beijing for discussion tonight.' After Rubel had read the contract, he was beside himself, spluttering with fury. 'Why is it conditional?' he screamed. 'Where is the conditionality? Where is it? Where is it?' The shouts came out against a vague background noise of fists drumming on a boardroom table some eleven thousand miles away.

Of course, the raging of the other directors could not change the facts. There was already a commitment to invest about twelve million within twenty-one days whether they liked it or not. Eventually, exhausted by the force of their own remonstations, they signed off. An uneasy truce was declared. Pat had broken the logjam and further investments followed quickly. It was a smart move at the time but it did nothing long term for the relationship with our colleagues in New York.

On 8 September 1994 the twelve million dollars were wired into Shi's bank account in Ningshan. Late that day, I took a long walk up to the Great Wall and stared out northwards towards Mongolia over the ancient parapets. We had made our first investment. I felt exhausted, exhilarated and apprehensive all at the same time. It had been a bruising process. Would it all be worth it?

Once the initial logjam had cleared and we'd figured our way through the bureaucracy, we were able to close other deals quickly. By the end of the year, we had invested the whole of the hundred and fifty million dollars in seven factories all over China. In the following year, 1995, IHC raised a further two hundred and sixty million and we invested that into more factories making components. We also used it to expand into another industry when we bought up three large breweries in Beijing. In the space of eighteen months, we had come from nowhere to be one of the biggest financial investors in China, right at the height of the China boom. We were fast becoming the nexus between the vast capital resources on Wall Street and the greatest growth story ever. Others had gone out and raised money, but no one had raised comparable amounts. Many of the funds that raised capital failed to invest it; their money was still parked uselessly in Hong Kong years later. No one else had managed to invest so quickly. It looked as if Pat had created his machine for bringing money from Wall Street to China.

In the space of two short years, we had grown from three

people sitting in a dingy office in a second-rate hotel in Chaoyang District on the east side of Beijing into a company with twenty businesses across China and twenty-five thousand employees.

Pat seemed like a man on the brink of greatness.

I was walking on air.

Six

山雨欲來, 風滿楼

Wind in the Tower Warns
of Storms in the Mountains

> *Tang Dynasty Poem by Xu Han:*
> *'Coming troubles cast their*
> *shadows before them.'*

They called themselves factory rats, those knarled old engineering types with beer bellies, checked shirts and nicotine-stained fingers. Before we found them, they'd spent the whole of their working lives as foreign expatriates, grappling with metal-bashing factories in developing countries all over the world. We hired them to form an operating team to get our factories in China really humming; twenty-five of them, grizzled and oily, tough old bastards who claimed they could hear the clink of a badly adjusted metal press a hundred yards across a factory floor. They didn't exactly fit in with the Wall Street types, but the idea was that they'd be there to guide the Chinese factory directors and help them improve each of the businesses while we got on and raised more money. But somehow it never quite worked out like that.

By the middle of 1995 we had completed our third round of fund-raising. With more than four hundred million dollars under management, we were the largest financial direct investor in China and we were bursting with optimism. After we raised the capital, we ended up visiting nearly two hundred factories throughout the whole country. Since that covered almost all the sizeable components businesses in China, we knew that we had invested in the best.

During the money-raising process, Pat and IHC were clear about the strategy of buying up factories and consolidating them into the largest components company in China. The investors identified with the story. It had happened in the States so why not in China? Pat had told the investors that we would go for size; we would only use their money to buy stakes in businesses that were in the top three of their markets.

As we trawled through all these factories, we found that Old Shi, with his business up in the hills of Anhui, was an exception. There were hardly any other privately owned businesses that had managed to get to the top of their markets; most of the other big components businesses were state-funded. Many appeared to be stuck in a time warp back to the 1950s and 1960s when the planners had first provided the funds. The problems surrounding state-owned companies had been at the top of the government's agenda since the country had started to open up in the early 1980s. For years there was no profit motive so most state-owned businesses were hopelessly inefficient, incapable of developing new products when markets changed and massively overmanned. It made no difference to the factory directors whether the business made profits or losses; they still got the same miserable wage. Many state-owned operations were dying, drowning in a sea of debt and weighed down by thousands upon thousands of excess workers.

But there were exceptions; some businesses made money and had a respectable market share. They were still over-manned and inefficient, but these problems had been masked in the boom years during the early 1990s when sales grew rapidly. Some had doubled in size in each of the three years before we invested; that meant that in the space of three years, their sales had grown by a factor of eight. We knew that they'd need a lot of work, but in the new climate of reform we thought that the factory directors would be receptive to new ideas. So we hired the factory rats and they started drawing up vast checklists for 'in-process quality control', whatever that was, and putting in computer systems. It looked as if they were getting to grips with the factories, so we left them to it. Pat went out to raise more money; by that time he had the cement, float glass and packaging industries in his sights.

The results in the first half of 1995 hadn't been good, but the optimism about the Chinese economy endured and there was little reaction from America. After all, it was only the first year of operations and the new working arrangements were bound to take some time to settle down. We'd delivered what we had promised: Pat had raised the capital, we'd invested it in good factories and had found a team of experts to run them, so there was no cause for complaint. I had no particular concern, but gradually I began to notice difficulties between our operations team and the Chinese factory directors. It was below the surface at first; just a vague feeling that they weren't getting on, or that there wasn't quite the right degree of trust between the two sides. But I still wasn't unduly anxious; the factory directors maintained their optimism; and I felt that, with their years of experience all over the world, our old factory rats were bound to be a jaundiced lot and would take some time to grow to trust their new Chinese colleagues.

But it didn't work out like that. As the months rolled on, the factory directors continued to be reluctant to change the way that they ran their factories and a kind of resistance set in. Again, we didn't take too much notice; it wasn't entirely surprising – no one likes change. 'Give them a few more months and it will sort itself out,' I thought. But the situation became worse and the first signs of seriously choppy water appeared in the autumn. The business-planning sessions for the next year were under way between the operating team and the factory directors. By the end of the year, it seemed as if the simplest decisions, like purchasing testing equipment for a few thousand dollars, often resulted in protracted and acrimonious rows. Our factory rats began to get frustrated and angry. I increasingly found myself being dragged into disputes. Pat gradually became fed up with all the arguments. He was impatient to get on and when the operating team found it difficult to get the Chinese factory directors on their side he became annoyed.

The first serious warning came in the springtime of 1996. We had invested in a factory in Sichuan that made gearwheels for motorcycles. The factory director, Mr Su, came up to Beijing with a plan to start making gearboxes and the operations team had told him not to. I thought that they were right. Making simple gearwheels is one thing, but I knew from my visits with Mr Che at the gearbox factory up in the hills two years earlier that making gearboxes is a much more difficult business. It required sophisticated technology and designs that we didn't have. Su agreed to stop the project until he had done further market research, found a technology partner and prepared a new proposal for discussion. A couple of months later, we went down to Sichuan for the board meeting, supposedly to listen to Su's new proposals. I was a little apprehensive; Su was stubborn and would probably argue for his gearbox project but I couldn't see how we'd ever be able to agree; it was far too ambitious. I hoped that the discussions wouldn't become too contentious.

When we arrived at the factory, Mr Su took us for a tour of the site. I had been there many times before so I knew the factory well. As we walked round a particular corner of a workshop, I expected to see green fields rolling gently down to the river at the bottom of the valley, but they had disappeared. On the other side of a hastily erected fence there were two colossal workshops, hundreds of yards long, extending into the distance, a vast new factory complex with chimneys, new power lines and rows of gleaming heat-treatment equipment. It had only been three months since I had been there last and there had been no sign of building then. Ai Jian stood rooted to the spot, pointing inarticulately towards the building whilst Pat went the radiant pink of a Chongqing sunrise. I eventually managed to stammer, 'Er, Mr Su, what's that?' Mr Su, beaming from ear to ear, announced proudly, 'It's the new gearbox factory.'

At the board meeting later on, he said that he had used the Chinese partner's money to build the gearbox factory in order to 'save time'. Now he wanted us to agree that the joint venture would buy the new factory buildings from the

Chinese partner, doubtless at a mark-up, and launch into gearbox production. It was a knotty problem: how could we spend money on a business when we didn't even know if we could even make the product? But on the other hand, it was a *fait accompli*; the prospect of a disgruntled Chinese partner setting up a new factory in the middle of ours and heading off in a completely new direction was hardly appealing.

Pat completely lost patience at this stage. 'These operations guys just aren't getting it done,' he said. The 'gearbox incident' and others like it had brought matters to a head. After several rows the leader of the operating team resigned. His replacement was also an expatriate and fared no better. The wrangling with the factory directors got worse and worse until, one morning, Pat blew up. He called in the entire operating team and sacked the lot of them. He made me the President of the company and we took on the job of dealing directly with the factory directors ourselves.

In the first half of the year the businesses continued to fall behind budget but I still didn't see any great cause for alarm. I knew that the factory directors were difficult to deal with but I felt up to it. With a bit more straight talking, I thought that I could bring them round. They maintained their optimistic attitude and it seemed more like a slight bump in an otherwise smooth ascent rather than any serious stalling of the engines. We asked the factory directors to come to Beijing where we went through the numbers together. They were all confident of being back on budget by the year-end so there were no particular alarm bells. But I never felt as though I had got the whole picture. There were nagging inconsistencies in the description of the overall market from the various factory directors. Whenever we asked questions, they seemed to throw up a smokescreen of perplexing detail that was difficult to assemble into a coherent story. Unperturbed by our confusion and rising exasperation, they sat on the opposite side of the table, smiling and slurping their tea out of big glass jam-jars at each meeting until they suggested lunch at eleven-thirty.

Over the coming months, as Pat and I struggled to gain control over the course of events, I experienced a slow but relentless realization that an almost superhuman effort was needed to bring about the slightest change. In Beijing, we had invested nearly forty million dollars in a factory that made engine parts that helped control pollution. Much of the money was used to build a brand new facility with state-of-the-art equipment so accurate that, in theory, it could drill a hole through a human hair. It was an impressive facility, all computer screens, complicated graphs, and control panels; one investor had toured the workshop and left after commenting that he thought 'it looked like the engine room of the *Starship Enterprise*.'

But the product that came out at the end of the process had endless quality defects. One of the problems was that the shift managers were 'saving money'; they refused to use the new air-conditioning. During summer, when it was hot, they simply threw open the windows, telling us proudly, 'No matter how hot or cold it gets, our workers will struggle through any hardship to meet production targets.' This was lunacy: the slightest temperature change caused minute distortions in the machines; the smallest particle of dust or grit could ruin the tiny precision drills. Even after we persuaded them to turn on the air-conditioners, we couldn't get them to improve the lighting in the workshop. They stuck to the poor lighting because 'bright lights waste electricity'. On they struggled, with their eyes straining in the gloom.

A few months later I received a call from another factory about sixty miles outside Beijing where we had one of the most modern ductile-iron foundries in China. It made brake parts; there was a huge furnace, called a 'cupola', rising up in a great column of refractory brick out of the factory floor and wrapped in a 'water jacket'. Vast ladles for moving the molten metal hung from gantries high up in the roof and two electric 'holding furnaces' kept the iron liquid until it went into the moulding line. I loved going there to watch them pour iron. With the smoke and the flames and the fiery streams of molten iron, the black-faced workers shovelling through vast heaps of coal, the roar of the furnaces and the intense heat inside the workshop it was like some romantic image of the nineteenth-century mills that powered the Industrial Revolution. But now I was informed that 'they had dropped the cupola.'

'The cupola? How can you "drop" a cupola? It's about a hundred feet high and must weigh tonnes!'

'Yeah, I know, but they were moving it around in the workshop and it fell over.'

'Fell over! What do you mean, it *fell over*? That thing must be worth a couple of million bucks! Anyway, what the hell were they doing moving it in the first place?'

I never got a straight answer to that question; the factory directors were always moving equipment. The constant rearrangement of machines seemed almost a self-fulfilling activity and I never understood why it was necessary.

There was a stubbornness about the factory directors that at times was truly breathtaking. They were absolute masters

103

of obfuscation. Constructive suggestions to improve productivity were brushed aside with the standard line: 'You don't understand China!' Requests for an account of the new machinery purchased with our investment brought forth blank stares. Pleas to collect cash from customers resulted in elaborate excuses which presented the customer in the most favourable light and made us feel that the mere suggestion that we should actually go out and collect cash from them was irresponsibly partisan.

Planning sessions for the coming year with the Chinese factory directors ended up in arguments about obscure details. There were endless circuitous discussions that wandered off the point in question without us ever quite noticing the exact moment when we lost the thread. We faced enormous difficulties in getting accurate information. Schedules of figures were presented at one session and then amended at the next. The factory directors would often talk for hours on end without getting to the point and then suddenly demand an immediate decision on purchasing millions of dollars' worth of machinery without any analysis, insisting point-blank that the decision had to be made there and then.

By the end of the year, with profits still nowhere in sight, it was obvious that the task ahead was much more difficult than any of us had imagined. But with more than four hundred million in the balance it was hardly the time for doubts.

About this time, board meetings in the States started getting seriously tetchy: the honeymoon period was over. Naturally, the American directors expected profits and they grew impatient as time went on. I started to feel squeezed between two powerful opposing forces: the Americans chafing for profits while the clock ticked away and ate relentlessly into their returns and the Chinese, utterly undisturbed by any sense of urgency, proceeding serenely forward with an almost ethereal timelessness that drove us all to distraction. At times I felt that the factory directors must have been on tranquillisers.

With growing pressure from America and painfully slow progress in bringing order to the factories in China, I thought that the time had come to lay down the law. At first I found it difficult to get Pat to focus on the Chinese factory directors. Michael had been convinced early on that they were the source of our troubles and he had won me round to his view. But Pat still felt that they would come through in the end and he remained optimistic. The market hadn't grown as fast as predicted, but he was confident that the situation would right itself in the end. He'd seen these kinds of cycles before on Wall Street, and with the four hundred million, we had enough capital to get through these temporary difficulties. Pat even thought that the downturn might do us some good. 'It'll weed out the weaker opposition,' he said.

But my doubts grew; I wanted to start challenging the factory directors more directly. Pat thought that I was too impatient, always spoiling for a fight, anxious to inflate small arguments. He wanted to keep everyone focused on the big picture and not worry about all the skirmishing.

'You're just like the Young Bull,' he'd say.

'The Young Bull?'

'Yeah, the Young Bull. Haven't you heard that story?'

'No,' I said.

'Well, you're the Young Bull. And I'm the Old Bull.'

'Oh yeah?'

'Yeah.'

'So what happens?'

'Well, the Young Bull, he sees a field of cows down in the valley and he runs up to the Old Bull, all excited, and says, "Hey, Old Bull, Old Bull, look at that field of cows down there, let's run down and fuck one of them." And the Old Bull, well, he just looks up slowly, takes in the field of cows, thinks for a minute and then says, "Nah. Let's just walk down and fuck all of them!"'

'Take it a step at a time,' Pat would say. 'Don't get so excited. Just take it a step at a time.'

I could certainly see how someone who had been successful on Wall Street might feel optimistic about the world.

After a few more months, it was obvious that conflict was unavoidable.

Our first serious fight was in Harbin, a city in the farthest north-eastern reaches of China, just a few hundred miles inland from Vladivostok. If I'd had any inkling beforehand that the fight would become so embittered and so entrenched, I would never have taken it on. But we were all new to the game and the experience taught us that in China iron had to be met with steel. In retrospect, when we locked horns with the Factory Party Committee up there in Harbin and tried to win just by being reasonable, it was as if an elderly Chinese gentleman armed with a couple of chopsticks had arrived in the States for the first time and taken on the 101st Airborne Division.

In late 1994, we invested several million in a factory up in Harbin that made electrical components. Pang Yuanweng, a short and wiry man who had moved to Harbin fifteen years earlier from Beijing, ran the factory. It had been founded in the 1960s and made electrical components:

horns, switches, ignition coils and the like. It was a typical state-owned business: old-fashioned, battered and over-manned. However, Pang had managed to borrow money from a local bank and had built a new modern facility on the outskirts of town. He had proven himself to be a capable salesman and had managed to build up the largest market share in China for car horns. The company's other products were also in great demand. The business had been growing steadily and seemed set for further expansion as its customers partnered with the European car-makers coming to China.

The Factory had originally been set up by the ministry in Beijing that ran the 'machine building' industry in the years after Liberation. Pang had a very bad relationship with the officials from the ministry. He felt that they interfered with his business without really understanding it. Although Pang was notionally in charge, it was still a state-owned business and he had to get the approval of the Party Committee for management changes. The Ministry controlled the Committee. So without the ability to hire-and-fire as he wished, Pang felt hemmed in; he couldn't run the business as he wanted and it was slowing him down. He wanted to escape from the Ministry's influence and doing a joint venture with us was his way out.

So we invested and, after a brief period of profits, in startling contrast to the radiant future that Pang had foreseen in his projections, there were massive losses. Much more alarming were the rapidly dwindling bank balances as cash poured out of the business. Basic things were missing. Pang never seemed to collect money from his customers, but paid his suppliers in advance. There was never any serious analysis when he wanted to buy new equipment.

Pang became more and more difficult to deal with; he talked in great ellipses, never really getting to the point and blowing up minor details into major rows. Whenever we asked questions, he took them as a sign that we didn't trust him and flew off tangentially, or worked himself up into truly shocking rages that left us completely exhausted. He was particularly bad at dinners after the *baijiu* came out. He would launch into monologues about how we didn't understand China and that we were making his life impossible by constant interference. It was absurd; far from being interfering, I felt that we were having no effect whatsoever. I began to think that Pang viewed us in the same light as he did the Ministry: we were there to supply cash when he needed it but we shouldn't think that we would have any say in actually running the business.

The relationship deteriorated even further throughout the autumn. Pang had insisted on buying some specialist equipment through an import company in Beijing but wouldn't explain why we weren't buying it directly from the supplier in Germany. I naturally asked the question whether there might be murkier reasons for using the intermediary, but of course there was never any proof either way. We were approaching the end of the second year, with profits nowhere in sight and with the business still haemorrhaging cash. Something had to be done.

The crisis came in the early winter when Pat called a meeting of all the factory directors in Beijing to coordinate sales across the country. Pang stood up in front of the group and in a long, rambling speech announced that he saw no benefit in coordinating with anyone else and that he had already set up his own sales network all over China. We were appalled; he had never discussed it with us and he had made us look like fools in front of the other factory directors who, of course, found the spectacle highly entertaining. We decided that we had no option but to remove him.

Pat told Ai to go up to Harbin and tell Pang that he had to go. Ai went up to Harbin together with an official from the Ministry. We took that as a sign that the Ministry wanted to get rid of Pang as much as we did. But we found out that matters were more complicated.

Ai called me from Harbin and said that the discussions with Pang had been difficult. I didn't doubt it, but I dug my heels in and said, 'Don't come back until you've got Pang's resignation.' A few days later Ai came into my office with a dispirited expression on his face and a crumpled handwritten note from Pang. It asked the Board of Directors to accept his resignation. Pat called a board meeting for 4 December, three weeks later, and we put the issue to the back of our minds.

Late in the afternoon of 3 December I walked into my office and found a fax from Harbin. It was from Pang. He had withdrawn his resignation and told us that the Chinese directors refused to come to the board meeting the next day. This was a problem: without at least one Chinese director present, the Board could not form a quorum. It looked like deadlock.

We checked our contract with Pang. It stated clearly in both languages that if the Chinese directors refused to turn up to a board meeting on three occasions, then we could exercise their votes in their absence. So Pat just sent out the formal letters to call a second board meeting; if they refused to turn up again, we could just call another and exercise their votes. It seemed that we were off the hook.

At the third board meeting, when the Chinese directors once more failed to turn up, we duly voted to accept Pang's resignation and appoint a temporary replacement until a time when we could all sit down together and sort out the mess. Our hopes soon faded. Pang received a copy of the Board resolution, but he just refused to leave the factory.

The Board decision had appointed a man called Jiang – 'Ironman Jiang' – to act as temporary replacement for Pang. He had earned the nickname during his fifteen years of running a stamping workshop at First Auto Works and he wasn't a man to mess with. He went up to Harbin to take over the factory, but with Ironman Jiang and Pang sitting in different offices and issuing contradictory instructions the middle managers and workers didn't know what to do. We thought about physically removing Pang from the factory, but that was risky; he was still Vice-Chairman of the joint venture and according to the contract only the Chinese Partner could remove him from that position. But with Ironman and Pang at loggerheads, the factory rapidly descended into chaos.

I should have guessed that it might come to a fight. Harbin is a tough place to live and the inhabitants can be a grizzled lot. The city sits on the Songhua River, which, in the short summer months when it is not frozen, flows through the marshlands to the Sea of Okhotsk. It is not surprising, given its proximity to Vladivostok, that Harbin had a slightly Russian feel about it and there was still the occasional painted wooden-framed house with tall shuttered windows set into steeply sloping eves. The city had been chosen as one of the centres for industrial development under China's State Plan in the 1950s and the shattered hulks of idle factories blighted the landscape. Steam engines were still a familiar sight and I often watched them straining at the front of long lines of wagons piled high with coal, disgorging vast clouds of black smoke into the wintry sky.

Harbin was famous for its 'Ice Festival,' where life-sized statues and buildings, even castles, were carved out of great blocks of ice and lit up from the inside. For a few weeks around Chinese New Year, the city had a carnival atmosphere: acrobats walked around on stilts, juggling, while Chinese opera singers, their features exaggerated with grotesque pink and purple face-paint, wailed in the background. Street peddlers milled through the crowd selling *tang hu lu*, long sticks of red sticky sugar-coated crab apples. The sticks were pushed into bundles of cloth on the back of the bicycles so that they looked like enormous pincushions.

The festival probably gave the people of Harbin a welcome distraction from everyday life; for the rest of the year, getting by was a struggle for most of the locals. Work was scarce and there wasn't much around to keep up the spirits with temperatures below freezing from late October until the April thaw. In the depths of winter, it could reach forty degrees below and a bottle of beer solidified in minutes. On my first trip up to Harbin, I noticed that the ice on the pavements wasn't slippery: the extreme cold had hardened it to rock. At times it seemed to me that the air itself had frozen as I saw the smoke from the factory chimney stacks hanging in great black funeral wreaths over the city.

A few weeks after Ironman Jiang came to the factory, Pang decided to counter-attack. He embarked on a campaign of disruption aimed at pushing us out of the factory. He called suppliers and told them that the joint venture had run out of money. They stopped sending us copper wire and production ground to a halt. He called customers and told them that we'd soon be out of business. If they delayed payment until we went bust they might never have to come up with the money to pay for goods they'd already taken. Cash dried up and the business stalled, but Ironman managed to hold it together into the spring. Then, just after Chinese New Year, we received a writ: Pang had lodged an arbitration claim in Beijing. His claim asked the China National Arbitration Commission to overturn the board resolution and reappoint him as Factory Director. This only served to stoke up the differences between the rival factions in the factory. Pang started to use the Factory Party Committee to pressure the workers and held meetings where individual managers were forced to declare in favour of 'the factory or the foreigners'.

By this time, it was obvious that I had hopelessly underestimated what we were up against and, after months of fighting, the business became dangerously unstable. The banks started calling in the loans and production was squeezed. There was a growing sense of crisis among the workforce. In China there is no social security so the workers had to rely on their 'work unit' for survival. If the factory collapsed, they would have nowhere else to turn. I went up to Harbin to try to stabilize the situation and met with the banks, the local government and the management team. There was a clear consensus that Pang had to go. But no one knew how to get rid of him.

I went to the local Municipal Government offices in Harbin and noticed again the Russian influence in the high ceilings, ornate cornices and chandeliers down the hallways. While I was inside, meeting with the Foreign Investment Bureau, there was a large demonstration outside in the square in front of the government building. It was blocked by hundreds of angry workers. A business had collapsed and the workers had been left stranded. After nearly fifty years of Communism, it wasn't surprising that they looked to the government for rescue. We had to leave by a side gate.

The meeting had been awful; the local government wouldn't get involved because they were nervous of the Ministry in Beijing. By that time, the Ministry had turned against us. We had unwittingly become enmeshed in a bizarre triangular dispute involving Pang, the Ministry and ourselves. In fact, the Ministry had wanted to get rid of Pang as much as we did. But when they saw us at loggerheads with him, they figured that they could divide and rule and grabbed what they reckoned was an opportunity to regain control of the factory. We didn't know at the time but they had never authorized Pang to let us have a majority in the joint venture; now they wanted to regain control and wouldn't help us get rid of Pang unless we agreed to give up some seats on the Board. It was a complete mess.

Sucked deeper and deeper into the mire, and appalled at the sight of the factory sliding towards bankruptcy, I flailed around trying to find a way to save the business. Finally I heard that one of the local banks had claimed that they had a mortgage over the land that Pang had supposedly agreed to put into the joint venture. It was a total deadlock.

Back at the factory, I tried to rally the management and gave a speech standing on a little wooden platform next to Ironman Jiang in a workshop at the top of the factory block. It was the only room big enough to fit in the whole management team. The room was battered, its walls covered with shabby peeling paint. Everyone wore thick padded coats even though they were inside. It was an uphill battle; I did my best to conceal my growing sense of despair. I had seen earlier that many of the workshops were in a shocking state, with piles of semi-assembled parts on old wooden tables and uneven stone floors disintegrating underfoot. I knew that the workforce's morale was at rock bottom, but I tried to raise their spirits and appealed to them to get back to work and unite around Jiang. If we all pulled together, we would be able to weather the crisis and they should not worry about the court case in Beijing. I was encouraged by some of the comments afterwards but became dispirited again as I left the factory in the extreme cold of the late afternoon. I had caught sight of Pang's pinched face squinting through a grimy window. He was hunched up over a desk, haranguing a group of workers who were sitting dejectedly opposite.

In the coming months, as the business sank further into the mud it started trading on barter. Lack of cash was a common problem in China at that time and many businesses began to exchange product instead. The knock-on effects passed from customer to supplier and spread throughout the country at an alarming rate. Reinforced by a multiplier effect, soon whole industries were illiquid, trapped in a mesh of 'triangular debt'. At one stage, the problem threatened to bring down the entire economy and the Central Government was forced to intervene with a massive cash injection.

I remember that many of the larger truck manufacturers were so tight for cash that they had to hand over trucks in lieu of payment for components. Several of our businesses had large truck fleets parked inside the gates. But this made the situation even worse as component suppliers, desperate for cash themselves, dumped the truck fleets on to the market at a discount, forcing the truck makers to lower prices even further.

Many businesses, particularly in north-eastern China, became like 'the living dead', clean out of cash and just limping onwards from day to day in a zombie-like trance without any real plan for the future. Suppliers kept sending raw materials without much prospect of getting paid except with components, factories shipped goods to customers without expecting anything in return but trucks, and the workers kept turning up to make product without any prospect of being paid in cash. I heard that one factory down the road in Harbin had been paying its workers in hair shampoo. The Factory Director had accepted a shipment of soap and shampoo in payment for goods and passed it on to the workers who then sold it in the local markets for cash.

Throughout this time, I had to go back to New York for quarterly board meetings. I had come to dread them; the mood by that time was invariably black and they often ended in 'scenes'. The meetings took place on the fifty-sixth floor of a glass tower in midtown New York, right at the heart of Manhattan Island. There were six directors on the Board representing IHC and a big pension fund. By then, the pressure from the Board for profits was intense and there had been strident demands for cost cuts, including radical reductions in the workforce. But that was completely impractical at that time in China because these was no social security. So the meetings became more and more difficult. My main mental challenge had become figuring out how to convey accurate news from the Orient without provoking mushroom clouds and streams of molten lava on the other side of the table.

Early in the spring of 1997, as I sat in a little side office and stared out of a window, high up in the clouds, waiting for the meeting to start, I gazed past the crush of colossal towers of polished glass and marble on Sixth Avenue towards Central Park. I could see the yellow cabs inching slowly along the straight lines of the streets far below. I thought fleetingly that those vast towers seemed to exude the same feeling of overwhelming power swamping the individual that the Stalinist colossi in China did. But then my mind flew back to the factories and smokestacks and the knots of bicycles. The two places were on opposite sides of the world and, at that moment, they seemed further apart than ever.

I was soon called into the meeting room. After a brief attempt to compose myself, I walked in with what I hoped was a cheerful smile and said, perhaps just a little too loudly, 'How y' doing!' I took in the familiar room with its serious faces, the pinstripes and pink ties and the tortoiseshell glasses and I settled down on the far side of the vast table. It stretched 'the whole nine yards' either side of a sleek speakerphone in the middle. Line prints of tall ships hung on the wall and there was a sideboard at the end of the room, laden with muffins and Danish pastries for breakfast. The smell of coffee filled the room.

'Diet Coke's in the fridge if you wannit,' someone said.

I went into the kitchen in the annexe at the end of the room. The fridge was huge: a hideous white monstrosity that seemed to be about the same size as an apartment back in Changchun.

I went back to my seat and looked through the agenda. I was down to give the Board an 'update on the issue in Harbin.'

'Issue?' I thought. 'Seems more like a knuckle fight in sub-polar temperatures with a Chinese car-horn salesman.'

Whatever: I was relieved to see that I was on just before

116

lunch. With a bit of luck that might distract the others' attention.

The meetings followed a set pattern, with Pat starting off. He gave a broad-brush summary of the economy in China and any major political developments, plus an overview of what might happen in the next quarter. Then it was left to Michael to go through the actual results. He often had a hard time explaining the numbers. Translating Chinese accounts into something intelligible on Wall Street was no easy feat.

One of the directors from the pension fund obviously fancied himself as a hardball player: he was huge, with an enormous pendulous neck that rolled from his ears down to his shoulders. He seemed to have established the dominant position when it came to tearing apart Michael's numbers. Every so often, when he'd scored a particular point or sensed some squashiness in the figures, he'd say, 'Now, let's all just push back on that one, shall we?' Taking his lead, with perfectly choreographed timing, the heads of all the six directors on the other side of the table would go down. All six leather chairs would roll back silently in unison. A long silence would follow until Hardball signalled a change in the mood; he'd move back in, hunching over his binder with a frown as the other five chairs rolled inwards to the table with synchronized motion.

'Michael, what we need here is traction! You gotta get traction!' It was the buzzword of corporate America at the time; Michael and I often wondered what it really meant. But neither of us ever had the guts to pretend we'd misunderstood it for 'tractors' and say that we didn't need them because we already had fleets of trucks in the joint ventures. That particular morning there were no memorable scenes, and the discussions droned on in the background as I went through my presentation in my mind.

As I stood up to go through the Harbin dispute, lunch was wheeled in. I figured that for the next few minutes the 'Fat Directors' would be much more preoccupied with choosing between pastrami sandwiches on rye bread or tuna mayonnaise bagels, so I hurried through the difficult bits. But I knew from experience that this was the time when the 'Thin Directors' were at their most dangerous. They had spent the first two hours of the meeting looking through their diaries, calling their secretaries, receiving important messages and checking their air tickets, but by the end of the morning, they had exhausted the distractions and they were concentrating. I saw the one with red hair stirring towards the end of the table. He was smart, that one, always asking the most difficult questions, so I held my breath. Further down, Rubel was scratching his palms, fidgeting about, cleaning his glasses on his tie and rummaging through his papers. He was wagging his foot so hard that I thought that it might fall off if he carried on much longer. I pressed on but inevitably ignition point was reached soon.

'Goddammit, look at these numbers. You're hosing out cash and you've got negative gross margins. That means every time you make another one of those things – what are they, ignition coils or horns or whatever – you're losing money. We may as well just write the whole lot off and close the thing down. How much did we put in there, anyway?' he asked, tearing through the schedules.

'Er, well, yes, it is problematic, I admit. But we've got our man in there and–'

'But what about the other Chinese guy, Pong or whatever he's called?' said Rubel.

'Pang.'

'Pang?'

'Yeah, Pang. Er, he's still in there as well,' I replied sheepishly.

'Well, why don't you just fire him and have done with it?'

'What?'

'Fire him!'

'Yeah, fire him!' the others joined in, passing congratulatory glances among themselves.

'Well, we tried, but he just stayed in the factory.'

'Fire him!'

'It's not as simple as that!'

'Fire him! Fire him! Fire him!'

The chant seemed to take on the rhythm of some primeval war dance, bodies swaying back and forth to the same beat.

'Fire him! Fire him! Fire him!'

When it eventually died down, one of the directors said, 'Well, what does his employment contract say?'

'His what?'

'His employment contract,' he repeated slowly, spitting every syllable through his teeth. 'What does it say?'

Of course, we didn't have employment contracts with any of the factory directors. What conceivable use would an employment contract have been up in Harbin? We'd got a cast-iron joint venture contract that had been approved by the Government and Pang had completely ignored it. But how was I going to explain that? As my mind raced through all the possible escape routes, I thought fleetingly of telling them that they should just be grateful that they didn't have to accept dividends in shampoo.

After the board meeting in New York the whole edifice in Harbin collapsed. Ai Jian had just returned from a trip together with someone from the Ministry to try to sort out

119

the mess with the banks. He had to get through demonstrations at the factory gates and, once the news spread that someone from Beijing had arrived, a group of workers tried to get into the meeting room. There was a struggle as some of the middle managers tried to block their way in, and a glass door was smashed. One of the workers broke free of the managers restraining him and his shirt was torn off in the process. He burst into the meeting room half-naked and bruised about the face and picked up a very heavy old-fashioned projector from the middle of the table. As he raised it above his head, apparently to throw it against the wall, he accidentally struck the ministry man a heavy blow on the side of the head, which sent the official reeling to the floor, concussed. Everyone in the room froze with the shock; there was absolute silence for a long time. No one dared move. The silence was eventually broken by the sobs of the worker as he sank down slowly onto the table.

Later that day, the demonstrations became ugly after an old woman died on the picket lines. I had heard that she had died from natural causes but Ai would never tell me exactly what had happened. He just felt that he was lucky to have got out of the factory and wanted to put the whole experience behind him.

Throughout those long months, the arbitration ground slowly forward in Beijing and at the end of the year the decision came out. We won hands down. It ruled that the Board decision to remove Pang was valid and that he should compensate us for assets that he had failed to put into the joint venture. We had won. Pang left the business, we appointed a new factory director and Ironman Jiang was able to came back to Beijing. But it was a Pyrrhic victory and it did us no good. The business had been so severely damaged by the dispute that it never recovered. Years later it was still struggling on, trading on barter and living from day to day under the constant threat of collapse.

I felt an appalling guilt at these developments. We had handled it badly, that was for sure. In retrospect I could see that we had missed opportunities to draw the ministry on to our side or moments when we might have negotiated our way out of the mess. But who would have guessed that the situation would ever get so complicated or so severe, or that Pang would go to such lengths to protect his own position? Or that the contract would have been so useless? It didn't make sense. All we had wanted to do was to build a strong business where all parties could benefit but we'd ended up achieving the exact opposite. I felt confusion and anger – and a deep sense of frustration that such an opportunity had been wasted by our inability to rein in one individual. All I could do then was survey the wreckage: the broken buildings and the broken lives, up in the ice and the cold.

During the time that the dispute in Harbin was rumbling on I had my first disagreements with Pat. Tension crept slowly into our relationship as he continued to push forward full steam with new investments rather than sort out what we had already got. He wanted to start investing in other industries like float glass and cement. I felt that it was as if the whole of China had been reduced to a business-school case study; as if we were dealing with the abstract, a place where theory remained undisturbed by reality. Pat had never tried to learn any Chinese and I felt that this kept him more remote from what was actually happening in the factories. None of the Chinese ever dared to tell him what was really going on, and he had no way to wheedle it out of them. Of course, he was meant to be leading from the front; part of his undoubted charisma was that he'd never take 'no' for an answer. But sometimes I was confused by this optimism. I remember once reading in the *South China Morning Post* that he had announced that we were planning to go public on the Hong Kong Stock Exchange the following year and raise another hundred million. 'We need at least $100 million to ensure adequate trading volume,' he said. It was the first that I had heard of the plan, and we were bleeding red ink in every direction.

As time wore on, the types of businesses that Pat wanted to buy became increasingly bizarre. He had met a Madame Yu who had several businesses in southern China. She was looking for four million to invest in an auto-repair shop and a bonded warehouse. I thought that it was too removed from our core manufacturing business, and we had several rows before Pat insisted on doing the deal. I was eventually ground down and went along with it reluctantly.

Several months later, I went down to Shenzhen to take a look at the premises for the first time. When we were picked up from the hotel, the driver said that the repair shop was a fifty-minute drive outside the city. 'What?' I said, 'Who's going to drive nearly two hours out into the country and back to get their car repaired?' On the way over, after about forty minutes, we came across a large checkpoint across the road and we had to show our passports. It was the border of the Shenzhen Special Economic Zone so not only did it take a fifty-minute drive but local Chinese needed a special travel permit to get to the repair shop from the city.

When we finally arrived we found something that had quite obviously been designed as an office block; it was a six-storey building in the middle of a rice paddy. I was told that the repair shop was on the fourth floor. It was reached by an

122

extremely narrow circular ramp that required specially trained drivers to manoeuvre the cars round. The walls of the ramp were covered with colourful marks scraped off the paintwork on the cars of previous customers. I wasn't remotely surprised when, in our first year, the repair-service income came out at about 5 per cent of budget.

The bonded warehouse was even worse. It didn't have a licence to import goods into China, which rather defeated the object. The Chinese customs authorities strictly controlled the licences and we couldn't start trading without one. A year later Madame Yu finally obtained customs clearance and we held our first board meeting. She told us that in the time since we had signed the contract rampant smuggling in the region had affected the business case for the warehouse since it undercut our pricing. 'However,' Madame Yu continued, 'if we could all agree to compete more directly with the others in the market, we will definitely make money.'

I missed the point at first, but Pat knew immediately what she meant. He held up his huge hands in the shape of a big 'T'. 'Time out, Madame Yu. Our shareholders are major US financial institutions and we're not going into smuggling, period, the end!'

We agreed to dissolve the joint venture instead.

By this time, some of the investors, as well as the Board, had started asking unpleasant questions. Dogged at every step by self-doubts in such a complex and alien environment, and feeling intense stress, I was caught between Pat's fearsome optimism, driving ceaselessly forward, and the awful reality at the factories as they spun off in a thousand different directions. As I tried to rein in both sides, lurching across China from one mess to another, the pressure started taking a physical toll as well. Then, just before Christmas, an incident occurred that felled me in my tracks. It happened at a factory in the south of China, in a new town on the coast, just across the border from the Portuguese colony of Macau.

Seven

八字衙門朝南開,有理无錢莫進來

The Magistrate's Gates Open Towards the
South, but With Only a Good Case and
No Money, Who'd Bother Going In?

Traditional rhyming peasant saying
about corrupt court officials

One clear winter's morning in Beijing, as I stared out at the perfect blue November sky and the mountains in the distance, I was interrupted by a phone call. I was faintly annoyed; blue skies in the Beijing winter are a rarity.

It was a call from Zhuhai. The previous year we had invested in a factory down there in the new town on China's southern seaboard next to Shenzhen. The factory made brake pads. One of its managers called me with the news that Wang, the Factory Director, had gone to America just after the Mid-Autumn Festival to attend a trade fair in Las Vegas. But that had been nearly a month earlier and Wang had not returned as expected. His wife had lost contact with him ten days ago and she was worried. The last time that he had called home he had been in New York and had seemed very agitated, as if he was frightened that someone else might have been listening. The management team down in Zhuhai didn't know what to do and wanted our help. We contacted Wang's host organization in the States but they were none the wiser, so we filed a missing-person report with the FBI. Another three days passed with no news; Wang's family were beside themselves with worry.

I was anxious too. Wang appeared to me to be rather naïve; he hadn't travelled much beyond the mainland except to Hong Kong. As well as soft features and clear skin that made him look younger than his thirty-seven years, he had a slightly hesitant manner as if he was seeking approval all the time. But it was difficult for me to get the real measure of him. He spoke in the local dialect, Cantonese, which I could not understand. My immediate worry was that he might have been mugged or had his money stolen in the Big Apple. I wasn't sure that he'd know what to do in an emergency and I had heard that he was alone and without translators. A few days later, we sent a letter to Wang's family and the employees of the joint venture telling them that we were working with the authorities in America and that we would bear any costs in the event that Wang had been hurt. There wasn't much else that we could do.

I hadn't thought of it at first but someone suggested that we should check the bank account at the joint venture, just in case. We called down to ask for the accounts department to check the balances with the bank and get them to confirm it directly to us in Beijing. The confirmation duly came over the wires; there was still a large balance of US dollars in the account. No problem. Attention shifted back to tracing Wang.

The following day another call came in from Zhuhai. It was the finance department of the joint venture. They said that they had received a second fax from the bank and wanted to send it up to me. I said, 'Fine, go ahead, you know the numbers.' But the voice said, 'No, this is an important fax. You need to go and take it from the fax machine yourself.'

I walked down with Michael to fetch the fax. It was already slowly whirring out of the machine. I saw the bank's letterhead and the first few lines in blurred characters referring to some letters of credit. That was the first alarm. A letter of credit is like an unbounceable cheque. They are used in international trade when the seller doesn't know the buyer well enough to send the goods purely on trust. All the seller needs to do is take the letter to his bank, together with proof that the goods have been sent, and the bank has to cough up the cash.

I stared at the list as it ground slowly out of the machine. There were four letters of credit for equipment that I didn't recognize – 'scorching machines', whatever they were. The total came to just under five million. Michael and I looked at each other. How could we have issued all these letters to buy this equipment without knowing? The fax was still churning laboriously out of the machine, along with one of the contracts. I saw that it had been signed and chopped by Wang and was an agreement to buy scorching machines and presses from a company called Solarworld based in Hong Kong.

'Solarworld? Who the hell are they?' said Michael, rapidly scanning across the page. 'Oh, look – here, at the bottom of that page.' He pointed out a note to the contract. It said: 'Eighty per cent of the proceeds to be paid to Che Lap Hong Company, attention Mr Max.' We stared at each other. 'Che Lap Hong?' My heart sank. 'Isn't that one of the shareholders of the Chinese partner?'

'Yeah, I think so.'

'So isn't this just hooking money out of China and straight into one of the Chinese partners' bank account in Hong Kong?'

We stared at one another.

It was a scam.

Zhuhai is a modern city that sprang up just after Old Deng's famous Southern Tour. It is rather like a miniature Shenzhen with modern high-rise apartment blocks, smart restaurants and multi-storey shopping centres. Its streets are broad and lined with palm trees and it has one of the best golf courses in China. And right next to Zhuhai, across a narrow canal, about forty miles from Hong Kong, lies the old Portuguese colony of Macau.

By the estuary of the Pearl River, where the sluggish muddy waters spill lugubriously into the South China Sea, there is a little bay on the coast of Guangdong. Portuguese merchant ships have dropped anchor there since the early 1500s. The early trading outposts on the hilltops around the natural harbour gradually grew into a colony known as Macau, or *Ao-men* in Chinese. Portugal administered it until 1999 when it went back to China, just two years after Hong Kong. On the top of the hill there is a stone fort with extinct cannons still pointing out to sea. Just below, standing out from the twisted alleyways leading up and down the hillsides, stands the gaunt frame of a wrecked church. The front façade remains intact but nothing besides still stands.

Macau's position, squashed up between its brash new neighbour Zhuhai and the sea, seemed to emphasize the Portuguese influence on the old trading settlement, with its winding lanes and ochre-painted villas. At the old Bella Vista, Macau's famous hotel that stood on the hill behind the harbour, they still served *olla podrida* and *vinho verde* on the veranda overlooking the bay. The hotel had seen better days but it still retained a faded colonial magnificence, with its columns, arches and stone-tiled floors. Every Saturday night an opera singer, slightly overweight and well past her 'sell-by date', stood belting out her arias under a glass chandelier that had most of its pieces missing. She stood swaying to the music with a large gin in one hand and the other resting on the top of an upright piano that hadn't been tuned for years. Down below, in the broad Market Square, there was a handsome town hall with green-shuttered windows and with stonework all in terracotta tones. Inside, tiles of white and blue lined the staircase that led up to an ancient library.

The hundreds of tiny inlets and coves along the coast meant that the border between Macau and China was almost impossible to police. Smuggling was rife, and secret criminal societies thrived during the mid-1990s. China was booming and Portugal had little incentive to control the gangs since the Portuguese had only a few more years in which to govern.

There was a particular problem in Macau. The southern Chinese are notorious for their love of gambling. After Liberation it had always been illegal in China. However, under Portuguese rule there had never been any restrictions in Macau and there were scores of casinos on the seafront and in the large boats moored to the quaysides. Towards the late 1990s, as passports for Chinese nationals became easier to obtain, Macau became a favourite destination for Chinese businessmen. Gradually, more sinister activities grew on the fringes of Macau's gaming industry: loan sharking, extortion and prostitution.

For the Triads, the secret 'black societies' that control

these rackets, the geography of the region was perfect. The southernmost province of Guangdong had always been difficult to administer from Beijing due to the huge distances involved and both Hong Kong and Macau were governed by remote and distracted European capitals. With these three different legal jurisdictions, effective policing was almost impossible. If the authorities came too close to the trail of the gangsters in one place, the criminals would just hop over the border safe in the knowledge that coordination between the different police forces was very difficult.

The seriousness of the problems came into the open in 1997 when Hong Kong went back to China. The Triads knew that two out of the three territories had now been unified and the third, Macau, was soon to follow. So in the run-up to the handover of Macau in 1999, gang warfare broke out as the rival factions struggled for control of the territory before it reverted to China. Murder of the most brutal kind, often involving lightning attacks in restaurants by mobs wielding Chinese meat-choppers, became commonplace; the newspapers didn't even bother to report the regular fire-bombings and armed robberies. The situation improved slightly after the arrest and jailing of 'Broken-Tooth' Wan, who was convicted of a host of Triad-related crimes in 1999.

But back in 1995, long before the handover, and long before the worst of the Triad activities became obvious, we had seen no particular reason to shy away from investing in Zhuhai. Macau had still appeared calm; it seemed as if the two parallel communities were neatly segregated on either side of the ancient Portuguese gateway, the Porto de Cerco, that still guarded the border.

In April, 1995, we were introduced to Mr Wang Jinwen who ran the brake-pad factory in Zhuhai. He needed investment to increase his production. Sales to the local car manufacturers were going well and he was convinced that there were huge potential export markets. After about six months of negotiations we agreed a deal and signed up to invest about eight million in a three-way joint venture with Wang and a big US-based car parts company. It was a small investment for us but it looked as though the business would grow rapidly. On Christmas Day in 1995 the business licence was issued and the cash was wired in shortly afterwards.

The factory was on the coast about five miles outside of Zhuhai in what used to be a tiny fishing village. The locals had long since given up their nets and there was a bustling business community with many small manufacturing plants dotted about in the gently rolling hills that faced the sea. Palm trees lined the narrow rocky beach while further out, towards the horizon, the vague and ponderous shadows of huge container ships moved sedately up the coast to Hong Kong. The sea breeze was clear and fresh and the local seafood was good. The brake-parts business had only been running for five or six years so it had none of the problems of our former state-run operations up in the north. Wang seemed happy with the way that the business was developing and was keen to push the export markets. Then, after the Mid-Autumn Festival the following year, he went to America to attend that fateful trade show in Las Vegas.

When we saw the fax from Zhuhai that freezing November morning, we realized immediately that Wang had somehow committed our money to pay for machines that we'd never ordered. It looked as though the money was being channelled through one of Wang's partners. Faced with what looked on the surface suspiciously like a fraud, we threw ourselves into a burst of activity.

The first thing to do was to establish the facts. Then there would be lawyers. And I'd have to tell the Board, of course. I shoved that prospect to the back of my mind for the time being. I could imagine the response I'd get, given the recent scenes when I had told them about Harbin.

The fax specified shipping dates for the goods and the vessels that would be carrying them to China. One should have set sail from Rotterdam, 16 November on a Panama-registered ship called the *Amazonite*. The easiest way to find out whether we had a fraud was to see if there really were any goods on the way. I contacted a friend who worked in a shipping line and asked if he could confirm the whereabouts of some ships for me. 'Sure, send me the vessel's name and last port of embarkation and I'll find it in no time.' So we sent a fax confirming the details and he called back in an hour and a half. He was puzzled. He said that there was indeed a ship called the *Amazonite* registered in Panama with all the correct references.

'That's your ship, all right,' he said. 'But it left Singapore on 14 November, bound for Hamburg.'

At that, the last doubts evaporated. We had a fraud on our hands. From there on, it would just be a question of damage limitation.

I had just hired a new recruit. He had sent me scores of messages from the States and when I told him that we weren't hiring at the time he arranged to come out to China to see me.

Li Wei had been born in Fujian, the coastal province in the south that lies between Shanghai and Hong Kong. His parents both had posts in the Chinese Peoples' Liberation

Army. He had learnt his English at an army school which trained people to listen in to the wireless transmissions of the US pilots who flew reconnaissance missions up and down the coast of China in the 1970s. He was a fast learner and went to one of China's top language institutes in Shanghai. He eventually ended up with a PhD from the Massachusetts Institute of Technology. His PhD thesis was on the Chinese Government 'office systems', which ran parallel to the government and party structures and was much more focused on powerful individuals rather than organizations. The 'office directors' took care of high level officials' diaries and controlled document flows, just like a good PA in a Western context, but the role extends much further. It includes arranging domestic affairs for the official and his family, such as accommodation, travel, education for children and so on, facilitating secret communication between officials and undertaking much of the political in-fighting necessary for climbing the Chinese hierarchy. Consequently the relationship between the official and his 'office director' is one of the utmost trust and the office director can acquire enormous personal power himself if his master's star is in the ascendant. I realized that anyone who had completed a PhD on that subject must have a grasp of Chinese politics which we, at that time, so clearly lacked.

I liked Li Wei when I met him. He was certainly very bright and he had a touch of the humanizing air of a harassed academic. He told me that after nearly ten years in the US he felt it was the right time for him to return to China. He had spent hours and hours searching the web for the right opportunity. He thought that his language skills and experience in America gave him an ability to bridge the gap between China and the outside and he wanted a chance to have a role in something big where his contribution would matter. I could identify with that. When he stumbled on our website, he thought that he had found the right place. I knew from our failures up in Harbin, particualarly the clumsy way that we'd handled the ministry, that we needed someone who could guide us more skillfully through the bewildering maze of government offices and bureaux. I was also impressed by his dogged persistence, so I hired him and pitched him straight into the middle of our difficulties down in Zhuhai.

We immediately flew down to Zhuhai with Michael and Ai Jian and had Wang's office safe sawn open. It took two workers about twenty minutes hacking away before it finally yielded. Inside, we found the first clues of what rapidly developed into a real horror story. There were about seven handwritten IOUs, one from a 'Big Brother Qiu' for one point two million Hong Kong dollars. It looked as if Wang had been involved in loan sharking. We also found suspicious-looking travel permits, several company chops and two backdated cheques to Wang for just under four and a half million Hong Kong dollars. They were drawn on Che Lap Hong and a company called 'Poly-ways'. I had never heard of 'Poly-ways', but at the bottom of the safe I found a contract to build a hotel in Vietnam signed by a 'Mr Lam, for and on behalf of Poly-ways.' I groaned. It was already looking distinctly possible that the hotel might have been funded with our money.

The picture soon got worse. In Wang's safe, we had found two air-ticket vouchers for his flight to America in the previous month. One was for Wang's journey to Las Vegas, but who was the other passenger? By the end of the afternoon Li Wei had found out: he was the assistant bank manager of the branch where we had deposited the US dollars. It was the same branch that had issued the letters of credit.

Li Wei told me, 'I called the bank manager and he said that he came back two weeks ago. Said he was with Wang in Las Vegas but left when Wang went off to New York. He said he hadn't a clue where Wang was now but seemed terribly nervous and started asking lots of questions.'

'But did he explain what the hell he was doing on a trip to the States with Wang to sell brake parts in the first place?' I asked. 'He's a bank manager, not a car-parts salesman!'

'He was a bit hazy on that one,' said Li Wei.

'Hazy?' I exploded. 'HAZY?!'

The story was getting murkier by the minute. There was no way to keep it under wraps; I had to tell the Board.

The hastily called telephonic board meeting that night provided further scenes of chaos. I had told Pat about the problem earlier but he was in Germany with some customers so it was left to me to break the news. With the time delay, the crackling lines connecting people in six different locations around the world and tempers rapidly deteriorating as the complexity of the mess became apparent, it was a struggle to keep the meeting on track. As I went through what had happened, a confused mass of questions burst in from all different directions with three or four people all shouting at the same time. One of the directors kept on asking about bills of exchange and bills of lading, repeatedly confusing the two and getting furious whenever anyone pointed out that they were completely different. Some wanted to call the police to catch Wang, but another said it was a waste of time. One pitched in with the truly amazing suggestion that 'We should go directly to the Hong Kong Monetary Authority to have everyone's bank accounts closed down.' The hordes of lawyers attending the meeting from different parts of the States all gave contradictory advice, droning on about injunctions and Worldwide Mareva Orders long into the night and it wasn't until three in the morning that a consensus emerged.

It was Rubel who eventually got to the point. 'OK,' he said, 'we've got those letters of credit out there but the cash is still in the bank, isn't it?'

'Yeah.'

'So we just need to make sure it stays there and the L/Cs never get paid, right?'

'Right.'

He asked what controls we had in place over the cash at the bank. We had all the normal stuff, with sets of signature cards, just like everywhere else. For any payment out of our dollar bank accounts in Zhuhai, the bank had to get a chopped approval from Beijing; Wang's signature alone wasn't enough.

'So the bank shouldn't take the cash out of our account to pay for the letters of credit, unless we sign off in Beijing,' Rubel said.

It looked as though we might be safe. But two questions made us all deeply nervous about the bank: why had they agreed to open the letters of credit in the first place when they had no chop from Beijing? And why had the assistant bank manager been on the same Las Vegas flight as the missing Wang?

The Board eventually decided that we should try everything to stop the bank from honouring the letters; if we stopped them paying out the money to the fraudsters, whoever they might be, and kept the money in our bank account, we were safe, or so it seemed. They instructed me to insist on a meeting with the Chairman of the bank the next day and demand that he stop the payment. And then some bright spark said right at the end, just as the phones went down, 'But, anyway, it's all governed by Chinese law, so maybe we should get a Chinese lawyer.'

The following morning, Ai Jian and I went to the head office of the bank in Guangzhou. It was about a two-hour drive from Zhuhai so we didn't arrive until mid-morning. We had called on ahead and eventually found the Chairman's office. He was away, but the bank's President was there. We had asked for a meeting but received no clear response, so we decided to go and find him. The head office was located in a huge tower block in the business district of Guangzhou, the main city in Guangdong. It occupied fifteen floors of the building so it took some time to find the President's office. When we got there, I found his office manager and demanded a meeting. Then we sat down to wait.

To my surprise, the President arrived after about ten minutes. He looked like a man whose curiosity had been aroused. It was probably a novelty having an agitated foreigner turn up on his doorstep without any warning and insist on a meeting. We got straight down to business and I explained that we were a foreign investment company with factories all over China. His bank held the account of one of them in Zhuhai, and 'There is a problem.'

I went through the facts, as we saw them. Our manager, Wang, was missing; before disappearing he had opened four letters of credit with the bank; the bank had agreed to open the L/Cs without proper authorization; no goods existed because the ships were in the wrong parts of the world; it therefore looked as though there had been a fraud and the cash appeared to have ended up in a Hong Kong account linked with Wang; and 'the assistant bank manager of your branch in Zhuhai seems to have been on the same flight to the States as the missing Wang.' The bank's President listened patiently but became annoyed when I mentioned the assistant bank manager. 'Just because he was on that flight doesn't mean that he's done anything wrong,' he said hotly.

'I didn't say it did, but you have to admit that it's a bit unusual.'

'Why?' He stared at me blankly.

I decided not to debate the point but said that we wanted the bank to refuse to pay for the letters of credit. We would refuse to honour them. The President said he'd investigate, and the brief, slightly testy encounter ended. I set off back to Zhuhai and arrived at the joint venture in the early afternoon.

Li Wei, meanwhile, had been to see the Anti-Corruption Bureau of the Zhuhai Government. We wanted the authorities to investigate Wang and find out what had happened to the letters of credit. The meeting had not been a success. Li Wei had been kept waiting for hours and was eventually shown into a small office, with dirty ashtrays strewn about and a bleary-looking unshaven man slouched behind a desk: he was apparently the Deputy Bureau Chief in charge of cases involving foreign investors.

'I thought that he should be extremely busy,' said Li Wei. 'You'd expect the Anti-Corruption Bureau Chief in Zhuhai to be rushed off his feet, but he was sitting in his office smoking and reading the newspapers.' I heard later that he had listened half-heartedly to the tale and then, rousing himself with some effort, he'd said that he would set up an investigation, but that in order to do so we would have to give him 'a car and some working capital.'

'What? Are you serious!?' I asked when I heard the news. 'So the Anti-Corruption Bureau wants a car and a bag of money!'

Towards the end of the afternoon, as we struggled to come up with a clear strategy for stabilizing the business, Li Wei came in. He'd just got a call from the accounts department. They had tried to make payroll that afternoon, but the bank had refused to pay it. Now the workers had no wages. The bank said that the local Intermediary People's Court had issued a freezing order and that all our accounts had been closed.

'What the hell's a freezing order?' I asked. 'Can we get a copy and have some Chinese lawyers look at it? Please!'

Back in Beijing, we found a law firm that dealt with fraud cases involving the banking sector. Two lawyers came round to the offices for a briefing. Over the time we worked together, I became very impressed with them. I knew almost nothing about Chinese banking law, and certainly hadn't ever wanted to, but they were always extremely patient in explaining their convoluted logic. Their names were un-pronounceable in Mandarin so, as neither of them spoke English, we simplified matters by calling them 'Big Lawyer' and 'Little Lawyer'.

In the next few hours, as we went though the documents, it emerged that the Court Order freezing all our bank accounts had been obtained by the bank itself. In the few hours that it had taken me to drive back from Guangzhou to Zhuhai after the meeting with the bank's President their lawyers had drafted a petition asking the court to freeze the cash in the accounts so that we couldn't remove it and refuse to pay for the letters of credit. The Order had been issued the same afternoon. I was amazed. 'How can they do that?' I asked.

Big Lawyer explained that when I had told the bank that we would refuse to pay the letters, we had created a legal dispute that could be heard by a Chinese Court. 'But the payment was never authorized,' I said. 'How can they expect us to pay?'

'But it isn't a payment,' said Little Lawyer.

'Of course it is.'

'No, it's a commitment to make a payment, not actually a payment.'

'What? It's the same thing.'

'No, it's not. You've just told the bank that when they try to make the payment, you won't approve it.'

'What?' I said that I didn't agree with that argument but Little Lawyer just pursed his lips.

'And look here,' said Big Lawyer. 'That's the company chop, isn't it?'

I squinted at the fax. 'Looks like it,' I said.

'And here. The Court documents say that there was an approval for the letters by the juridical person.'

'The what?'

'Juridical person.' After several minutes spent searching through various Chinese – and English – dictionaries we managed to figure out that the 'juridical person' of a business in China, normally the Chairman, has the power under Chinese law to bind the company with a signature. In this case, the juridical person was Pat.

Little Lawyer said, 'If he's signed anything approving Wang's issue of the letters, you're on the hook for the whole of the missing five million.'

I could see that we were heading for a long battle through the Chinese courts. It emerged later that Pat had in fact signed a power of attorney that authorized Wang to act as

140

the 'juridical person for normal operations'. It was in Chinese so Pat, presumably not realizing the significance of the document, had signed it anyway. An argument then developed among the lawyers over whether buying five million dollars' worth of equipment was within the definition of normal operations. I thought that it was beside the point; I was convinced that the bank personnel knew the real nature of the transaction and therefore that they should never have agreed to open the letters of credit.

At this stage, the Board back in America briefly discussed just writing off the whole thing to experience and getting on with life. But what kind of message would that send to all the other joint ventures? If we just gave up and failed to pursue Wang and his accomplices, it would hardly be the best deterrent in the event that someone else was considering similar antics with a different business. Also, we had agreed a set of bank signatories and we felt that the bank had ignored them. That brought the whole banking system into doubt and we had several hundred million sitting in accounts all over China. How could we continue to invest in China and hold cash in Chinese banks if we couldn't rely on the controls over payments?

So the battle opened up on two fronts. Pat was determined to keep the business stable so that we could save whatever value was left. So he appointed a new manager to the joint venture, an Italian, Carlie Verlucci. He arrived, complete with sunglasses, trilby and a double-breasted jacket with two rows of gold buttons, which looked as if it had been borrowed from his much larger sidekick, Romanelli. Together, they arrived in January to take over the factory.

Next, Little Lawyer came up with a strategy for the court case. If we could show that the bank had known that the whole scheme was a fraud in the first place, then the court would judge that the bank should pay, not us. That meant that we had to find Wang. If we could get him to confess and show that the bank officials were in on the scam, we'd be off the hook, so we thought.

It took months to get an arrest warrant for Wang. I was surprised how difficult it was but, of course, it was right that the police would not issue a warrant without convincing evidence. The Chinese police issued a 'red warrant' as spring ended and Interpol followed shortly afterwards. The search for Wang had begun.

It was much easier to get action on finding the documents in Hong Kong and soon the police raided Solarworld's offices in Kowloon, retrieving boxes of documents. They revealed a baffling web of interconnected shareholdings and bank transactions together with evidence that Wang had brought the letters to Hong Kong and somehow managed to cash them. That meant that somewhere in the international banking system there were four letters of credit on their way back to Zhuhai that would eventually hit our bank account.

Over the coming weeks, we pieced together the money flows. Wang had found a local finance house, called of all things, Best Finance, and persuaded them to give him a bill of exchange for the letters in return for a hefty discount. He had walked into a bank, deposited the bill and, over the following few days, withdrew the money. In the space of a few short weeks, he had managed to get nearly four million dollars in cash. He then got into the plane at Kai Tak Airport, presumably with the assistant bank manager and 'a large suitcase', and that was the last that we heard of him.

Back in Zhuhai, the Anti-Corruption Bureau was making little progress. That was hardly surprising. We had realized what we were up against after the raid on Solarworld's offices in Hong Kong where the police had found documents showing that a former Zhuhai Government official was one of the shareholders of the company that had received the proceeds. Another shareholder was a Mr Lam, who had previously served a two-year prison sentence for letter-of-credit fraud. It looked as if we were dealing with at least one experienced criminal who could probably count on protection from high places.

Next we heard that the Chinese partner in our joint venture had held a board meeting in Wang's absence to try to figure out what to do, but that it had broken up in disarray. One party, 'the Village Committee', which looked after the little fishing village, tried to take back the land at our joint venture but the others wouldn't agree. It then came out that Wang had also defrauded the Chinese partner by 'pledging' their bank balances against a loan from another bank and then disappearing with the proceeds. Any amusement I felt at the sight of the Chinese partner falling into the same trap as we had was short-lived. I found out that Wang had also dragged us into that mess by using our assets to guarantee the Chinese partner's loan. Since he was now missing and the Chinese partner claimed to have no money, it looked on though we might have to pay that as well.

I was relieved when Big Lawyer told me that the guarantees were against Chinese Company Law. I thought that at least we could escape from that mess. But when I met with the bank manager and told him that the guarantee was invalid, he thanked me profusely and left the room saying that he had never really understood the Company Law and that he would immediately instruct his staff to check whether there were any similar arrangements with other customers! And then, a week later, we received another writ: the bank had sued us to enforce their guarantee even though it was against Company Law.

The first court hearing was held in Zhuhai in the summer. Pat had to give evidence and he said that he'd been impressed with the process. Evidence had been heard and the lawyers had had the right to ask questions and cross-examine the witnesses from the bank. We had been lobbying the Zhuhai Government through the embassy to ask for a proper hearing and the case had attracted some interest from the Central Government, so I was confident that we'd at least get a fair trial. There was so much evidence that the bank had been careless – reckless, I thought – when they'd opened the letters of credit and that they had broken their own internal controls and manufactured documents after the date. It seemed difficult to believe that the court would rule that the bank couldn't have had any suspicion at the time that it was a fraud.

I was slightly perturbed when I heard that the judge had said that he had found the case 'confusing' during the trial and had then visited the bank later to ask further questions. It seemed a bizarre reversal for the judge to be going to the bank rather than demanding that they appear in his court. But I shrugged it off and looked forward to the verdict.

So it was to howls of protest that the court issued its verdict six months later. We had to pay for the whole amount of the letters of credit, the guarantees and our legal costs. The bill was more than ten million. Detailed reading of the written judgement rubbed salt into the wound; the judgement included new evidence that had never been heard in the court. Moreover, some of the documents that the court had demanded had been 'lost' by the bank and only photocopies were supplied. One of these photocopies was of a document where the police had found the original in the raid on Solarworld in Hong Kong; on the 'photocopy' supplied to the court, several parts had been altered.

The judgement then became a hot political issue. We had been keeping the US Embassy in Beijing abreast of developments and the staff there had been very supportive. Once the judgement came out, it transformed the issue from a commercial dispute into a question of the reliability of the Chinese courts. In the following months, letters flew between the top levels of the governments concerned, raising the case and asking China's Prime Minister Zhu Rongji to investigate. We decided to appeal to the Supreme Court of China.

Although Michael had handled much of the work on this case, I was exhausted. The fight in Harbin had been going on at the same time and we had increasing troubles in our breweries in Beijing. I had been travelling almost continuously for nearly a year, putting out fires and trying to get to grips with the factory directors. I had an ear infection that affected my balance and I had lost a pair of glasses so I couldn't see properly. I couldn't sleep either. We were making such slow progress. So it was in a black mood that I went to France for a much-needed rest.

Eight

泰 山 壓 頂 不 彎 腰

Crushed by the Weight of Mount Taishan

> *Traditional saying: Taishan is*
> *one of China's five holy mountains and*
> *represents enormous force or weight*

In France that year the snow just fell and fell. Up in the mountains, wooden chalets disappeared, swallowed whole underneath a great white cloak. Streams were caught mid-flow; trees sagged, their branches drooping under the great load of snow until, suddenly, they'd cast off the burden and snap back to attention. Occasionally, the creaking, crunching sound of an avalanche drifted down through the mists. The skies were leaden and heavy; the snow seemed to deaden all sound as we trudged up and down the slopes. Clouds, rotund and mournful, rolled up the valley. All was grey. The weather matched my state of mind. I seemed imbued with a sense of heaviness that had soaked into my bones.

I couldn't sleep. For several nights, as I twisted about in the sheets and wrestled with jet lag, I felt breathless, as if a heavy weight was pressing on my chest. And the headaches: not

146

even Mayor Huang's *baijiu* had made me feel like that. As I lay there in bed, great stupefying depth-charges boomed at the centre of my brain. I tried to kid myself that it was all caused by the altitude and rolled over, sweating. But on the third night I woke up with a pain in my chest that I could no longer ignore. My hands became clammy as the pain waxed and waned. Slowly, it grew in intensity and radiated through to my back and down to the fourth finger of my left hand. I sat for an hour on the edge of the bed, vainly attempting to deny the truth, and watched the first cold fingers of light creep across the sky. I tried an aspirin; but it wasn't that kind of problem. We called a doctor.

Fifteen minutes later, three men arrived in what looked like firefighters' outfits. I was confused. They seemed to have brought an oxygen bottle and wanted to carry me out. I insisted on walking. We drove for ten minutes to a local clinic where a doctor shoved a needle into my arm and strapped monitors to my chest. I couldn't understand what anyone was saying. I was irritated by all the fuss; if they carried on that way, I'd end up missing the morning's skiing. So I was in a filthy temper by the time they'd strapped me to a stretcher, dumped me into the back of an ambulance and driven me down the valley. Fuming silently, I lay on my back in the ambulance, watching the tops of the fir trees at the edge of my vision turning back and forth against the dull grey sky as the vehicle wound slowly down the mountain road.

The gentle rocking sent me to sleep. I was exhausted. I must have been in a deep sleep when we arrived at the hospital. I remember vaguely someone putting a probe on my chest again and a big monitor, but nothing else. I found out later that I had been sedated.

I woke up with a start in a room that I didn't recognize. Gas bottles and monitors crowded in on me. There were charts on the wall. A nurse came in, looking hassled. She leant over the bed and, with a slight sideways glance, whispered, 'You're in intensive care.'

She waited as it slowly seeped in.

And then, 'You've had a heart attack.'

At first I really had no idea what she meant. How could I have had a heart attack? I was thirty-eight and ran three miles a day. They'd got the wrong guy! I thought briefly about the *baijiu* and the Red Pagoda Mountain cigarettes: not enough there to cause problems, surely. So I sank back into a fitful sleep and waited.

I was fitted with all sorts of drips and monitors and oxygen gauges. The nurse told me that they'd put me on heparin, a blood thinner that might give me a headache. If it got too bad, I should tell them.

The next day was uneventful, but the following morning I woke up with a crashing pain in my head and called the nurse. She adjusted the heparin dose and went away. Gradually, the pain came back in my chest. I struggled against a rising sense of panic. I felt my heart stopping and restarting again with a great thump inside my ribcage. But much worse than feeling these breaks in my heartbeat, I could *see* them as well! I stretched my neck sideways and backwards, craning to watch the green point on the monitor screen that registered the heartbeat. As it moved silently and relentlessly across the screen, there were long depressions in the wave followed by a sudden burst of activity before it flattened out again. The heart rate on the monitor screen fell from sixty down to fifty-five and through fifty. The pain increased. I felt great stabs through my chest and a dull all-consuming ache in the temples. My head span. Down through forty-five to forty. At thirty-eight, great squashy blotches appeared in front of my eyes. As I passed out, I remember hearing, as if through a long tunnel, the frightened voice of the nurse calling for a doctor for '*le jeune anglais*'. And then all was black.

I woke up feeling like death.

For a long time, I didn't move. My arm hurt. I looked down and found that my body was covered in repulsive bruises right down to my feet. Great black veins on my arm stood out half an inch. I had been given an emergency treatment with a powerful drug that turns blood to water, a risky crisis treatment for someone actually having a heart attack. It dawned on me that this might be for real.

I lay there for six days, drugged and drifting in and out of sleep. On the sixth day, I was loaded into a tiny jet and flown back to Oxford. I had been given a letter to take with me. It was in French and I had it translated afterwards. It described all the symptoms and the diagnosis, concluding that my problem was an 'inferior subendiocardial infarct in a young man with no risk factors except stress.' From where I was lying that meant trouble.

I had an angiogram at the hospital. I was frightened before I went in. They had told me that it wouldn't hurt but that they needed to push a tube up through a vein in my thigh into my heart while I was still awake. They promised to knock me out a bit while they were doing it; 'gin and tonic' said the surgeon. Luckily it was stronger than that. I don't remember much except that my feet were very cold; I discovered afterwards that while they were doing the procedure the fire alarm had gone off and I had been wheeled out into the car park for ten minutes until it was safe to go back inside.

That afternoon the surgeon came in with a smile on his

face. 'Good news,' he said. 'Your pipes are as clean as a whistle.' The diagnosis had been wrong so he sent me home with an aspirin.

I was completely shattered. How could all this have happened? How could everything have gone so bizarrely wrong? For me personally the whole experience had been an utter disaster.

My nerve had held during the crisis. I had been too confused to think that I would die there and then, but as soon as it was over I collapsed completely. Thoughts of my children tore at me; my little one was only four months old. For days afterwards I wept silently and alone.

At first the doctors didn't know what had happened so they gave me test after test. Once they called me on the phone and told me rather lethargically that the problem might be a cracked aorta, but I replied that I thought that I'd be dead if that was the case. They seemed to agree and promised to look for something else. The tests eventually showed that I had suffered some weird viral attack that had inundated my heart and liver and had got into my joints. They said that a combination of my body's 'depleted batteries' and the altitude in France might have contributed, but that now the trouble was gone and I should rest for a few months and not worry about China.

I didn't think about China for a long time, but gradually my thoughts drifted back to the other side of the world. My first instinct was just to forget the whole thing. The problems appeared overwhelming. We were losing nearly twenty million a year while the factory directors careered off in every direction and we argued among ourselves about what to do. With this new blow to the solar plexus, I thought that the personal cost of continuing was just too high. I decided to quit.

But then, throughout the early spring in England – days, unusually, of sunshine – I thought more and more about what had gone wrong. Strangely, as time passed, the shock had had a calming effect. It put the business difficulties into perspective and, as the months rolled by, I felt that I could view things more objectively from England.

As I sat in the sunshine, listening vaguely to the birds in the hedges and thinking, I started to have my first doubts about just jacking the whole lot in. China seemed to have worked itself into my bones. It wasn't going to be easy to leave all that behind. And what about the people who had given us all that money? Didn't I owe it to the investors to at least try and sort out the mess? And the Chinese: for every Pang Yuanweng, there was an eager translator up in the hills, desperate to expand his horizons and embrace the outside world. For every Wang who had stolen millions from our joint venture in Zhuhai, there was a Mayor Huang and an Ironman Jiang and a Li Wei. What about the people who really believed in what we were trying to accomplish? Or Ai Jian who'd had the guts to leave the security of his job? No, here was something worth fighting for. I realized that I couldn't just run away.

And there was another, much bigger reason for wanting to go back. China was in a state of supreme upheaval as it fought to adapt. The pessimists gleefully predicted from the sidelines that the crisis was so deep that it might destroy China's existence as a unitary state. I didn't see it like that. But I knew that when Deng had opened up the gates he had unleashed centrifugal forces that sent millions reeling; billions and billions of dollars had poured into China along the coast in a great splurge whilst the neglected hinterland remained destitute. A confused tidal wave of people rose up from the country villages sending a hundred million itinerant labourers swirling towards the sea.

At the same time, with its resources exhausted, the government began wearily removing the props from the old state-owned factories. Staggering under the weight of bloated payrolls, these old factories began collapsing as though in a great domino pile, dragging down banks and savings cooperatives with them and toppling millions more out onto the streets. And – almost as a side issue – the newspapers routinely reported the execution of officials caught looting state coffers of millions of dollars and bank managers who lent astronomical sums of money to their relatives. In just one case, the Bank of China admitted that in their branch in Kaiping, a medium-sized town in Henan Province, they had lost $483 million dollars when five officials fled in 'a well-organized escape plan involving dozens of fake passports'. Meanwhile a cowed peasantry of nine hundred million toiled on the land while images of unattainable affluence beamed into the villages from outside.

The contortions required of the Chinese leadership in this immense social and economic balancing act were scarcely comprehensible. For certain, China had to change in order to progress and the Government had to relax its grip to let that happen. But if central authority should collapse, the population movement would affect the whole world. So, for me, this was a chance of a ringside seat at a spectacle of massive historical importance. There wasn't a choice. I felt that I had to go back.

So what had I learnt? From my eight years at the coalface in China, I knew that I was dealing with a society that had no rules – or, more accurately, plenty of rules that were seldom enforced. China seemed to be run by masterful showmen: appearances mattered more than substance, rules were there to be distorted and success came through outfacing an opponent. The irony was that the entire nation seemed to be shadow-boxing with itself. Whereas to most foreigners China seemed too centralized, with an all-controlling Party brooding at the hub of a vast monolithic State, everywhere I had looked there had seemed to be a kind of institutionalized confusion.

I'd realized during the dispute in Harbin that there were two completely separate power structures in China: the Government and the Party. The idea was to provide checks and balances. But every senior official in the Government was also a senior Party member. Most senior Party members had held top Government positions. They constantly switched jobs between Party and Government so that real power ended up in the hands of the individual rather than the office. Responsibilities overlapped, which resulted in protracted and pointless power struggles, but elsewhere the system left no one in control. Ministries fought over territory whilst the army expanded into commercial activities such as manufacturing medicines or investing in hotels. I remember hearing that the police in Guangzhou were running a chain of cake shops.

The result was a society with some areas of rigid control where the Party delved deep into narrow vertical sections. But these sections seemed roped off from each other, leaving great voids in between. That was where the Chinese entrepreneur learnt the ropes, where officials routinely manipulated badly written rules: a place of writs and freezing orders, fake letters of credit, judges who did not understand a case but passed judgement anyway, officials from an Anti-

Corruption Bureau who asked for cars and bags of money. One thing was for sure: if you played by the rules you were finished. I realized that if I was going to go back, I would have to unlearn everything.

I knew that we would have to find a Chinese solution to a Chinese problem. As I thought through what had happened and tried to anticipate the battles ahead, one remark kept coming up again and again. It went round and round in my mind. It had been made when Pang Yuanweng had told the managers up in Harbin that they had to choose between 'the factory or the foreigners'.

The factory or the foreigners. That didn't sound good.

I had sensed early on that Chinese people understandably had exceptionally negative feelings about the country's colonial history. Conversations often came up about the nineteenth-century Englishmen who arrived with their gun-ships and their Indian opium. I knew that Chinese people had not forgotten that long period of national humiliation. It was too much part of their heritage: part and parcel of Mao's audacious promise that his new People's Republic would 'reverse the reversal of history'; the reason why Deng was never going to let Hong Kong remain British.

I turned Pang's remark over and over in my mind. But, as I thought about what had happened up in Harbin, I still couldn't characterize it neatly as a straight fight between Chinese and foreigners. Despite the slogans and 'the factory or the foreigners' remark, I still hadn't felt any real racism creeping in. Even when the fight was at its most intense, I hadn't seen the closed-mindedness, the chauvinism or the essential lack of self-confidence that fuels true racism. When anger spilt over, as it did in 1999 when NATO bombed the Chinese Embassy in Belgrade and demonstrators threw rocks at the US Embassy in Beijing, it seemed natural that these emotions should have found direction most easily along nationalistic lines.

But ours was a much more familiar story; it was just another fight between two groups of people over power and money. And Pang, when he tried to stoke up ethnic differences, was using every weapon he had and it hadn't really worked. No, I felt that the Chinese were too practical, too self-confident and too curious about what was going on in the world outside to fall into any negative racist trap. They wanted to catch up.

I hoped that this might give me a chance of reaching across the cultural divide, a chance of appealing to common values. If it came to a struggle with the factory directors, I had to convince them that I was fighting them not as a foreigner but as a businessman. That way, I might have a chance.

Chinese people have a deep sense of 'Chineseness', which I felt I had to break through. This 'Chineseness' extends well beyond patriotism, nationality, citizenship and loyalty but includes all of those ideas. I wrote that when I first came to China almost ten years earlier, I had found something so vast and so old that it took me right out of myself. Over time, I tried to clarify those hesitant first impressions into something more distinct. I had developed a sense of some special bond between the people now living in the country we call China and the immense and ancient culture of their ancestors; ancestors who lived on that land for five thousand years and wrote down their history in an unbroken chain. 'Bond' is the right word: a binding, restraining force that includes the concept of owing as well as receiving. I think that being part of that exclusive five-thousand-year-old club gives the Chinese a sense of separateness and self-esteem. It can occassionally develop into a sense of superiority, but no more than anywhere else. And the legacy has its costs. The price that China paid came from the burden of history. Until recently, China couldn't change.

'Chineseness' is innate, something that you are born with. It can't be changed by something as ephemeral as a passport or a mere lifetime spent abroad. Once, as I sat chatting under an old wisteria in the Beijing spring sunshine with Old Liuzi, the conversation turned to adoption. I'd known Liuzi for several years and I told her that I had just come back from Changsha in the south where I had seen a group of about thirty foreigners all carrying tiny Chinese babies. Every year in China, thousands of unwanted babies are abandoned so the Government set up an adoption service to cope with the problem. We talked a bit about the 'one-child' policy – most of the unwanted babies are girls – and Liuzi told me that she thought that it was probably a good thing that so many were being adopted abroad. But when I mentioned that Chinese babies adopted by parents in America or Europe would not necessarily grow up just naturally speaking Chinese, she didn't believe it. She would have none of my theory that language depended on environment. She was convinced that speaking Chinese was hardwired into the genes. This almost physical connection with their culture that Chinese people feel was something that was slowly dawning on me.

Language is central to this sense of 'Chineseness' and the written Chinese characters are central to the language. They provide a link with the past quite unlike that provided by European languages. The characters represent complete ideas rather than sounds so they are different to an alphabet in that they resist changes over the years or between regions. Pronunciation of Chinese words might change over the

156

centuries, but the written character remains constant. The character 香 may be pronounced *xiang*, *heung*, or *hong*, but it always means 'fragrant'. Separate from the sound and recognizable across thousands of years, the characters keep history alive. When China's earliest philosophers recorded their ideas on bamboo spills as far back as the sixth century BC they used characters, many of which are still in daily use. It's as if, with a little effort from the reader, the words of Plato or Aristotle leapt from the page in the original.

The link in China between daily language and the past is strengthened further by a lack of tenses. In Chinese, there is no verb change depending on time. 'Mao Zedong is a good leader' and 'Mao Zedong was a good leader' are not distinguished in Chinese. Things that in our language are extinct remain alive in Chinese. Without the separation in language or thought between what 'was' and what 'is', China's past seems to merge into its present.

Until the last century, this connection was strengthened by a traditional dating system that provided no simple way to gauge relative historical periods. Dates were defined by the Emperor's reign: AD 1817 was Jiaqing 18; AD 965 was Taizu 5; there was nothing to indicate that one of the dates precedes the other by 852 years. The past seemed to merge into cycles that lacked a clear timeline mapping stages in development or an origin where $t = 0$.

The heightened awareness of history inhibited change and created a great tension. The language provided a permanent rigid connection to a past that looked backwards but at the same time there was a realization that China was in a struggle for its survival where success depends on the ability to change. The Chinese seemed caught between a great reverence for the past and the need to move on.

*　　　*　　　*

My own journey through the language had taken many wrong turnings and, as hard as I searched, I found no alternative to rote learning. Chinese children have to do the same thing; hours and hours and hours spent writing the same character again and again until it sticks. Repetition is the only way in. For an English-speaker learning French, there are prompts. Police becomes *police*, garden becomes *jardin*. But a foreigner has no such guide into Chinese: police is *jingcha*; garden becomes *huayuan*. And not only *jingcha* and *huayuan*. For every word, you have to learn three components: the sound, the character and the tone.

In Chinese, the pitch of each word affects its meaning. *Mai*, for instance, with a falling tone, means 'to sell'. But *mai* with first a low falling and then a rising tone means precisely the opposite, 'to buy'. Even Chinese people find it confusing. At the Shanghai Stock Exchange the brokers used slang to make sure that they don't mix up buy and sell orders.

Many words sound exactly the same or confusingly similar. Often Chinese people have to go to great lengths to define a character taken out of context. For example, it would be perfectly normal for someone to introduce themselves with 'Hello, I am Deputy Section Chief Li, that's the *Li* with the sign for tree on the top and a seed underneath,' or 'Hello, I am Madame Wang, that's the *wang* used in "boundless oceans" not the one that means "king".' Without further explanation, a character lacking a clear context is often impossible to identify with certainty if one relies merely on its sound.

As a result, Chinese people often have to give lengthy explanations to convey accurately meanings that would be quite obvious in English. Once, as I waited at Nanjing airport with Ai Jian, we went into a small restaurant. I ordered a beer but when Ai asked for some boiled water the waitress hesitated. Remember, there is no tense in Chinese.

'Does this man mean "boiling water" or "boiled water"?' So he expanded: 'Cold boiled water!' But that made it worse. She looked completely blank. I could see the concept of cold boiling water slowly developing in her mind. So he gave the full explanation. 'Please can I have some water that was once cold and then was brought to the boil and has been left so that it has become cold again, so that I can be sure that the water is clean.'

'OK,' the waitness said flatly and without the remotest change in expression.

Then there were further complications. Ai Jian had used the expression *liangde kaishui*, meaning 'cold boiled water'. But it sounds almost the same as *liangge kaishui*, meaning 'two cups of hot water'. So it took another round of negotiations to sort out that he only wanted one cup. No wonder bottled mineral water is so popular in China. The alternative is just too exhausting.

I loved to eavesdrop when large groups of people became embroiled in these states of confusion, especially when there was a chance that a foreigner, exasperated beyond endurance by endless unintelligible discussions over simple questions, might finally lose his temper.

Top of my collection of 'Chinese cross purposes' occurred in a Chinese medicine shop close to Qianmen, the front gate of the ancient city of Beijing just south of Tiananmen Square. I'd heard that some of the old Chinese remedies there contained a high concentration of cannabis and, although the particular remedy that I had discovered appeared to be a laxative, I was willing to have a go. So I went down to the old Chinese medicine shop, *Tong Ren Tang*, which was founded in 1669 and still resides in a three-storey building with enormous red columns, rickety staircases and dusty Chinese lanterns.

Inside, I found row upon row of ancient wooden shop counters containing every conceivable vegetable and animal part, all neatly ordered and packaged and categorized by function; there was the 'thinning blood' section, several counters for 'revitalizing the *qi*' and the 'department of wind control'. It was bemusing, so I asked for the medicine, *huo ma ren*, at the front desk. They directed me past display cases stuffed with dried sea horses, anti-obesity tea and 'slices of multi-flowered knotweed tubers'. I climbed the stairs towards a dispensary at the back of the shop. There I found one of the illest-looking shop assistants I had ever seen. Thin almost to the point of translucence, she was deathly pale with papery skin stretched over a face anchored down by a set of outlandish dentures and crowned with a great knot of dried-up hair. She looked as though she was about to fall over. She wore a badge which read 'Shop Assistant Number 14' pinned on to her white overalls. I asked for my medicine and, as she fussed about with a pair of ancient weighing scales, I was distracted by a disturbance down at the other end of the long wooden counter. A large woman with a headscarf and thick glasses and wearing blue factory overalls tucked into a pair of enormous boots had clumped in. She was loudly demanding senna. I had obviously stumbled on Constipation City.

Once the woman had stomped off with her bags of senna, the second shop assistant (Number 8) turned to the next customer. He enquired politely whether they sold ants. Number 14 called across from the weighing room and asked, 'How much d'you want, then?'

'Well, how do you sell 'em?' the customer replied.

Ants: I wondered. Maybe by the ounce? By the litre? By the hill?

The discussion on ants fast became the focus of attention,

and another customer barged into the conversation with the question, 'So what do ants cure, then?' Shop Assistant 8 was immediately highly indignant. She flounced off back to the weighing counter, complaining loudly to Shop Assistant Number 14 about customers asking such idiotic questions and announcing hotly that she really had no idea. The customers appeared taken aback by this response. They were, after all, in a medicine shop. But I was sensitized to the confusion and twigged immediately. When the customer had said, '*Ma yi zhi shenme, ne?*' – 'What do ants cure?' – Number 8 had misheard it for '*Ma yi chi shenme, ne?*', which sounds almost identical but means 'What do ants eat?'

So everything comes back to the ideographic character. Written down, 'cure' – 治 – and 'eat' – 吃 – are immediately distinguishable. It's the sounds *zhi* and *chi* that confuse. Without seeing a character, or having it laboriously described by context or shape, it is not possible to be absolutely sure which one is meant.

About a hundred years ago, there was a move to abolish characters. There was a brief reform movement and the government was trying to modernize the country. The writing system was seen as archaic, something that was holding China back, so they proposed the idea of replacing characters with a phonetic representation. The characters for China, 中国, would be replaced by a spelling of its sound: 'chung kuo'. Beijing, or 北京, would become 'pei ching'; the underlying characters would be done away with.

A professor at Beijing University wrote a short, nonsensical but intelligible story in response. It told of a poet, called Gentleman Shi, who lived in a stone house and became addicted to eating lions. He went in search of them and found ten in a market, but realized that they were all

161

dead when he got home. The professor published his story without any comment.

Transcribed into the phonetics that the government had suggested,

施氏食狮史

石室诗士施氏，嗜食狮，誓食十狮。氏时时适市视狮。十时，氏适市，适十狮适市。是时，氏视是十狮，恃十石矢势，似是十狮逝世。氏拾是十狮尸适石室，石室湿，似侍试拭石室，石室拭，氏始试食是十狮尸，是时，氏始识事是事实。

试释是事！

became:

Shih shih shih shih shih

Shih shih shih shih shih shih, shih shih shih, shih shih shih shih. Shih shih shih shih shih shih shih. Shih shih, shih shih shih, shih shih shih shih shih. Shih shih, shih shih shih shih shih, shih shih shih shih shih, shih shih shih shih shih shih. Shih shih shih shih shih shih shih shih shih. Shih shih shih, shih shih shih shih shih shih, shih shih shih, shih shih shih shih shih shih shih shih, shih shih, shih shih shih shih shih shih shih

Shih shih shih shih!

Every character in the professor's story is pronounced *shih*. The last four mean something like 'Go on, check that it's true!' The professor's point was clear; like it or not, Chinese can't be reduced to an alphabet. The characters are here to stay.

Modern Chinese characters are highly developed pictograms. Sometimes it is possible to make out the root, but for most it is not. 'Horse', for example, still looks vaguely like the animal. With a bit of imagination, the mane, the back, the four legs and the tail in the hook on the right hand side are still visible.

馬

But then tiger,

虎

or snake,

蛇

give no obvious clue to their meaning. Rain can be seen in the picture of a cloud and cascading water droplets,

雨

and umbrella – well, it's an umbrella.

伞

In other characters, vague hints can be given to the meaning and sometimes the sound, but never enough to be sure. For instance, three droplets at the left-hand side of a character imply water, thus:

river,

江

lake,

湖

waterfall,

瀑

the wistful sound of the rain pattering through the leaves,

潇

and snot.

涕

To make matters even worse, Mao tried to simplify the language by modifying the characters. The idea was to make them easier to learn, but his changes can add to the confusion. For instance, the character

体

has an alternative form

體

but has a completely different meaning from

休

which *looks* almost the same.

So this was my third reason to go back. With all its comic imprecision, the mesmerizing poise of its characters and its mysterious capacity to reach back into the depths of history and bring thoughts resonating across thousands of years, I had unwittingly fallen for the language.

As I started to think about what to do next, I felt that the core problem was that we had somehow completely failed to get the Chinese on our side. We had invested vast sums of money into China; that was unusual in itself. There were some global giants who had invested more, but not many. We were the only foreign investor to have put such huge amounts into the inner provinces where money was most needed but where few investors were willing to go. Su's gearwheel factory, for instance, was in a tiny village in Sichuan. When I went there in late 1993, I was the first Westerner ever to visit. When we wired in our investment of fifteen million, it was held in escrow by the Prefectural Bank for four days while they confirmed the amount with the remitting bank. It was the largest transaction that they had ever handled and they assumed that there had been a clerical error with the amount.

Later we invested in a Third Line factory in Shanxi near where Ai Jian had lived with the peasants. When we arrived, the factory had nothing. It was a huge iron foundry originally built to supply parts for tanks, but they had never had enough money to get it up and running. Some of the buildings, which had been started in the 1970s, were still not complete. There was hardly an unbroken window in the whole factory. In winter, it was freezing inside; at dinner, they couldn't afford beer and in the surrounding fields people still lived in caves. But when we eventually invested twenty-five million in the factory, we still didn't seem to get them on our side.

There seemed to be an almost total mutual incomprehension. According to our world-view, we thought that we had something enormously valuable to bring to China, which would enable the factories to prosper and develop. But the factory directors had seemed to be quite uninterested in building something together with us once the money had arrived. It was as if some things hadn't changed in the two hundred years since George III first tried to open up China for business.

In 1793, the British king had sent an emissary to the Chinese Court to negotiate trade relations. The mission lasted two years and involved seven hundred people – doctors, musicians, painters and soldiers among them – all loaded up with telescopes, porcelain, fabrics and chronometers, models of gunships and a planetarium as gifts for the Emperor. The emissary arrived in Beijing but was only granted an audience with the Qian Long Emperor after months of bickering over whether he would *kow-tow* by banging his forehead on the ground nine times before addressing the Emperor. Britain, at the time, was an advanced mercantile nation, on the brink of industrialization and with the most powerful navy on earth so George III, understandably, considered himself an equal when dealing with the Emperor. But that was utterly removed from the Chinese picture of the world. It never occurred to them that George III would consider himself anything other than the petty administrator of some distant vassal state and prostrate himself before the Emperor. After months of haggling, a formula was eventually agreed where, according to the emissary, as representative of the King, he went down on one knee. But after he had been finally ushered into the imperial presence, he was handed an edict by Court officials that had been prepared weeks beforehand. It read:

Although your country, O King, lies in the far oceans, yet, inclining your heart towards civilization, you have specially sent an envoy respectfully to present a message. We have perused the text of your message and the wording expresses your earnestness. From it your sincere humility and obedience can clearly be seen. It is admirable and we fully approve.

It went on to deal with the King's key request – that permission be granted for trade representatives to reside in China – as follows:

> The Celestial Empire, ruling all within the four seas, simply concentrates on carrying out the affairs of government properly . . . we have never valued ingenious articles, nor do we have the slightest need of your country's manufactures. Therefore, O King, as regards your request to send someone to remain at the capital, whilst it is not in harmony with the regulations of the Celestial Empire, we also feel very much that it is of no advantage to your country. Hence we have commanded your tribute envoys to return safely home. You, O King, should simply act in conformity with our wishes by strengthening your loyalty and swearing perpetual obedience so as to ensure that your country may share the blessings of peace . . . this is a special edict.

The British eventually responded by blowing up Nanjing. But at the time, the emissary returned to England, completely mystified as to why the Chinese didn't want the benefits of trade and technology that he could bring from Europe. The Chinese probably never gave it another thought. To be sure, almost two centuries later Deng had ripped open the doors and let in the outside, but there were still times when I felt traces of this traditional thinking, the sense that China had endured temporary invasions for centuries but had eventually absorbed the invaders; that it didn't need to accommodate a better relationship with foreigners but just take what might be useful at the time and continue on its own chosen path.

There was no point in trying to change China. We had invested the money there and we had to learn to play by its rules.

On the other side, I found the Wall Street world-view almost as immutable as that of China. I had little faith in being able to persuade the Board back in New York to meet the factory directors on their own terms. When Wang Jinwen had taken out the letters of credit that eventually exposed us to a bill of ten million dollars, the money was still in the bank. We just knew that there was a commitment that would eventually come home to roost, but it could have taken months to find its way back to Zhuhai. The Chinese solution would have been to transfer most of the money out of the bank account quietly and in small amounts, until the bank noticed and froze the account or until there was no money left to argue about. We had done the exact opposite and precipitated a crisis by blustering into the bank's head office. As soon as the bank's senior people knew that there was a problem they made a couple of phone calls to the local court and froze our money while we were embroiled in all-night board meetings with hordes of lawyers discussing injunctions and Worldwide Mareva Orders. There had been a knee-jerk reaction from the US to hire battalions of private investigators and lawyers in a highly sophisticated response that was completely useless in dealing with the actual problem. Our whole case in Zhuhai rested on our belief that the bank had not been properly authorized to issue the letters of credit. But we subsequently discovered that, even though he had no authority to do so, Wang had chopped some of the documents with the company seal or 'chop'. Chops are little round seals, which are rubbed on red inkpads and are needed to approve virtually every type of document in China from train tickets to declarations from the Politburo. Under Chinese law, a red chop can authorize a document regardless of whether or not the person who actually chops the document has any authority to do so. This had made no sense to us as Westerners used to seeing signatures as approval. In China, the system of using chops can lead to a separation of responsibility and power since no one can prove which individual actually chopped a document. Li Wei used to describe it as a kind of 'collective irresponsibility' but the system has been around for thousands of years and it is not about to change.

As a final irony, Wang was arrested in the States several years later and convicted of some minor related offences. The last I heard, he was serving a prison sentence in California, but I was told that when he gets out, he can't be extradited to China because conviction of the theft of such a large amount carries the death sentence and the US considers the Chinese judicial system to be unreliable. Who knows, he might even get to stay in America. The money was never found.

Wall Street's theory of 'private equity investment', investing in private companies like we had done in China, was based on two principles. Firstly, that the system of law and other controls are reasonably effective in dissuading business managers from helping themselves to the cash and secondly, that a management team will work hard over long periods for clear incentives. Under these conditions, the theory goes, the management team can be left reasonably free to run the business and report to a Board of Directors that sets budgets and reviews progress. We had applied this model in China – and it was obviously not working. Zhuhai taught us a lesson about the first assumption and I was starting to realize that the second was too simplistic.

Pat's world was dominated by the endless search for capital and, in the States, this was supposed to occur through open competition. But it wasn't the same in China. Pat had a way of looking at our factory directors that he often wrote about and mentioned in speeches. He'd talk about a 'management gap' in China. His analysis was that, after the founding of the People's Republic, China had essentially been closed to foreigners and there had been no true competition in the socialist economy. So managers in China had just been allocated capital and told what to make. There had never been any pressure to respond to a market or develop new products. Capital was simply assigned to whoever worked their government networks most successfully. There was no market regulation to funnel capital to the best managers and no pressure to perform. Once Deng took off the handcuffs, the natural Chinese entrepreneurs suddenly burst out into the open. The problem, Pat thought, was that managers seemed to go to either extreme. 'If the management is too bureaucratic, you can't get anything done,' he'd say, 'But, on the other hand, if they're too entrepreneurial you can't sleep at night. You may be in the components business one day and find that you are in the hotel business tomorrow.' Or gearboxes. Or smuggling.

It was true. Some of the factory directors were so stodgy that we couldn't do anything with them. Early on, when we had tried to motivate them with increased salaries and a new bonus system, I had found that many of the factory directors were actually reluctant to take the pay increase. During the salary negotiation with a certain Kang, who ran one of our businesses in a remote country village in Sichuan,

170

it felt as if our positions had been completely reversed. I started by offering him two hundred thousand *renminbi* a year, a big increase at the time, but he would only take a hundred. I eventually bargained him up to one hundred and fifty. Then, when I wanted to backdate the rise to January, he wouldn't take it. After about twenty minutes of arguing around, we compromised on April. Living in an isolated factory up in the hills, Kang was unwilling to take a large salary rise. Everyone worked and lived together in the confines of the factory and Kang was not ready to break the old established mould.

On the other hand, the more entrepreneurial managers were incredibly quick on their feet. Their thinking didn't conform to a big picture; they were focused entirely on the short term. In China, new businesses often sprang up and withered in a matter of months. There might be a shortage of some particular product so factories were built in mere weeks, often creating a glut that caused many of them to fail. This short-termism might derive from there having been so much turmoil and reversal in China's recent history, particularly during the Cultural Revolution. The extreme degree of uncertainty about the future might motivate people to grab what they can while they can. It not only creates the Wang Jinwens, who may take your money while you're not looking, but also the Sus, who might erect a huge new gearbox factory without discussing it with anyone beforehand.

So it was true. Most of the factory directors were either wild men, or so stodgy that they drove us to distraction. In both cases, we weren't really in control. We owned the controlling stake in each business but we weren't in control. Maybe we should have been firmer at the start, but by this time we just had to find some way of taking back the businesses, either by establishing trust with the existing factory directors or by booting them out and replacing them with someone else we could rely on. We had tried that up in Harbin, and it had been an abysmal failure. The next steps would require more caution, more intelligence, more guile.

And then, of course, there was the other side to contend with. As losses mounted, more and more impractical demands came beaming in from the States. Headcount reductions became an obsession. Almost all Chinese state-owned businesses were heavily overmanned, but significant lay-offs were virtually impossible. There was no social security, so what were these discarded people supposed to do? But still there was a knee-jerk reaction to headcount figures. 'Three thousand workers? Cut the payroll!'

I once received a note from one of our Chinese factory directors in the southern province of Hunan. Li was one of our best managers, a rare example of a factory director comfortably in the middle of Pat's management spectrum, and we trusted him. He had attempted to implement cautious workforce reductions at the factory and provide some continuing payments for those who had to leave. But the message from Hunan told me that 'Yesterday a worker arrived at the house of Mr Li with some bombing materials.' Apparently a worker had strapped explosives to his chest and had barged into Li's flat at the factory while his family were eating lunch and threatened to blow the whole place up if Li made him redundant. There had been a stand-off lasting four hours, with police outside, but it had eventually been settled amicably and the worker had gone home. Our factory director was shattered and resigned from his post.

I heard afterwards that the police had not taken any action against the worker. Dynamite, apparently, was reasonably easily available because it was used to blast irrigation ditches in the countryside and the authorities were terrified of provoking further unrest. Eventually, Li agreed to stay on, but there were no more workforce reductions. The episode was quite an education for me. The lack of a government social security system and the years of reliance on the work unit in socialist China meant that real redundancy plans were almost impossible to implement and they raised tough moral questions as well.

Nevertheless, I felt that the directors back in New York were starting to think that I was full of bullshit when I went through these types of difficulties. I sensed that they thought I was throwing up roadblocks and making excuses for not getting things done. I began to think that it was only a matter of time before my own head would be on the block. One thing was clear: there wasn't much time.

So I went back to China in the spring of 1998. I knew that there were some heavy-duty fights ahead and I knew that they couldn't be won with teams of lawyers sent in from the States. Harbin had been a disaster; this time we would have to be less gentle and fight with more cunning. The stakes were high, but strangely I felt calmer about the prospect. The shock of sudden illness had left me feeling that I should go back and do my damnedest, but if it didn't work out, so be it. There were other more important things in life that I wasn't prepared to lose.

Nine

強龍不壓地頭蛇

The Battle of Ningshan:
The Mightiest Dragon Cannot Crush the Local Snake

From 'Journey to the West',
an unattributed sixteenth-century
Ming Dynasty novel

As soon as I got back to China, I went down to Ningshan to see Shi. After we made our first investment down there, he had proven to be extremely resourceful and the business was our best performer. Shi had surprised us all at first when he managed to get the government chops so quickly after Pat signed the contract, but we soon got used to his energetic, buccaneering style and since the business made money we left him to get on with it.

But on this trip to Ningshan, after a three-month absence, I was met by a group of agitated people. They looked nervously around and quickly drew me into a side doorway. In hushed voices, they gave me lurid descriptions of a second factory that Shi was building some miles down the valley. They had heard that Shi had ordered a large batch of moulding machines. 'That means that he must be trying to set up in competition with us,' they said darkly. 'If you don't stop it now, you'll have a monster on your doorstep.'

Back in 1993, on my first trip to Ningshan, I had landed at Hangzhou airport in an old propeller plane in the drizzle and mist. Everything was grey, cold and damp. There didn't seem much point in visiting West Lake to take in the scenery, so we made straight for the mountains.

It was the first time that I had been to Anhui, but I knew that this landlocked inner province in central China had vast mountain areas surrounded by dense bamboo forests that were still inaccessible by road. One of China's holy mountains, *Huangshan*, the Yellow Mountain, was in Anhui. For a thousand years, it had inspired watercolours of rocky pinnacles with twisted pines and peaks stretching high above the clouds in the valleys far below. Further north, the steep-sided hills and bamboo forests gave way to gentler slopes that rolled down towards the Yangtse. The sixty million inhabitants of Anhui spoke with a thick accent, which was difficult to follow, but I had heard that they shared the northerners' taste for good food and strong liquor and never passed an opportunity for a party.

The tiny village of Zhongxi in Ningshan County sat high up in the mountains, miles from anywhere. At first the road to the factory crossed dreary flood plains, flat and monotonous, but gradually the road approached the foothills and we wound our way upwards through rolling countryside. Tea bushes with stiff dark green leaves covered the hills in neat rows up to a certain altitude where, over time, they gave way to lighter bamboo tints. As we climbed, the road deteriorated and the journey became slower. We frequently stopped to wait for local farmers to clear the road of huge piles of bamboo. The hillsides became steeper and rockier and the valley sides closed in. It was a wilder landscape than I had seen the year before when we'd visited Che's gearbox factory in Sichuan.

After about four hours, on the brow of a hill, the driver stopped for a cigarette. It was the highest point and marked the border between the provinces of Anhui and Zhejiang. The sky had begun to clear. We gazed down the stepped terracing in the valley in front of us. There was complete silence except for the sound of a man scraping about with his hoe some two hundred yards across the valley. A little stream fell down over the rocks and stones as it made its way under ancient stone bridges. The air was clear and odourless, a relief after the smog of the city. In the surrounding fields, I could see hundreds of winding paths worn flat by cloth shoes.

We got back into the car and followed the stream down to Thousand Autumns Pass where there was a little group of houses. The chimneys perched over the slanting tile roofs showed the faintest traces of smoke. We drove on while scores of people laboriously planted and dug and sifted in the soil. The only signs of mechanization were the odd three-wheeled tractors hauling great loads of rocks up the valley. At last, over the brow of a hill, through the thin mist, I could see a stone causeway and, beyond it, a little hamlet between the steep sides of the valley.

Zhongxi Village had maybe a hundred battered houses scattered around the stone road, a bank and a handful of shops. The buildings were basic. They looked damp and in a state of disrepair. The pavements were clogged with debris and young men sat loafing about on broken old chairs, smoking and idly watching the world go by. In the centre of the scene was a group of buildings protected by a high wall and with a large gateway facing the main road.

As we went through the factory gates the sun shone down on to a perfect lawn surrounded by a stone pavement swept spotlessly clean. Pots of brightly coloured flowers were arranged in rows and circles. A short avenue of twisted 'dragon-claw' scholar trees led to a three-storey office building covered in white mosaic. The river flowed through the compound and, on the opposite bank, behind another expanse of lawn, there was a huge factory building set about with cranes and scaffolding. The faint whirr of machines rose from the workshops closer at hand. The path between the buildings was lined by rows of mature magnolias, almost in flower. Outside the workers' dormitories, the gardens were divided by box hedges and there were miniature fruit trees dotted about. At the base of each tree, concentric rings of little pebbles, probably taken from the river, had been sorted by colour. There were rings of grey, fawn and white. On that first trip back in 1993, I had wondered who was behind this patch of ordered neatness up in these distant hills and I soon discovered a story of epic struggle.

The factory started in the mid-1970s as a tiny workshop making plastic sheets. For years, a handful of workers sweated blood to make ends meet, eking out the most basic existence. Then one day Shi arrived in the village, a stranger from the distant flat-lands near the coast. In little more than a decade he had built a business that transformed the tiny hamlet and, by the time I first went there, it provided job security to the three thousand workers who lived in the village and the surrounding fields.

* * *

Old Shi was born in Jiangsu in 1947 in the low-lying coastal region just north of the Yangtse Delta. In the early 1940s Japanese invaders had smashed this whole coastal area but the occupation collapsed shortly before Shi was born, leaving chaos in its wake. I never heard Shi talk about his early days but they can't have been easy. By the time he reached his twenties, the turmoil of the Cultural Revolution was at its peak. The local gossip was that Shi had met with some trouble in Jiangsu and had been sent up to Harbin where he had been locked up in a freezing cell. When I first heard the story, it was long before my first trip to Harbin, so I didn't know that the winter there was so cold that many people freeze to death each year. The conditions in a Harbin prison in the Cultural Revolution are hard to imagine. When Shi finally got out, he came to Zhongxi as an outcast in search, so he said, for the peace to read. I think that it must have been more to escape and forget.

Back then, the locals had absolutely nothing but for the clothes they stood in, a few cooking stoves, the plastics workshop and some wretched houses. Getting enough to eat was a constant worry and life was unremittingly harsh, especially in winter. The only source of work was farming or the tiny factory. Shi was interested in the business and soon the workers asked him to take over. He agreed and took out his first loan. It was five gallons of diesel to run the old generator. Electricity had not yet made its way up the valley.

Several years later, Shi struck up a friendship with an old Japanese man who had retired but, for some reason, wanted to help a struggling Chinese business. With this newly acquired know-how, the tiny business signed up customers in China's mining industry. Rubber seals were a

178

particular problem on the hydraulic supports used in China's deep coal mines. The whole mining industry in China had a terrible safety record and Shi soon found willing customers. In a short time, he was able to persuade the local Agricultural Bank to lend him thirty thousand *renminbi*, which, at the time, was about six thousand dollars.

Once Shi had access even to these meagre resources, the business grew rapidly. Shi was a born optimist and his engaging character was perfect for a business leader. He was a great storyteller, always had a quick answer and he inspired his workers with his optimism, his theatrics and his appetite for risk. He was entirely self-educated; all the schools had been closed during the Cultural Revolution. He read voraciously and his conversation drew on the poems handed down by the ancients. He was in his early fifties when I first met him and he had a slightly wild appearance, with unruly hair and rather staring eyes. He seemed to lean forward at an odd angle when he talked to you. He smoked continuously, fretting about his health at the same time. In earlier years, he was given to wearing a jacket and trousers with enormous checks that didn't quite match. Years later, after we had made our investment, these outfits raised the odd eyebrow on Wall Street and they disappeared quickly afterwards.

By the mid-1980s business was good and Shi started to make a bit of money. The little business borrowed to buy more technology from a Japanese company introduced by his old friend. This was progress but there was a problem. The rubber available in China was of poor quality. It wasn't good enough to make the new products and difficulties in importing good rubber threatened to strangle the business. At that time, China's economy was tightly controlled and access to foreign currency was restricted. No one abroad would accept *renminbi*. As a solution, Shi set up another factory. In a hook of the river, a stone's throw downstream, he built a new factory that made simple car jacks. Although they would never make fat profits, the jacks could be exported to America for much-needed dollars. Through his jack factory, Shi had ingeniously created a currency exchange.

In the following years, the business won many awards for quality and Shi's reputation spread far beyond the valley. By 1990, sales were several million dollars a year and he started to export to his old friends in Japan.

Then, after Deng's Southern Tour, when the State banks opened up the coffers, Shi grabbed the opportunity. With a hugely ambitious plan, he tried to quadruple the factory's output at a stroke and started building a gigantic facility on the opposite side of the river. He did this by taking out short-term loans that could be approved locally under China's bizarre rules of central planning. These were meant only for working capital, but Shi invested the money in a huge building and lots of new equipment. By early 1994, just at the time that we raised our first fund, it looked as if China was overheating and the government took fright. It tried to rein in the exploding economy and called in short-term loans. Shi had to repay the money. He was caught with his checked trousers round his ankles and embarrassing discussions with the bank commenced. This gave us our chance. We had the cash to give him a way out.

The negotiations to buy a share in the business were straightforward. Shi always knew his mind and made quick, precise decisions. He was flexible and only dug his heels in on two points: our cash had to come quickly and he was to remain in charge. After a couple of meetings, we agreed a handshake; twelve million for 60 per cent of the new business. Accountants and lawyers were dispatched to work out the details. That was the time when Shi suddenly came up to Beijing and persuaded Pat to sign the investment contract.

Despite the explosions from the Board in New York and the mess with the accountants and lawyers, it had all been sorted out in the end. On 8 September 1994, we made our first investment and the money was wired across to Shi's account in Ningshan.

We got off to a good start. The joint venture was officially opened with a fusillade of Chinese firecrackers that lasted several minutes. After a tour of the factory, during which one of our factory rats dropped a cigarette on the ground and Shi pointedly bent down and picked it up, we withdrew to hold the first board neeting. Shi was relaxed and in good form, but at precisely the moment when he declared the meeting open a huge landscape painting, twelve feet in length, fell from the wall and crashed to the ground. There was an uncomfortable pause.

1995 was a happy year and the honeymoon endured as the seasons turned. 1996 was even better. Newly acquired plant and machinery had been put to work. Revenues doubled, profits trebled, new products started to flow and everybody was happy. On visits to the factory, I could feel the place humming. Shi bought himself a Mercedes and was enjoying his success.

The careers of local Party officials often benefited from a big foreign investment and ours was by far the largest in the whole prefecture. As his friends in the Government rose up the political hierarchy on the back of his achievements, Shi's reputation grew. He was appointed as a People's Deputy in the Provincial Assembly. The road between Zhongxi and Ningshan, the main town of the county, was repaired and Shi gave a handsome donation to the Village Committee for a new office building. His influence waxed and, stirred by these successes, the seeds of wider ambitions grew silently in his mind.

During the summer, there are often heavy rains in central China and that year was no exception. The river that ran through the factory compound rose to dangerous levels and finally burst its banks in the small hours of the morning of 16 July. Muddy water surged into the dormitories and the factory buildings, submerging large areas and damaging equipment. For several days beforehand, the workers had desperately shovelled sand and ballast on to the banks but finally the flood had been too much. Exhausted, they retreated up the hills and waited miserably until it receded.

The next day, one of our junior managers telephoned Shi from Beijing and pressed him on details of the insurance cover. I was horrified when I heard. It made us look indifferent to the human side of the disaster and as though we were only interested in recovering our losses. Pat asked Ai to visit Shi in an attempt to atone for the blunder and he found him greatly upset. His niece had been badly hurt in a traffic accident on the road up into the mountains and her friend from the village had been killed. Ai Jian met with Shi very early in the morning in his office. A tear had appeared as Shi turned his face to the wall and said *waiguoren meiyou renqing gan*: 'Foreigners have no human feeling.' It had been a dreadful blunder.

1997 saw slower growth but we were preoccupied with the problems in Harbin and Zhuhai. The business in Ningshan was still profitable after all. But I had an ominous conversation in April. Shi had received permission from the Central Government to take his company to the stock market in Shanghai. This might net him a huge profit but in order to list he needed more than 50 per cent of the business. He had already sold 60 per cent to us so he wanted to know if he could buy back some of the shares. When I declined the conversation became tetchy. He complained vigorously about the performance of the other factory directors. 'Most of them are just old state-run bureaucrats, like Pang in Harbin,' he said, 'but the others, you foreigners don't know how to control them. Now that Wang has stolen your money in Zhuhai, you don't trust any of us.' When Shi had signed up with us, he thought that he had found a strong financial partner who could give him all the money that he needed. He had readily bought into Pat's strategy of buying up many businesses in China and building a national company but by then he felt that he was being dragged backwards by the problems at the other businesses.

Although the relationship was a little strained on the surface, whenever I spent time with Shi he was immensely reassuring. The business was running smoothly and Pat brought in a large US partner with modern technology. Shi seemed happy and the future still looked promising.

Then, suddenly, Shi arrived in Beijing. He said that the rubber business no longer needed his undivided attention. Several senior officials from the Prefectural Government had recently paid a visit and they needed his help. Many of the state-owned businesses in the area were making losses and unemployment was a big headache for the Government. They hoped that Shi might buy some factories and turn them around; the government might even get some cash in the transaction. Shi was interested in a paper factory in the nearby town of Guangde but he needed money. Would we buy another 20 per cent of the joint venture from him? He was looking for $10 million.

As the months rolled on, we talked round and round. There was a dilemma. If we refused, we might further alienate Shi. He was our best manager so switching horses at that stage was not an option. But if we bought more of his shares, he would only be left with 20 per cent and he might lose interest. After much debate, we agreed to go ahead. The price was eventually bargained down to six million. But we had one absolute condition where we would not compromise: Shi had to sign an agreement promising that he would not use the money to compete with us. The papers were drawn up and on 17 December we became 80 per cent shareholders. By the end of the year, Shi had another six million in his bank account. We were pleased with the result. We had kept our management team happy and motivated, and we had an extra 20 per cent for a good price. The future looked rosy and any uneasiness about Shi was put on the back burner. A couple of months afterwards, I went to France.

When I went down to Ningshan after recovering from my illness and first heard about Shi's second factory, I wasn't sure what to believe; there were plenty of stories but not much hard evidence. I raised it with Shi, but he was blandly reassuring. 'China is always awash with rumours,' he said, 'but you should be able to work out the truth.'

When the time came to leave the factory at the end of

that trip to Ningshan, I remember that the car was a little late. I walked out on to the perfect lawn in front of the factory. The green of the grass was cool and almost luminescent in the late-afternoon sunlight. I looked around me and took in the neat office building, the workers' dormitories, the rows of magnolia trees, the clipped hedges, the sound of the river, the mountains and the birds around me. The scent of viburnum drifted over from the river bank. I felt a profound sense of calm and order. Workers in uniform chatted contentedly as they went quietly about their business. In the distance, the garden of Shi's apartment was bright with the blossoms of the fruit trees. I dismissed the rumours. Nobody could be so stupid as to risk all this.

Pat went to Ningshan a month later and came back saying that the meetings had gone well. However, I heard later from Li Wei that Pat had arrived at the factory at about one o'clock and wanted to meet Shi as soon as he got there. But Shi had left instructions that he didn't want to be disturbed from his lunchtime nap until three. He kept Pat waiting and when Shi eventually walked into the room his hair was uncombed and he yawned and stretched ostentatiously. It was not a good omen.

Six months on, again without warning, Shi arrived in Beijing. We all met with him in Pat's large semicircular office. Shi said that he had been thinking about the future and that he was no longer so interested in the rubber business. His whole demeanour had changed; his manner was impatient and bored. It was as if he found talking to us a laborious chore and he made little effort to conceal his feelings. As he spoke, he pointedly lapsed into the familiar form of address in Chinese and said that he would be prepared to carry on but only if we changed the arrangements. He would pay us some interest on the money that we had invested, but he would keep the profits. From then on, we would have nothing to do with managing the business but he would send us the occasional set of accounts. 'It's the norm nowadays in taking over state-run companies,' he said. He then announced that if we didn't agree, he would simply leave and his people would go with him. We would be welcome to the empty buildings. Then he left.

I was shocked and angry but I knew that we had to react cautiously. After several anxious discussions, we decided to stall for time. Li Wei and Ai Jian went down to Ningshan to commence phantom negotiations. We had to put Shi to sleep and buy some time to think.

We were in a hole. We had eighteen million stuck up in the hills, in the clutches of someone who was by then in open revolt. I wasn't sure what to do, but I knew that we couldn't let this become another Harbin. With all the other factory directors watching from the sidelines, there was no way we could buckle in to Shi's demands. It would lead to similar claims from all our other factories across China and then we would have a revolution on our hands. I needed a man of steel, a man of unbending obstinacy, tough enough, maybe even reckless enough, to take on Shi on his own ground.

I met Chang Longwei through an agent. She sent me a copy of a two-page article from *Time* magazine, about the reform of China's state-owned enterprises up in the northern rust-belt city of Shenyang. A local bus factory had been chosen as the example of a success story. It was called the Jinbei Bus Factory.

In the early 1990s, after years of massive losses, Jinbei

had been taken over by a Hong Kong group and, just after Deng's Southern Tour, it became the first Chinese company ever to list in New York. The bus factory used the money from the Stock Exchange to buy new technology from Toyota and its new minibus had grabbed over half the Chinese market in three years. The man behind the turnaround, so the article said, was Chang Longwei.

Chang was born in Beijing in 1946. In his late teens, he had been sent to Datong to work in a state-owned gearbox factory. Datong was in Shanxi Province, not so far from the place where Ai Jian had worked with the peasants. I had been there when I had been studying at the university in Beijing. I remember an overnight train journey that seemed to move several hundred miles northwest and fifty years backwards. Outside the train station there were rows of people squatting around red plastic buckets and eating. When I got close, I saw that they were gnawing on rabbit heads. Datong is in China's interior coal-mining region so not only was it poor, it was black. Coal dust had worked itself into every pore of every face. It clung to buildings and windows, it hung in the stairwells and clogged the drains. Chang had emerged from the gearbox factory after twenty years with iron in his soul.

The *Time* article included a picture of Chang over the caption: 'New Revolutionary at his Jinbei Factory.' It said that 'when the plant, burdened with seven thousand workers making shoddy cars no one could afford, foundered in the early 1990s, a Hong Kong company took over. It went out looking for a mainland manager and found Chang.' Chang was quoted as saying: 'Management is the key. Subject to the Board, I can make all the decisions. I don't always have to listen to the Government.' Workers were shocked when he downgraded the first lazy mechanic. 'If you don't work hard here,' he said, 'you can work hard finding another job.' His managers also had to shape up and he sent them on training courses at Toyota. The article reported that corruption still plagued the Jinbei plant, but also said that Chang was determined to stamp it out. 'If I hear of it, I fire them,' he said, 'no matter if they are a Party member or whoever. The highest cadres can't be corrupt, because if they are the rest are.' When he was asked about the Party, he replied, 'Oh, our work has no relation to all that!'

I didn't take to Chang on first meeting. He was like the Chinese equivalent of a northern mill-owner and seemed to treat me with an earthy disregard despite the fact that I was meant to be interviewing him. Gradually I became more impressed. I could detect an immense strength of will in his rugged features and lumbering gait. He seemed an extraordinary mixture of obstinacy blended with a thirst for learning new things. More importantly Jinbei was a well-known company, a success story and the biggest problem with removing Shi was coming up with someone who would be remotely credible as his replacement. We needed a real heavyweight. Although Chang was clearly a handful, I thought that he was just the man we needed at Ningguo. So we drew him in, and finally he agreed to go up to the mountain valley. It was quite a coup.

The stage was set. We held a planning session in Beijing in great secrecy. As at Harbin, our contracts allowed us to dismiss Shi if we could hold a board meeting, but for that to happen Shi would have to attend personally. If his suspicions were aroused, he might refuse to come.

In the middle of November, we formed a team of eight

to take over the factory. Chang had persuaded a few loyal colleagues to move over from Jinbei, including an engineer called Yang Bai. She was thirty-six when she came down to Beijing to meet with me. During the interview, I asked her whether she thought that a woman might have particular difficulties managing workers in a place where traditions remained strong. She looked at me scornfully and asked whether I really thought that a bus factory in Shenyang was so easy. I liked the reply and she joined the next week.

The team carefully laid plans for seizing control of bank accounts, stabilizing workers and lobbying the local government once Shi was out. The whole operation required meticulous attention to detail. We drafted several different notices for posting on the factory gates, each one anticipating different reactions from Shi: one in case he agreed to resign, one in case we had to fire him. We even hired our own transport in case Shi ordered his drivers to refuse to take us to the factory – or, worse, to take us off in the opposite direction. Finally the date for a board meeting was set. It was 2 December 1998.

We had insisted on holding the board meeting in Hangzhou in order to avoid confronting Sha on his home ground. We had to pull him off his mountain perch. After a very bumpy flight, we arrived with our nerves frayed. The air around Hangzhou was extremely turbulent and the aircraft shook violently before going into an unusually steep descent immediately prior to landing.

Characteristically, Shi came alone. I remember catching sight of him in the restaurant the night before the meeting and feeling an irrational twinge of sympathy for this solitary and complex figure. In spite of what he was trying to do to us I could not completely suppress my admiration for what he had built.

The meeting was held the following day in a little side room containing a slightly greasy table and a few cracked teacups. Pat said that he hadn't slept all night but I felt curiously calm now that the moment had arrived after so much planning. Shi arrived early and we chatted away about nothing in particular before the others arrived and we got down to business.

Shi started with a report about the state of the business, blaming the poor results on a general downturn in the rubber industry and high import prices. No one was listening, but a tape machine turned silently on the table in front of us. When we came to the restructuring of the business that Shi had proposed, the mood changed abruptly. Pat said that we had thought about his ideas but that we had made an agreement in 1994 and we should stick to it. We weren't going to be pushed out. The first signs of puzzlement came across Shi's face but he didn't react except to light up another cigarette. Pat went on but Shi soon lost patience. He repeated the same threats that we'd heard in Beijing. There followed a long silence as we stared at each other across the table.

Eventually Shi broke the quiet and asked us what we would like to do. Pat said that Shi should resign to run his own business and that we should find someone else to run our factory. Shi would just remain a shareholder. There was absolutely no reaction. He just sat for what seemed like an hour, wreathed in smoke, silently brooding. Eventually rousing himself from his thoughts, he asked whether we had a replacement candidate in mind. This was the first time that Chang's name was mentioned. Again Shi sat absolutely motionless, his hand in front of his mouth, eyes narrowed as he drew slowly and silently on his cigarette. He asked where Chang was from and when we told him that he had been the General Manager of Jinbei, Shi seemed to crumple slightly. Then he once more sat absolutely motionless for what seemed like an eternity with smoke curling up around him.

Shi eventually hit back with a comment that Jinbei was a badly run company and that we were taking too much of a risk. By then he was stalling for time as his mind raced through a thousand calculations. After another five minutes, we gave him a simple choice: resign or be sacked. He extracted the odd concession and signed his resignation letter. We agreed to meet again the next day up in the factory to make a joint announcement to the workforce and so the meeting concluded.

We subsequently discovered that, after effectively signing his own dismissal notice, Shi had been driven at lightning speed back to the factory, screaming down his mobile phone. His black Mercedes flew through the villages and fields as our wretched minibus laboured up hills and we checked the maps. As we drove into Zhongxi Village at dusk with Chang and his team, we saw that Shi had gutted the factory. The dormitories, which would normally have been alive with the sound of the evening's cooking under way, were dark and silent. There was nobody there. The entire management team had been ripped out and sent down the valley. My heart sank. That night, just before I went to sleep, I was called with the news that the boilers on the other side of the river had been busy all afternoon. It looked as though a large number of books and ledgers had been burned.

Next day at an early breakfast, the electricity suddenly failed. All the workshops and houses throughout the entire village were stranded in the watery grey daylight of an overcast dawn. At eight o'clock the workers arrived, but by now the word was out and everyone stood in doorways, gawping and gossiping. Notices had appeared all over the factory overnight announcing a four-day holiday and the workers gradually drifted away.

Pat and I wandered over to the big moulding workshop on the opposite bank of the river where I had seen the cranes at work on my first visit four years before. It was dark and empty like the rest of the factory. Our prospects looked bleak. No electricity, an absent management and the workers sent home. As we walked past the deserted workshops along empty paths, great snowflakes began to fall mournfully from the leaden skies.

After the initial shock we rallied. There was no way we were going down without a fight. The first thing to do was to demand our electricity back. Talking to the Village Committee would be a waste of time. They had been in Shi's pocket for years after he had paid for some medical expenses for Madame Ye, the Committee Secretary. We went for the higher authority, the Government of Ningshan, which was located at the railhead some thirty miles down the valley. Pat headed off to dig out the Party Secretary whilst I stayed at the factory and ransacked the offices for the chops.

I was to get to know the Party Secretary of Ningshan County quite well in the following two years. Secretary Wu was a rarity in the Chinese political system in that, to the extent possible within that world of constant intrigue, he appeared to say what he thought. In a tight spot, Chinese officials often disappeared from the scene for urgent meetings that were mostly imaginary. Although the events up in

Zhongxi Village could become a real hot potato for the local government, Secretary Wu made no attempt to hide. The removal of Shi, a prominent local businessman with friends in the Provincial Government, was a sensitive issue. He was a powerful People's Deputy well connected in the provincial capital of Hefei. But on the other hand the joint venture accounted for a good proportion of local tax revenues, so he couldn't risk a fight with the foreigners. Wu was in a difficult position and he knew it.

Unusually tall for a Chinese, Secretary Wu had a presence about him that was only slightly diminished by hair that absolutely refused to sit flat and an enormously long finger-nail – which seemed to be reserved for ear-scraping – on the little finger of his left hand. He poured some tea and listened politely to Pat's explanations. Deftly sidestepping the real issue, he replied that the choice of the manager of any business was up to the Board so he couldn't comment on the specifics. However, as the leader of the local Party Committee, he had a duty to protect foreign investors. Therefore we could have our electricity back.

Back in Zhongxi Village, an agitated crowd of several hundred had gathered outside the gates of the factory, milling around among the potholes and craning their necks to read the notices announcing Shi's resignation. Reactions varied from angry disbelief to barely concealed glee but the underlying anxiety was palpable.

Shi had disappeared and throughout the day his brooding presence loomed in the background as we tore through the offices in search of the chops. Eventually we found them, and, by close of play, we had at least secured the bank accounts, although we found out later that several million *renminbi* had been wired out within a few hours of the board meeting.

At dinner that evening, as we sat glumly over our chopsticks and mulled over the situation by the light of a few candles, the electricity suddenly came back on. This development was greeted with a huge cheer and shouts for more beer. Maybe things weren't quite so bleak. Later someone called to ask if a delegation from Shi could come to negotiate with us, but in a moment of bravado we replied that there wasn't anything to negotiate. We went to bed with our spirits lifted.

Early the next morning Shi himself called to ask for a meeting with Pat. Shi arrived at the factory looking tired. He mumbled that the change had come as a great shock and some of his people had overreacted, but now he wanted to get back to business. By the time we left, the managers and workers were slowly drifting back. Round One had gone to us.

Over the coming weeks, an uneasy stand-off prevailed. Shi and Chang developed an immediate loathing for each other but Chang appeared to be in control despite the sullen stares and disobedience of the locals as Shi lurked in the shadows, plotting revenge. On the surface all was normal, but underneath tempers were frayed.

News started to trickle in about Shi's rival business down the valley. Chang had driven past and told me that it was impressive, at least from the outside. It was much bigger than I had feared and that convinced me that conflict was unavoidable. There was too much at stake for both sides. At the end of December, Chang had taken one of the cars from Zhongxi Village and driven up to the gates of Shi's new factory. The guards thought that they recognized the number plates and let him straight in. Chang had strolled around the workshops, asking the odd question, taking detailed photographs of the machinery and production facilities and, after about fifteen minutes, he calmly drove off again, waving cheerily to the guards as he left. I couldn't believe his barefaced cheek. He might have been severely beaten if he had been caught. But we now had proof that Shi had broken the agreement that he had signed that he wouldn't compete with us.

By this time, Chang was spoiling for a fight. He felt that some of the locals were using blocking tactics against him and he became testy. Just before Chinese New Year, I came down to the factory to talk to the management team. On the way up to the factory, the driver complained almost continuously for the whole drive about what we had done to Shi. I told him that he didn't know the full facts and that I planned to talk to the whole workforce. But he said, 'If you speak a thousand words it won't be worth one from Old Shi!' so I knew that it was going to be tough.

Even so, we convened the meeting. I felt that the managers should be told directly why we had kicked Shi out and have a chance to ask questions. I tried to win them over but Chang was having none of it. He launched into a monologue, his already huge voice amplified by a set of outlandish speakers that were hopelessly outsized for the small room. He bellowed, 'I'm the General Manager now, and I won't tolerate anyone who won't listen to what I say!' As he started to list the various departments at fault, one man in the audience stood up and started shouting back. Chang demolished him in the ensuing shouting match, called him into his office and sacked him on the spot.

The Chinese New Year holiday that year was an anxious time. I knew that Shi would not just go away, so we waited nervously for his first move. On 5 February he finally struck. All 138 members of senior and middle management, except for eight people, left the business *en masse* and went down the valley to Shi. I received despairing calls from our people in the empty offices. They couldn't see how to carry on, but Chang seemed completely unperturbed. 'We can get new people,' he said. 'I've still got my core managers and most of the sales force has held. What we need is a morale booster.'

It was soon the fifteenth day after Chinese New Year, traditionally a time for fireworks. Chang did two things: he bulldozed the factory gates and ordered a colossal firework display. In China, imposing gateways were still taken as a sign of wealth and social standing. Chang had described the gates of the factory as *tu-qi*, meaning 'earthy' or 'peasant-ish'. He was right; they were a bit shabby. It was strange that Shi had cared so little for the gates when he'd paid so much attention to the environment inside. Traditions were still strong in the village and the demolition of the gates and the posters of the new ones had quite an effect. The firework display brought in from Shanghai was the largest the valley had ever seen and lasted nearly forty minutes. Huge crowds came in from the surrounding countryside and gathered in a carnival atmosphere on the bridge across the river. The fireworks worked wonders for morale. Nerves were steadied by Chang's cool defiance of Shi, the local warlord, and several people returned up the valley.

Shi had clearly expected the business to collapse when he took out the management and had said so publicly. 'One kick and the whole factory will come down,' he had boasted, so the survival of the business surprised everyone in the valley and by then we knew that Shi had problems of his own. We guessed that he had planned to bleed the joint venture for some time as his own business grew, so when we kicked him out he lost a source of financing. There were rumours that he couldn't make payroll in January. The atmosphere in Zhongxi changed. When the presses still pressed and the mixers still mixed, there was a growing sense that we could win. One lad, who must have been worried about job security, said to me, 'Your enemy is now a frozen snake. Don't let him thaw out.'

For weeks we tried to get the government in Ningshan to enforce the non-competition agreement, but that would mean squashing a successful self-made local and, on a more practical basis, it could have meant more unemployment in this remote, underdeveloped and isolated region. After all, the dispute affected more than five thousand people. From the outside, the Government appeared indifferent to our arguments but somehow, despite the tangled relationships and cross-allegiances inside the local Party, a consensus slowly emerged. Secretary Wu had exerted enormous pressure on Shi to come to terms with us and, in early March, I was summoned to Ningshan.

Shi and I met, in an atmosphere of great tension, to try and straighten things out. Chang, Li Wei and I arrived early and were ushered up to the top of a building in the centre of Ningshan. As we waited for Shi to arrive, I gazed out over the rooftops to the hills in the distance. It was a lovely spring morning, the air was warm and the hillsides in the distance had lost the tired look of winter as the leaves began to unfold. Closer at hand, I could see the blue tiles on the roofs of the dormitories in Shi's new factory. The layout of the trees and shrubs in the surrounding gardens, and the rings of coloured stones at the roots of the trees were quite unmistakable.

*   *   *

Secretary Wu arrived with the Mayor and told us that they would both personally attend the discussions. This was a good sign because it meant that the government was anxious to broker a settlement. Shi came in, looking nervous and irritable but during the discussions I could feel that his mind was still working very quickly. He peered at me over the table with a look of intense concentration. Secretary Wu had explained privately that he thought we could persuade Shi to swap his new rubber factory for the old jack factory. We might have to make a balancing payment, but it seemed like a sensible plan. We would end up with a bigger rubber business, free of the local competitor, and rid ourselves of the jack factory and the burden of its one thousand employees. I hesitated in giving a firm reply, but it seemed like a perfect solution so I made positive noises.

On my return to Beijing, a sharp disagreement surfaced. I wanted to try to reach a deal with Shi and get rid of the jack factory. It was only useful as a currency exchange, but now we had dollars. But Pat insisted that we needed the export volume; the jacks were being sold to America. I thought that there was no way to survive in the long term with such a simple product and I was depressed when I lost the argument. I dutifully sent a note to Secretary Wu rejecting his proposal. Years later I heard that the news of this blunder had been greeted with gleeful incredulity in the Shi camp. It enabled both Shi and the local government to say that they had tried their level best to achieve a compromise but that the foreigners would not come to terms. It was a very close escape for Shi. We had let 'the frozen snake' thaw out. The local gossip was that we couldn't have read Sunzi's *Art of War*. We had opted for Sunzi's worst option: a long war of attrition on enemy ground. Round Two had gone to Old Shi.

* * *

About that time, we all had to troop back to the States for another quarterly board meeting. I knew that this one was going to be tough; the Board had set up an Advisory Committee and invited a couple of retired business leaders to attend as expert advisers. It was another knee-jerk reaction from New York. 'We have operating problems; *ergo* we need a couple of experienced operators to tell our guys in China how to get it done.'

It sounded sensible on the surface, but these new advisers were veterans of multinational companies, a bit like high-flying factory rats. One had ended up running a huge chemical factory in Holland and the other had run HR for one of the biggest global companies on earth. I'm certain that they had been good at what they did; but at the board meetings, they naturally came up with questions suited to running chemical factories or the personnel function of a well-oiled global business machine. They just couldn't grasp that we weren't in control and droned on about installing 'six-sigma' quality controls and 'constrained manufacturing', whatever that was. At that stage I was more worried about making sure that the electricity wasn't cut off and the accounting records weren't thrown into the furnaces in a factory where our most sophisticated HR strategy was to invite everyone to an enormous fireworks party.

'EBITDA' became an obsession. It's a kind of financial performance measure that tries to mix profits with cash flow, and we were tracking seriously behind budget. The Advisory Committee wanted to know why and they weren't impressed with the explanations. I didn't think that there was any point in squeezing out the last drop of EBITDA from a factory that was convulsed by a major battle between its shareholders. I wanted to keep the business stable and, in China, that meant keeping the workers busy even if we had short-term losses. If production stopped, we would be finished; Shi would be the only option for the workers and they'd all move down the valley.

We were tracking behind in exports as well. Pat had come up with a hugely ambitious plan to increase exports to $22 million in that year and we were already hopelessly behind. The meeting became acrimonious after one of the directors said that there was no point in messing around with Excel sheets and taking 'a foolish stab at numbers.' Pat countered by saying that he had to maintain a sense of optimism and so we went round and round, in the same sort of circuitous arguments that I'd had in China, with the familiar frustration steadily rising on both sides. After one session, again on exports, it got so bad that we were barely on speaking terms and there were long pauses in the board meetings as both sides glowered at each other or shuffled about with their papers. Once, at the end of a prolonged argument about exports, one of the directors from the pension fund looked up at Pat and abruptly adjourned the meeting.

In a low voice full of menace, he said: 'You wanna be Mr China,' and after a deathly silence continued, 'And Mr China ain't gett'n it done in China!'

It was awful. Pat had looked deflated afterwards but tried to brush it off. He muttered that the director who made the remark was supportive behind the scenes but had to appear tough in front of Rubel and the others from IHC. I was skeptical; it looked much more like the old Wall Street maxim coming out where, as they say, 'You're only ever as good as your last deal.' It didn't matter how many successful deals Pat had done in earlier days. By then they needed a whipping-boy and it seemed to me that the other directors from IHC had conveniently erased the fact that they too had spent months analysing China and doing due-diligence before we all made the joint decision to go out to raise the funds. I felt that, at that stage, there was no point in wasting time in internal arguments that had nothing to do with the real problems in China. There wasn't the time. We were at the key moment in the first struggle that we might actually win. We knew what we had to do in China and we were out on our own.

Back in Ningshan, a storm had burst about Chang's head that almost overwhelmed him. First a key delivery of raw materials disappeared. The rumour was that a truck from Shi's factory had secretly entered the docks in Shanghai at night. The Customs officials allowed them to load up eight tons of raw rubber that we were due to collect the next day. Chang reacted quickly and airfreighted rubber from Malaysia. It was money well spent.

Shortly afterwards, there was a strike. It had been organized to coincide with one of my weekly visits in an attempt to embarrass Chang but he just walked into one of the workshops, picked someone at random and told him that if he wasn't back at work within ten minutes, he would fire the entire section. By the time I left, they were all back at work.

Three days later, the Deputy Mayor of Ningshan arrived with a posse of local policemen and, after several hours of stormy meetings, removed some key equipment. He claimed that it belonged to Shi. We cobbled together a new workshop consisting of a series of simple drills and presses set up in a tent in the truck park. The makeshift facilities enabled us to limp on.

Next a hailstorm of writs hit the company. Shi had persuaded certain suppliers rumoured to be relatives of his wife to take court action to recover monies due from us. It felt as if I was back in Zhuhai when the local courts issued freezing orders over our bank accounts even though we had been paying normally. I made what I thought was a threatening telephone call to one of the suppliers in Shanghai accusing him of paying kickbacks but he just laughed and put the phone down. Chang quickly opened a number of undercover bank accounts outside Ningshan and diverted customer receipts, so we managed to avoid the freezing orders.

After several orders were cancelled, we found that Shi had a warehouse in Shenzhen with a large store of faulty and defective goods. There were rumours that his people had taken defective goods and packaged them in our boxes and shipped substandard goods to our customers, but it sounded rather far-fetched to me.

Back in the valley, the Village Committee stepped up its propaganda campaign. Chang was incensed by a pamphlet that Shi called 'The Everlasting Beacon of Zhongxi'. The article had all the overblown outmoded rhetoric of the Cultural Revolution, praising Shi to a degree that was both embarrassing and ridiculous. Some of the locals were taken in but I told Chang to forget it and get back to work.

By late April, confidence was returning. We had started a recruitment drive at the local universities in Hefei and Hangzhou for graduates to be trained into management jobs. We had been quite successful and around eighty students had signed up. A slow but steady trickle of people started to return up the valley. We had recovered our balance.

My meetings with the managers in Zhongxi became a little more relaxed. I felt that confidence was slowly returning. After twenty years in a gearbox factory in Datong,

202

Chang had no time for pretty words but he knew how to work an audience. He made a speech to the whole factory and I saw him warm up as he spoke. 'Shi,' he bellowed, 'the Peasant Warlord, with no law and no heaven had boasted that he could sweep us away with one blow. But the "Seven Crushing Blows of Ningguo" have fallen and we are still standing.'

When he finished a ragged cheer went through the audience. We had survived the strike, mass defection, rubber stolen from the docks, writs, the Village Committee propaganda, confiscated machinery and the faulty products in Shenzhen. Now it was time to counter-attack.

Chang's speech was important; all battles in China are won or lost on propaganda. Forced to take on Shi head-on, we had to hit back, so we decided on a publicity campaign aimed at unsettling his bankers. To get their attention, we had to come up with something big; something big enough and bad enough to frighten them away from giving him any more money.

We spent days in an upstairs room in Zhongxi Village sifting through boxes of papers, trying to come up with a case against Shi. Our eyes strained as we tried to decipher the scribbled notes of Shi's accounts clerks. The long hours were sometimes punctuated by a burst of excitement as someone found a particularly incriminating slip of paper. We were all absorbed in the work as we broke open cupboards and tore through dusty boxes together. The paperwork was in an appalling state but there was strong evidence of a horror story of machines transferred out to Shi's new business, quantities of missing rubber and moulds, and spurious expenses. We also found further orders to transfer out a large batch of equipment on 6

December. Our dismissal of Shi on the second day of the month had been in the nick of time.

In the end we cobbled together a claim for missing assets and damages from the non-competition agreement, more than a hundred million *renminbi* in all. It was a fantastic sum, big enough to pull Shi under if we won. After Zhuhai we knew that many of the claims would be thrown out by a court. But that was not the point. We were playing by the Anhui rules and perception was reality.

We lodged a court case in Beijing and produced a booklet with screaming headlines about American investors pouring millions into China's inner provinces to help modernize industry only to be ripped off by one of the locals. We included samples of scandalous documents and sent the whole lot to Shi's bankers. It worked: his loans were frozen and the applications for more money were rejected. However, with the luck of the devil, Shi had just taken a large loan from a local quoted group arranged by his friends in the Prefectural Government. He survived. It seemed as if Round Three had been a stalemate. I knew that Round Four would be decisive.

Our legal battle slowly ground forward through the autumn and the first hearing in Beijing went well. Morale improved further some weeks later when we won two smaller court cases in Hefei. But this, in a sense, was a side issue. The real outcome would be determined somehow from within the Provincial Government but, of course, winning the legal cases would help in the propaganda campaign. At that point, we needed to get our message across more effectively to the top levels of the government so we found a retired General from the People's Liberation Army to help us.

When Deng achieved ultimate power in China by resigning his offices so that others were forced to resign too, the only position that he kept was Chairman of the Military Affairs Commission. This shows the importance of the army. Mao has often been quoted as saying that 'political power grows out of the barrel of a gun' but that was only part of his maxim. He went on to say, 'So that is why the Party must always control the army.' There had always been some tension in that relationship, particularly when the Party started converting the military factories up in the hills to civilian production. The army had responded by going into hotels, resorts, trading companies and manufacturing businesses, until Jiang Zemin, after a long struggle, put an end to the free-for-all and forced them to give up their investments.

The General was right at the edge of the very small group of people who control China and he could find a way into most government departments. He was a big, stern-looking man who didn't smile much and rather stood on ceremony. I never felt comfortable with him; I always worried that I might inadvertently offend him. But he certainly understood business and enjoyed the odd bottle of *baijiu* at lunchtime. After listening to our case, he agreed to talk to the Provincial Government and over time the combination of improving government relations and the relentless pressure of the court cases started to have an effect. Throughout the following winter, Shi began to tire of the fight and, by the following spring, the decisive moment arrived.

On a lovely clear spring morning, on the way to work, Chang and Yang Bai were just about to go through the gates of the factory when a car drove up at high speed. Two men leapt out from the kerbside. Chang and his companion were shoved into the back seat and driven off. Just before Thousand Autumn Pass, some twenty miles down the road, on a sharp bend, Chang and Yang Bai leapt out of the car and took refuge in a local house. They found a man with a tractor and made off. Returning down the valley, they saw that the factory gates were covered with notices proclaiming the formation of 'The Committee for the Protection of the Investors'. It had seized control of the factory and was allegedly headed by Madame Zhao. Madame Zhao was the old accountant whom we had hired some years before. She was a sweet old lady, a grandmother over retirement age who had spent several weeks in hospital at the time of Shi's removal because her nerves couldn't take the stress. The idea that she was the mastermind behind an attempted coup was utterly preposterous.

It emerged later that the uprising had been led by a group of disgruntled managers at the jack factory where the workers had become worried about their jobs. Chang never liked the jack factory any more than I did, and, knowing him, he might have gone too far in saying so. When he arrived back at the village, Chang had tried to go to work but he was expelled a second time by a group of about fifty workers. He decamped to the Village Committee opposite the factory gates and waited. The Municipal Government down the valley was informed and Secretary Wu dispatched officials to try to calm the situation. Order was eventually restored and Chang returned to his office at the end of the day. That, so it seemed, was that.

There was a group of drivers from the transportation department of a supplier staying at the guest house in the factory. They looked disreputable, drank too much and had been behaving boorishly that night at dinner, hassling the waitresses and making offensive jokes. They had some friends with them who were much worse. Rumours spread around the factory that these people were members of the local Black Hand Society, a feared and detested Mafia-type organization. The rumours were that Chang's office manager had hired them to put down any further dissent. Subsequent investigations by the Government never reached a conclusion, but at the time it was like a red rag to a bull.

The following morning, a large group of workers surrounded the guest house and forced their way up to the third floor to confront the intruders. At the door a serious scuffle broke out. The people inside panicked and produced knives, which in turn led to calls for more workers to come upstairs. A huge fist fight ensued, resulting in broken noses and stab wounds. A knot of people struggled up and down the stairs in a mess of broken glass, torn hair and bleeding knuckles. Nine people finished up in hospital.

The fight raged up and down the stairwells and by the time it was over there was blood all over the marble floor in the entrance hall. We had a group of people from Beijing visiting at the time who were terrified and locked themselves in their room. Even from the inside, the noises were horrible: frightened voices and the sharp animal howling of people in pain. Eventually the intruders fled and the rage of the crowd turned against Chang, Yang Bai and the visitors from Beijing. The doors were broken open and they were all dragged outside. Marched out of the factory gates by a crowd of over a hundred, they were pushed and kicked the length of the main street of the little town.

The Village Committee Secretary, Madame Ye, with her pinched white face visible behind a megaphone, tried to restrain the crowd but the mob was intent on revenge. They continued over the bridge and into the jack factory. The workers slammed the gates and the small group gathered into a knot in an attempt to avoid the blows and punches. Yang Bai seemed to be a particular target and she was taken alone to the back of a warehouse. She has never talked about what happened there.

After a few minutes, the police arrived and Chang and Yang Bai got into the police car. Before it had time to leave, the car was overturned with Chang, Yang Bai and a couple of terrified policemen still inside. The car was then bounced out of the factory gates.

By this time the Prefectural Government, alarmed by the serious civil unrest, authorized the use of the military and an army detachment was sent from Xuan Cheng. This news cooled down the hotheads and the crowd dispersed. Chang escaped to the Village Committee.

Late that night, up in Beijing, Michael and I met Pat in his office and got through to the Village Committee. Chang's voice came over the line, sounding exhausted. He said that the violence had been an attempt to frighten us into removing him from his post. With an absent management, it would be pretty obvious who would be there to fill the vacancy. Chang was shaken and talked in a low voice as if there were others listening. He said that his back was 'blue and bruised' but that he wouldn't leave.

I heard months later that Chang had shouted at the mob in the jack factory that he would 'rather die at his post than at home'. Wild rumours were circulating in the fraught atmosphere saying that we had already agreed to remove him. He said simply, 'If you support me, I won't run away. If you don't, I'll go now.' I felt a tremendous wave of loyalty towards Chang at that moment. We had asked him to fight a battle that was not of his own making

208

and he had put himself through fire for us. We all told him that we were relying on him and, to his evident relief, we promised to put through a call to Secretary Wu. We left in the small hours of the morning reasonably confident that the final crisis had been weathered. It had been a close call.

When I saw Chang a few days later, he was withdrawn. The frightening events had shattered his normal ebullience. In the end his true feelings came out: 'It seems so shaming to be beaten by your own people.' He had always prided himself in winning the hearts of his employees, but up in the hills the memory of Shi was too strong. As I watched Chang struggle with his deeply wounded pride, the unfairness of it all left a bitter taste; and all for that wretched jack factory.

After the final storm, events came neatly to a conclusion. The court in Beijing issued a ruling that Shi could not compete with our joint venture. Although I knew from Harbin that it would be almost impossible to implement the court order in practice, it dramatically increased the pressure on the Local Government to find a compromise. In the absence of a fair solution, we could try to blow up the whole dispute and go to the Central Government. No one wanted that.

In fact, my immediate reaction was to do nothing. We had moles inside Shi's business so we knew that he had thrown himself into a flurry of activity, coming to Beijing to meet with his lawyers and flying to Hefei to lobby officials. But everywhere he went the message was the same. The judgement could not be overturned. Most of the officials were wearied by this constant struggle. They were bored with the story and suffering from battle fatigue. They told him to settle with the foreigners. They didn't want any more turmoil.

Eventually the phone call came. Would we like to meet up in Beijing? Secretary Wu was at the Cadre Training School near the Summer Palace. Maybe we could meet up with Secretary Wu and the General? That way we might be able to reach agreement.

Under a freezing blue sky in early December, Shi came to Beijing. We met in a hotel, on neutral ground. Despite everything that had happened I couldn't dislike him. He was so incorrigible, the performer who would never give up. As he walked in, head on one side as usual, he looked at me with mock surprise and said, 'Haven't I seen you before somewhere?'

There were several rounds of discussions with Secretary Wu and the General acting as referees. On the third round, down in Ningshan, I remember hammering Shi on some tedious point about accounts receivable where I had been particularly well briefed. He looked pained and walked out of the room. A minute later, a message came in; could Shi and I meet in a separate room?

We sat alone on opposite sides of the table, separated by two cups of hot water containing floating tea leaves, just as we had six years earlier. Shi gave me a cigarette and I took it. In five minutes we had a deal. No lawyers, no minutes, just two people on either side of a table. He would hand over his shares in our business and we would drop all our claims. A small balancing payment would be made.

That afternoon, in a haze of *baijiu*, Shi took me around his new factory. The same Old Shi was evident in the neat rows of machinery, the uniformed workers, clipped hedges

210

and perfect lawns. I asked him if he would come up the valley with me for a visit to the old business. On our way up, he told me that he had not even driven past the gates of his old factory for two and a half years. He hadn't been able to face it so it was a moment of bitter-sweet emotion when we walked through the gates together. As we toured the workshops, the atmosphere was electric. Chang had extended the shift by an hour and the workers craned their necks to catch a glimpse of the vanquished warlord's return.

Much of the dinner that night is a blur in my memory but I do remember that the whole Government turned out: Secretary Wu, the Mayor and four deputies. The *baijiu* flowed and even the General relaxed a little, reciting poetry with a few lines missing. I sat between Chang and Shi, just in case there was trouble, but even they managed to hold a civil conversation.

Through the window we could see Shi's old apartment and I caught him shooting several glances in that direction. He seemed happy enough, but kept moving over to sit alone on an old wooden sofa at the other end of the room. I discovered later that it was from Shi's apartment and that it had been moved there after he had been kicked out. At the end of the dinner, Shi gave me a huge seal carved from red granite. I was thrilled with it so after I returned I set about to find the best seal carver in Beijing. I was given an address: The Pavilion of Accumulated Literature, Glazed Tile Factory Street, Just South of Tiananmen Square. The woman in charge said, 'Old Master Xu's already stopped. He's eighty-six.' But she found me his apprentice. He was sixty-seven.

He carved the chop with a poem that Shi had taught me years before. It tells of petals falling from a flower into the soil below and adding colour to next year's growth, a poem of sacrifice and renewal from more than a thousand years ago:

'落紅不是無情物,
化作春泥更護花'

Falling Red is not without feeling,
It changes the spring soil better to protect the flowers.

After I collected the chop, I went over the road to buy a huge red inkpad so that I could use it. The shopkeeper recognized the character style of the carver.

'He's not bad,' said the shopkeeper, 'but he's still too young.'

I stared at him. 'He's sixty-seven!'

The shopkeeper just looked at me blankly and said, 'I know.'

In the end, I found that the Battle of Ningshan drew me closer to Old Shi. He had given us no option but to fight but once peace was restored the bitterness quickly melted and I could see my opponent as another human being fighting his corner. I liked what I saw: Old Shi, the risk-taker, the opportunist, the optimist, the showman, the loner.

The second battle was to be with a character of a very different kind in an ancient walled city set in the watery marshlands of central China.

Ten

上有九頭鳥,下有湖北佬

The Siege of Jingzhou:
Up in the Sky there are Nine-headed Birds;
Down on the Earth there are People from Hubei

> Traditional Northerner's saying
> about people from the
> Central Province of Hubei

I had already started to suspect hidden complications at our joint venture in Hubei when I heard the news that our factory director had been shot. Chen Haijing had been walking home from work as usual one evening when a dark figure leapt from a doorway, raised a gun and fired at point-blank range into Chen's right leg. Chen was immediately taken to hospital and remained there for several days. Michael flew to Shashi to visit him and found him in combative spirits. 'Give me a week,' he said, 'and I'll be standing by the factory gates as usual, watching the workers clock in, you'll see!'

Hubei is right in the middle of China, in an area of flat-lands cut in two by the Yangtse River. The Yangtse is the longest of China's three great rivers and the Chinese call it just that: *Chang Jiang* or Long River. It flows from the glaciers in the west to the sea at Shanghai and forms the main connection between China's leading business centre and the vast central hinterlands, which are home to four hundred million people.

In the extreme west of China, the river meanders across the Qinghai-Tibetan plain in shallow, pebbly bands until it reaches the edge of the plateau and descends rapidly through winding valleys. By the time it reaches the end of the upper section, the Yangtse has fallen more than three miles in altitude. The middle section stretches for about seven hundred miles and passes through the Three Gorges in Sichuan down to Yichang in Hubei. As the water rushes through the gorges the sheer limestone sides tower overhead like fantastic pinnacles and dwarf the boats that churn through the channel. In the narrowest sections, the walls seem to close in above and the eddies and currents are treacherous. The river waters there are the deepest anywhere in the world.

The Three Gorges have inspired poets and artists over the years as the dynasties rose and fell. Each gorge is said to have its own distinctive character: majestic steep crags, elegant forest-covered peaks, fog and spray, churning currents and whirling pools. Hundreds of thousands of tourists visit the Gorges every year, but for me the next section of the Yangtse, which flows through Hubei, inspires even greater awe.

When the waters reach the end of the third gorge, they spill out through a narrow pass into the vast open plain of central China, creating a huge system of lakes, marshes and channels. Although the river still has thousands of miles to run, the whole region lies at an altitude of only fifty metres above sea level and in ancient times it was known as The Endless Marshlands. The river grows sluggish and at first the landscape seems monotonous and drab. But after a time I found something intriguing about the vast tangled network of waterways, with their reeds and rushes, the dykes and ancient bridges, the little circular islands rising from the waters with their ancient ochre-walled temples. There was something untamed and wild about the landscape and I heard that there was still piracy on the vast network of canals. Boats hide easily in the quiet backwaters waiting to pounce from behind the tall reeds.

Although it has been used as a waterway for centuries, the river has never been mastered. Vast dykes were built along the banks to prevent flooding, but the river silts up so the huge embankments had to be raised in height again and again. There are sections now where the river bed is three metres above the surrounding countryside. In attempting to tame the river, the Chinese created a tyrant. Infinitely more dangerous here than in the confines of the Gorges, the Yangtse can burst its banks and inundate vast areas from its elevated position, disgorging limitless quantities of water across the land. Every year in early summer the people of Hubei look anxiously up at the skies, hoping that the 'Plum Rain' would be light and burning incense to pray that there would be no flooding.

On the northern bank of the river, in the middle of the marshes some eighty miles downstream from the Gorges, there is an ancient walled city surrounded by moats and waterways. The grey brick walls of Jingzhou were first built in the Ming Dynasty and are over seven miles around. Even in recent times the only way into the city was through one of the five magnificent gateways that stand opposite long arched marble bridges spanning the moat. The pavilions on the gateways, with their red lanterns, tiled roofs and upturned eves, created a classic picture of Imperial China. The atmosphere under the gates, where blind fortune-tellers rubbed shoulders with the persimmon salesmen, was only slightly marred by the bells ringing on hundreds of bicycles and the hooting of trucks as they lumbered into the city.

I first went to Jingzhou in the autumn of 1993 when Pat was in the States raising the first fund. I went to visit a factory in the nearby town of Shashi. In contrast to Jingzhou with its parapets and gateways, Shashi is a nondescript, dreary industrial town with one of China's largest fertilizer factories as the main scenic attraction. The broad streets were lined with plain trees and drab tenement blocks dotted the skyline around the lake at the centre of the town. There was an electrical motor factory there so I went to find out if they needed any foreign investment.

The factory was squeezed between a department store and a hotel which looked only half built. Behind the metal gateway there was a small compound with a shabby office building. The conditions inside were terrible. There was no heating and the offices were in need of a coat of paint. Spittoons stood at the corners of the passageways and the only light in the corridors came from forty-watt bulbs hanging on wires from the ceiling. The main meeting room contained a semicircle of ancient collapsing sofas, with shabby beige cloth covers. There were green plastic thermos flasks on the dusty sideboards. The man in charge of the business, Chairman Ni, kept us waiting for an hour or so. When he arrived, he seemed weary and his clothes hung loosely about his gaunt frame. His features were those of a young man, but there were deep lines of exhaustion etched into his face. His handshake was weak and lifeless and he spoke slowly, making rather listless movements as he gave us the history of the business.

Chairman Ni had been with the factory since it had been founded in 1965. It started as a state-owned electrical motor factory but developed into a key supplier of starter motors for petrol and diesel engines in China. But the product samples that Chairman Ni showed me had huge heavy cast-iron casings that would be hopelessly overweight for modern engines. It looked as though we had wasted our journey. As we toured the factory and saw the dilapidated buildings, bored workers and ancient assembly lines, I thought about cutting the visit short. But towards the end of the tour, Chairman Ni introduced us to the General Manager of the plant and told him to take us to Factory Number Two.

Factory Number Two was located outside of town, in a field nearer to Jingzhou than to Shashi. The General Manager was much more vigorous than Chairman Ni and displayed a sure grasp of his business as we sauntered along the walkways between rows of modern machinery.

Chen Haijing was the opposite of Chairman Ni in every way. His round, smooth face betrayed a healthy appetite and he talked excitedly, chuckling all the while, with quick nervous movements. He was thirty-seven when I first met him; Ni was sixty-three. Chen had graduated in engineering from Wuhan University, in the capital of Hubei Province, about two hundred miles downstream. He joined the factory, working his way up through engineering and product development before he took over the marketing. He had become General Manager of the factory two years earlier. I realized the business might be interesting after all, so I started to take the measure of Chen.

He seemed at ease with himself as we strolled around the workshops and he answered detailed questions confidently, without hesitation or notes. He was a man of regular habits. Every morning he waited by the factory gates at seven-thirty to chat with the workers as they clocked in. Every evening he was there to see them home. In winter he would deliberately gain weight during the cold months and shed it again in the spring. He drank moderately and didn't smoke. He spoke amusingly but not boorishly. His clothes were neat but not showy. In short, he had an assured manner and an even-tempered confidence that gave the impression of understated power.

Chen told me that the designs for factory's products had originally been transferred to China by the Soviet Union in the 1950s, before Khrushehev had recalled the advisers. In the early years they sold these ancient electrical motors to a local truck factory up in the hills but they were now hopelessly out of date. High-performance electrical motors are complicated so Chen had tried to get new technology from an American company. It had taken seven years of negotiations but eventually they agreed to transfer the technology. But Chen didn't have the money to buy the expensive new machinery that he needed. It seemed there might be a good case for us to invest. So we arranged a follow-up meeting.

The negotiations to set up a joint venture dragged on through the summer. Each time we went back to Jingzhou, the first day was wasted discussing things that we thought we had agreed during the previous visit. In September the negotiations fell apart. We were in the process of raising the second fund and we didn't have any time to waste. Any further interest in Jingzhou was put on the back burner.

The following January, Chen called. He wanted to restart the talks. He said that there had been some disagreements among the Chinese parties so it had been difficult to progress the discussions. However, he was now running the shop and he wanted to get on. By April, we had a contract and it was signed on 15 May. Our cash was wired in and, amidst the familiar roar of firecrackers, we became the holder of a 51 per cent interest in one of China's leading electrical motor factories.

I didn't visit Jingzhou for nearly a year after the deal was done but when I eventually paid a visit the progress looked impressive. Chairman Ni, the old Chairman, had been ousted after what sounded like a bitter, drawn-out fight and Chen was now firmly in charge. The changes outside the works were equally dramatic. Factory Number Two, the modern facility, had been in the middle of a field the first time that Chen showed me round. But a year on it was just one of a long row of modern factory buildings on the edge of a new highway linking the two towns of Jingzhou and Shashi.

Huge glass buildings towered on the other side of the road. A new Customs house, several banks and the local government building had shot up in less than twelve months. The road was broad, divided down the middle with a grassy verge and mature trees that must have been transplanted from elsewhere. The whole area had the purposeful feel of the modern commercial district of a prosperous provincial town.

The factory itself was full of new equipment, neatly arranged in lines. There were huge winding machines that wound thick copper wire around armatures as if they were wrapping cotton around a bobbin. The workers were all busy, moving about briskly in standard blue overalls, while noticeboards showed monthly targets for production, quality-defect control and sales, with red lines indicating actual progress. There were specially made trolleys stacked high with copper windings and when I stopped to talk to the workers they told me that they were happy and felt that the business was going in the right direction.

Chen had won First Auto Works up in Changchun as an important new customer. This was quite an achievement; selling from central Hubei up to the north was difficult due to local protectionism. Encouraged by his success Chen set his targets on an even greater prize: Shanghai. There was a buzz to the place, sales were going up and we were happy about the progress. There was only one problem: the business lost money.

I never understood why the business didn't make a profit. It was one of our larger companies in terms of sales, with good products and customers. It didn't make sense and Board meetings became tetchy as we struggled to understand the figures. We were never briefed properly; Chen just tossed vast tomes of badly photocopied Chinese figures across the boardroom table when we arrived. Whenever we asked questions, different explanations would come from different members of the management team. No one seemed to be able to grasp the overall picture.

Frustrated by the confusion, we insisted on hiring a new finance manager and after months of acrimonious discussions Chen eventually agreed to accept him. He didn't last six months. Ostracized and isolated in his separate office and with no one to talk to, he quickly became dispirited and left. It made me uneasy. It was difficult to recruit competent people to Hubei.

The first solid clue that something was seriously wrong came when we stumbled across a set of accounts for the Chinese partner on a routine visit to the tax office. The accounts showed that they were making huge profits. But the Chinese partner had put all of its assets into the joint venture. How could it be generating profits when the joint venture was making losses? I went to see Chen. He betrayed no unease at our meeting and told me that it was just a matter of accounting for some adjustments that related to the time before the joint venture. I was sceptical but he said that if I didn't believe him we could send in auditors to look at their books.

Shortly afterwards, we discovered an unauthorized transfer of a million dollars between accounts at the bank and demanded an explanation directly from the bank manager. After Zhuhai, we were nervous about bank controls, so I asked the bank to explain what had happened. There was a lengthy exchange of letters in which the bank would neither confirm nor deny whether the controls had been broken. Their replies took the natural aptitude of the Chinese language for vagueness to new extremes. Frustrated beyond endurance, we demanded that Qiu, the old accountant, should be sacked and after several months of bitter wrangling we insisted on putting in our own man.

Little Zeng was originally from Shanghai and he thrived on conflict. All of our previous appointees had resigned within a couple of months but Zeng was keen for the challenge in spite of Hubei's reputation for wildness and lawlessness. He was small and wiry and had a toughness that went well beyond the point of insensitivity. He was deeply suspicious of everything and he had an obstinacy that would never be deflected from his lifelong pursuit of accounting irregularities. His pallid complexion, the result of long hours spent poring over ledgers in dimly lit offices, was accentuated by his habit of dressing only in black. He had the appearance of the quintessential auditor and a sense of humour to match. In short, he was perfect.

Shortly after Zeng arrived in Shashi, it became obvious that something was seriously wrong. The operations and accounts of our joint venture were hopelessly intertwined with those of the old Chinese partner. Accounting records were conveniently merged so that an outsider could never really tell where cash receipts had gone. Managers held dual positions, money was transferred between the two companies and we found that some of the sales offices were still operating under the Chinese partner's name. That set off alarm bells. We'd had similar problems in Harbin and it was a classic way of syphoning off profits.

We all took the view that the problem started at the top: Chen Haijing was the general manager of the Chinese partner as well as of our joint venture. We told him it had to stop. There had to be a complete separation. 'You can't have a foot in both camps,' we told him, 'and you've now got a month to decide.'

After I came back from France, I went to Jingzhou many times. I had the job of hammering out a deal with Chen and I became familiar with the journey from Beijing. It's a two-hour flight to Wuhan and then a four-hour drive through the flat-lands and marshes to Jingzhou. In one stretch the fields surrounding the highway are dotted with scores of ancient oil rigs. In the evenings, as the car sped along the raised highway, I would watch the silhouettes of the oil derricks against the setting sun. The cantilevers on top rocked back and forth, drawing up the black liquid from far underground like some old woman stooping over a well.

That summer there was the worst flooding for decades. From the middle of July massive rainstorms lashed down in the upper Yangtse basin near Tibet. The water surged down the valleys at the eastern edge of the highlands, gathering momentum. The geography of the region magnified the floods. When the river was forced into the gorges it became compressed into successive peaks or waves, known as flood waves. In 1998 there were eight flood waves, one of which, at Jingzhou, was the highest in recorded history.

The flooding that year affected the whole country. A sense of crisis deepened when three key sluice gates east of the city of Harbin collapsed and the Central Government organized massive evacuations. Confronted with a growing national calamity, the Government mobilized more than a million soldiers of the People's Liberation Army and sent them to the flood regions to guard and repair embankments. The entire nation was transfixed by the tales of heroism beamed across the airwaves.

Throughout the long summer, the sixty-five million people on the Yangtse flood plain lived on a knife-edge. Due to the elevation of the river bed caused by the fragile dykes, millions of people were living in the surrounding countryside at an elevation *below* the level of the dangerously swollen river. In July, the Government declared an emergency and Jiang Zemin, China's State Chairman, called on the nation for a 'do or die' effort to control the waters.

In early August, a large section of the dykes collapsed downstream at Jiujiang City, flooding the town of half a million people. The soldiers deliberately sank eight boats and manoeuvred them into the 130-foot wide breach in an attempt to plug the gap. More than thirty thousand soldiers and civilians toiled arounds the clock and eventually blocked the flow by adding bags of cement, stone, coal, sand and even rice and soya beans around the sunken hulks. But the government officials barely had time to congratulate themselves before the grim news arrived that torrential rains in the upper basin in Sichuan had caused another flood wave to form. This, the fifth wave, was the largest yet so the government drew up plans to dynamite the dykes on the southern bank of the river.

This ancient method of flood control relied on the deliberate destruction of the dykes at key points in order to flood low-lying farm areas and relieve the pressure on the cities. It was a simple choice: destroy vast areas of farmland to the south or risk the waters bursting into the major industrial towns on the northern bank. Wuhan, a city of eight million people, one of the main industrial centres of China, lay on the northern bank further downstream.

More than three hundred thousand people were evacuated from the southern flat-lands, sometimes forcibly. At Jingzhou, the decision was made to blast the ditches if the water reached a height of 148.5 feet, but the final decision was reserved for China's State Council, or Cabinet. The Prime Minister himself arrived to inspect the preparations and the television showed dramatic footage of him plodding along the dykes and staring glumly out over the grey swirling waters. On the evening of 9 August, the river stood at 147.3 feet as the final peak water-crest surged out of the Three Gorges, eighty miles upstream, and poured out into the flat-lands. The authorities knew that in a few hours the peak would reach Shashi. During the night the water rose to within two inches of the limit, the highest ever recorded in history, but the government held its nerve. By the morning, the crisis had passed and the water began to subside.

More than two thousand people died that summer and forty million homes were destroyed, but the Government had responded to the crisis and an even more serious disaster had been avoided.

As the flood waters rose and ebbed, the talks with Chen dragged on. He came up with endless reasons to do nothing, chuckling all the time, showing his perfect white teeth and moving his hands around as he spoke. But there was one point that we weren't going to budge from. He had to decide which business he wanted to run: 'It's ours or the Chinese partner's but not both,' I told him. We slowly turned the screws and eventually, in September, he agreed to resign from his positions on the Chinese side. We had a small celebration after we reappointed him as General Manager of the joint venture. In the following months, the business turned to profit for the first time and even Little Zeng seemed to relax.

It seemed as if we were getting a new start but rumours soon started to filter back to Beijing that the Chinese partner was trying to go public on the Shanghai stock market. It was impossible to know what to believe, but the experience at Ningshan had taught us about the dangers of having a Chinese partner with independent sources of money. When I questioned Chen he assured me that it was all rumour but the word from Jingzhou got steadily louder and louder. There were stories that equipment had been transferred out to another site owned by the Chinese partner at Shihaolu. We had reports of long weekend meetings where the Chinese management debated how best to prepare for going public.

Finally I received a fax from Zeng that changed everything. It was a notice sent out by the General Manager of the Chinese Partner. And it was signed by Chen Haijing. He hadn't resigned after all.

A familiar story was instantly recognizable. If the Chinese partner managed to raise capital on the public markets we would have a competitor on our doorstep. But this time it was different from Ningshan. We were early enough to take pre-emptive action. The only option was to fire Chen and put in our own man. On the surface, it seemed an easier proposition than ousting Shi from the tiny village of Ningshan where he was like a local warlord. Jingzhou had a population of nearly a million.

But we still needed to find Chen's replacement. I had been interviewing an overseas Chinese manager throughout the summer. Mr Hou was in his late forties and was an engineer by training. I had heard that he had handled some difficult situations where there had been labour problems, but he did not strike me as being particularly tough. He had been in China for nine years and managed a number of automotive factories. He was familiar with the business and gave the impression of unflappable patience – which would probably be needed at Jingzhou. He came with a strong record of team building and had worked in operations for many years. He was certainly no Chang Longwei but he seemed calm and capable and willing to take on the task so we signed him up and started to plan.

Just as at Ningshan and Harbin our contract allowed us to remove Chen but we had to hold a Board meeting with the Chinese directors physically present. We had done that successfully with Shi but had let him strike back later. This time there would be no such limp-wristedness.

We had three people working in Jingzhou together with Zeng. Little Li and Cao Ping were in exports and Zhao Xun was in sales. We called the team together and went through a rigorous planning session. We prepared letters to change the bank mandates and agreed to post people with mobile phones outside the banks all over the city waiting for the signal to go in. Notices to be pasted up around the factory, were prepared, announcing the change, and arrangements were made to seal off the file stores, lock the gates and impound movable assets. It would take a team of twelve people so we drafted in reinforcements from Beijing. Zeng and his colleagues were relieved and excited that we were finally going to do something about Chen. He had made their lives miserable in Jingzhou so I was confident that there would be no leaks.

I flew down to Hubei a day early. It was my habit to go through the topics in advance with Chen so I kept to the normal arrangements to avoid raising any suspicions. It was surreal sitting opposite him and listening to his plans for reorganizing the factory; he described them excitedly but I knew that they would come to nothing.

I couldn't focus on the conversation and stared at Chen. I had no feelings of enmity towards him personally, more a sense of slightly bored confusion than actual anger. I stared at him again; why did it have to be this way? I was tired. I felt a kind of detached neutrality that would have been more fitting in a disconnected observer as I went mechanically through the first steps of throwing him out.

That afternoon I went for a long walk alone around the lake in the middle of the city and stared across the reeds towards the humpback bridges in the distance. There was a fine autumn mist in the late-afternoon as the sun cast its last weak rays over the ornamental rocks beside the lake. I wandered down the pathways over a wet mass of squashed black leaves towards the small zoo on the far side of the lake. I stared for a few minutes at the fat three-legged tiger limping back and forth restlessly behind his bars and then turned back over the raised embankments by the lake. I felt listless. We were about to fire Chen and throw him out of his job. It made no sense – but what alternative was there? I turned my face away from the setting sun and shivered in the early-evening cold. Quickening my pace, I pulled my coat more tightly round my neck and turned back towards the hotel.

I woke up early and, after a breakfast of fried twisted dough sticks and hot water-buffalo milk in a greasy restaurant by the hotel gate, Pat and I set off for the factory. The meeting opened in the normal way with Pat in the chair. The presentation of the results droned on in the background as blood throbbed in my temples. After half an hour, I looked at Pat and signalled that it was time. We stopped the meeting and asked Chen if we could meet with him in a separate room alone. Still apparently unsuspecting, he agreed readily and the meeting was adjourned.

We went into a little side room with dirty windows. An old desk with some browning newspapers on it and a few old mops propped up against the wall added to the tatty appearance. There was an old black plastic sofa and a wooden chair.

Pat and Chen sat on the sofa. It was a familiar conversation. Our investors needed to see some returns . . . not satisfied with performance . . . need independent management and so forth. Chen was clearly shocked and then asked if he could negotiate his personal settlement with me alone, so Pat left.

As we discussed Chen's deal, one of the cleaners came in and there was a brief exchange in the heavy Hubei dialect. I failed to catch its drift. The conversation went round for another ten minutes and then Chen excused himself to go for a leak. I wandered out and saw the other two Chinese directors disappear into the gents' after him. With my nerves already jangling I sensed a plot. With their mobiles, there was no knowing what they might do to avoid being ousted, so I ran the length of the corridor and pulled a startled Chen from a cubicle and back into the little side room.

I said, 'Resign now or be publicly sacked,' handed Chen the letter and said, 'You have fifteen seconds.' He signed it and I gave the signal to go into the banks.

Within ten minutes the bank accounts were changed, notices were posted all over the factory, the file store was locked and all the gates were secured.

The other Chinese directors, white with fury, took the news in silence. Chen tried to persuade them to sign the Board resolution removing him and appointing Hou as a temporary replacement, but two abstained and Qiu, the old accountant whom we had sacked the year before, put up a more respectable defence and voted against the resolution to remove Chen. It didn't matter: we had a majority and Chen had already resigned, so there wasn't much they could do.

We called a meeting of the middle management staff and Chen went through the agreed face-saving formula. He said that he had chosen to remain as the leader of the Chinese company and had resigned from the joint venture.

After the meeting broke up, Chen and I stayed in the room alone. I tried to persuade him not to fight. 'Old Shi came back at us after we had fired him and look what happened there. Two years of legal fights and damaged reputations, all for nothing.' He just mumbled that we'd made a mistake. Just then the office manager came in with the news that the file store was locked and that we had grabbed the chops. Chen gave me a wounded look. I just shrugged. There wasn't much else I could do.

Straight after the meeting. I went off to lunch with Wang Ping. He was a director in the Machinery Bureau of the Jingzhou Municipal Government. I had met him at the time we did the joint venture at some *baijiu* dinner. He had stuck in my mind as one of Mayor Huang's few rivals in the whole of China for consumption of alcohol. Affably useless as always, he was much more interested in getting half a bottle of *baijiu* down me than in listening to the story about Chen, and he repeatedly interrupted with toasts. I plugged on anyway and he eventually came up with the throwaway remark that it was really up to the Board to decide what to do – and why didn't I have some more bean curd? I left feeling thick-headed.

Back at the factory, everything seemed normal. Chen was nowhere to be seen. Cao Ping told me that as he was pasting up one of the notices an old factory worker had said *gai zao zuo* – 'It should have been earlier' – as he read the notice. I guessed that Chen was probably licking his wounds in private, so we said goodbye to Hou and drove off to Wuhan for dinner with the Provincial Vice-Governor.

As I drifted off into an uncomfortable sleep, with *baijiu* in my veins and a pounding in my head, the familiar flat-lands flashed past outside. As I dozed fitfully I felt pleased with the day and confident that we'd rescued our investment in the factory.

The weekend was quiet. No news from Hubei was good news, I thought. On the following Monday, I flew to Shanghai. We had a visiting Japanese delegation from a company that might be interested in selling us technology for piston rings. I was at lunch when a phone call came in to Li Wei. He looked worried but said nothing.

As we left, Li Wei drew me into a corner and told me that there was some trouble at the factory. Chen Haiping had arrived there as usual in the morning and a conversation between him and Zeng had turned nasty. Apparently they had exchanged insults loudly at the factory gates and had attracted a large crowd of onlookers outside the office building. Chen had been furious and had sent a letter to the Provincial Government complaining that he had been insulted. Like Shi, he was a People's Deputy and he sent a formal demand that a team should come down from the Provincial Government in Wuhan to investigate.

Apparently a similar confrontation had occurred after lunch. The two men had been screaming insults into each other's faces when Chen had suddenly turned green and collapsed. He had been carried into the office building. Hou became seriously rattled when efforts to revive him failed. Chen was rushed into hospital where he had been declared critically ill and put into intensive care.

The sight of Chen being carried out of the office building and the news that he was seriously ill caused a riot. The factory was a tinderbox after Chen's sacking, with rival factions forming to support or oppose the decision. When the news spread, a huge surge of rage swept through the factory and about a hundred furious workers surrounded the office building, baying for blood. Hou and his team were still trapped inside. I heard later that they had been in a third-floor office when a full bottle of beer crashed through the window and exploded on the wall next to Cao's head.

Zeng and Hou had been separated and no one knew where they were. The others were bundled into the Factory Workers Union Building where Ma Xiatong, one of Chen's assistants, leapt onto a table and, in front of a crowd of excited workers, delivered an impassioned speech saying that, 'The factory belongs to the workers who built it with their bitter tears and blood.' He urged the crowd to seize control and kick out the foreigners. Desperate calls to the police and local government met with no reply. The workers were trying to break down the heavy doors of the office building that had been locked from the inside. I gave instructions for the office in Beijing to try to contact the government and boarded the plane back to Beijing in a state of great agitation.

In the two hours that I was out of contact, the situation stabilized. Wang Ping had eventually arrived. The Government was trying to calm down the workers. I hoped that at least this remarkably witless man would bore them all into a trance – as he would if his conversation over the *baijiu* was anything to go by. I eventually got through to Hou and his small voice came over the line. He told me that there was no immediate threat but that there were still fifty workers outside who were demanding that he hand over the chops. I said immediately, 'There's no way we're doing that otherwise we'll lose everything. You know that you can't get at the bank accounts without the chops, so you won't be able to run the factory.' Inwardly I was confused. It seemed odd that workers would be demanding the

233

chops. I was surprised that they had realized their full significance.

Over the next hours there were many conversations back and forth. Hou was clearly very rattled. I told him just to sit down and do nothing. He wouldn't come to any harm with Wang Ping there so he should just wait until it was safe to go back to the hotel. He was clearly wavering so I tried to be calmly reassuring but as the evening wore on he became frightened out of his wits.

The conversation went round and round. 'Think this through. Just sit there and do nothing.' I said. 'The workers won't attack you with a government official in the room. You know that if we lose the chops we can't manage the business and we'll be finished. Just sit there and do nothing. I'll come down first thing in the morning. Just sit there and wait.' And so on long into the night.

Matters were eventually taken out of my hands when a miserable Hou called and told me that he was going to hand over the chops. I had one final go at dissuading him but he just replied limply that he had no choice. I eventually persuaded him to give them to Wang Ping for safe keeping rather than hand them over to the workers. He said that he'd see what he could do. I put the receiver down at three in the morning and suddenly snapped.

I threw the phone against the wall and screamed 'Shit!'

The news that awaited me in the office the next morning was even worse. Hou had been followed back to the hotel and his nerve had broken completely. He told the team to pack their bags and run. They were now on the plane back to Beijing.

I couldn't believe it! Handing over the chops was one thing but abandoning the post meant that we were completely lost. We now had no one at the joint venture and no one that I could send there. The workers knew that all they had to do was throw a few beer bottles around and the next lot would run as well.

I knew that all the other factory directors were watching events closely. I had to stop the rot otherwise the team might collapse entirely so when Hou arrived, I called him into my office and sacked him. I told the others we were going back in and we got on a plane for Hubei.

When we arrived in Jingzhou, Li Wei went to the factory and Ai Jian to the hospital. They both came back worried. Li Wei had managed to negotiate his way in through the factory gates and had met with Chen's deputy, Old Zhou. But it was soon obvious that Old Zhou was not in control. Halfway through the meeting, there was loud banging on the meeting-room door. It was locked from the inside but Zhou, obviously frightened himself, had taken some time to persuade the workers to go away. Ai Jian came back from the hospital with a couple of bruises. He had gone to ask after Chen but a large crowd had barred him from the room. There had been a scuffle and he had been kicked out of the hospital.

The next day we asked for a meeting with the Chinese partner. Old Zhou and Qiu, the old accountant, came over to the hotel. They said it was too dangerous to go to the factory. They looked ashen and frightened, but they were absolutely adamant that we should declare the board resolutions invalid and that Chen should go back.

Li Wei guessed from their anxiety that when we had dismissed Chen we had destabilized the loose coalitions within the Chinese partner. If they had been united, he would have expected them to be angry rather than worried.

He figured that with Chen absent and ill in hospital, no one was really in control and the prospect of serious unrest had terrified the other Chinese directors. I tried to use this as a tactic to get them to work together with us to stabilize the situation, but they refused and after a call came in to Old Zhou's cellphone the meeting ended abruptly.

Two hours later a fax arrived in Beijing demanding that we retract the board resolution and 'accept responsibility for the economic damage caused by the abnormal situation.' I had it faxed on down to me. It was signed by Chen Haijing. The signature was written in clear, bold characters. It did not look like the signature of a man who was critically ill. We decided to call the Government.

We trooped in to see the Deputy Mayor of Jingzhou in charge of industry. The meeting was in the new Government building opposite Factory Number Two. As I arrived, I noticed that a large crowd had broken into the ground-floor reception. There was complete chaos, with a scrum of people shouting and crying. I managed to figure out from the protests that a local state-owned business had collapsed. An old woman was howling that with the factory gone, there was 'no rice to eat' and that all her 'family had to run to outside places to look for work.' Several government officials were patiently listening to the complaints, trying to calm down the workers, asking them to go home and promising to report to the Party Secretary. We managed to get through the melée and I clambered up the stairs wondering how the hell we'd get any attention with that fracas going on downstairs.

Deputy Mayor Shang listened to our complaints and gave us the standard line that he would deal with the case in accordance with Chinese law. Old Zhou was there but he didn't say much. After the meeting closed we tried to leave the office but the workers were still milling about in reception, so we were shown out of a side door and went back to the hotel to wait.

There was absolutely no response. I was in Jingzhou for three weeks. Every day, we made calls to the Government but there was silence. Every day we sent faxes to the Chinese partner but there was no response. I couldn't even persuade Wang Ping to share a bottle of *baijiu* with me. After Hou's flight we were on the outside; Chen could safely ignore us. Just like at Ningshan, we'd blown it after a good start. Once again, we were engaged in protracted struggle on enemy ground. But now it was even worse. We couldn't get into the factory this time so we were on the outside looking in. The only cause for hope was that Hou had handed the chops to Wang Ping prior to his flight. Without the chops, Chen could not operate the bank accounts, so he couldn't make any payments. The business would slowly bleed to death. There was no alternative but to sit out a protracted siege until he was forced to deal with us.

I was genuinely surprised by the severity of the Chinese reaction. Sure, Chen was bound to have been furious when we'd kicked him out. But there was something of a pantomime about the dramatic illness, the immediate diagnosis of a critical condition, the worker's uprising and the flying beer bottles. It all seemed a little far-fetched to me. Something was missing; we hadn't found all the pieces of the jigsaw and something in the puzzle was eluding me.

Every day for those three weeks I walked the full circumference of the city on the little path between the walls and the moat, wracking my brains for a plan. A rhythm settled in as I tramped the path each day, waiting for the call from the local Government, hoping for some news of Chen. But there was silence as I walked. Over time, the sights of Jingzhou became routine and ordinary: the young boys climbing thirty feet to the top of the walls, pulling themselves up with their fingers gripping the cracks in the ancient brickwork; the damp odour and green moss under the gateways; the boats moving slowly and silently through the mist on the moats; the falling leaves and the fog; the baskets of persimmon in the orchards on the opposite bank. Seven miles every afternoon, racking my brains for a plan.

After we had been expelled from the factory there was almost no news of what was going on inside. But there were ominous signs. Chen had not reappeared and he remained in his hospital bed. But it seemed that he was controlling events from behind the scenes. There were rumours of a purge where anyone suspected of cooperating with us had been fired or demoted. I remember that one day, during one of my long walks around the moat, I received a call from someone in the accounts office. Little Dong was suspected of leaking information to us. She explained in a voice shaking with rage that she was a university graduate but that she had been reassigned from the finance department to machine maintenance. She had been moved permanently to a filthy old workshop at the back of the factory. She was given a toolbox and a huge spanner and told to repair two enormous old metal presses. We eventually found her a job at another of our factories and she went off to Shanxi a month later.

It was really Zeng's persistence that gave us our chance – that, and a bit of luck. Zeng had noticed that the serial number on one of the joint venture's land certificates didn't match the number on a building certificate that had been issued some years earlier. It all seemed a little esoteric to me, so I ignored him at first but he was like the terrier that wouldn't let go. I became irritated by his constant harping on the issue and told him to drop it. But he didn't.

Gradually I began to have my doubts as well. Land certificates are important in China because they are taken as conclusive proof of title to the land. Most importantly, the certificate can be used as collateral to raise loans from Chinese banks.

My suspicions deepened after another meeting with Old Zhou. Incredibly, he left the handwritten notes that he had used to prepare for the meeting on the table after he left. There, among the mostly indecipherable scribbles, at the bottom of the second page was a reference to some trans-ferred land certificates. Before Old Zhou came back we rushed to the next room where there was a photocopier. He returned puce in the face and out of breath, grabbed his notes and walked off, fuming.

It looked as though we might have found something that we could use to put pressure on Chen. But to uncover the truth we needed someone on the inside, someone who would be willing to ferret out documents from within the Government. I put a call through to the General.

Lawyer Xie had been a friend of the General for many years and readily agreed to help. He was in Changsha when we called him but said that he would drive over to see us. Changsha lies in Hunan Province to the south, some four hundred miles away from Jingzhou, and the roads were terrible. Xie arrived after sixteen hours in a taxi. Once he'd showered and eaten we looked through the documents together. We had taken copies of the original certificates at the time that we did the joint venture so I had them faxed down from Beijing. We could see that the serial numbers had been changed and didn't match, and Lawyer Xie was as puzzled as I was. Something was wrong, but the only way to unravel the mystery was to go to the Land Bureau.

Lawyer Xie spent hours on the phone with his contacts in Wuhan, the provincial capital. He eventually found the right person who agreed to try to arrange for him to have a private meeting with a low-level Land Bureau official who might be able to provide some clues. A call was made and Lawyer Xie set off.

There didn't seem much point in hanging around in the hotel so I went off for a walk around the city walls. I waited anxiously for a call on my mobile but I walked the whole distance without receiving any news. I was much too agitated to relax, so I went round again. When I finally got back to the hotel, it was past dusk. Lawyer Xie had just arrived back, carrying a bundle of photocopied documents wrapped up in brown paper. The copies showed that a large piece of land that was originally owned by our joint venture had been transferred out to the Chinese partner. There were copies of the old certificates in our name with a red chop that read 'cancelled' stamped across the face, a transfer document signed by Chen, and a new land certificate in the name of the Chinese partner.

The story was out. I saw why Chen had been so desperate. When he had tried to take his company to the Shanghai stock market, he realized that it didn't have sufficient assets. Chen had never intended to resign from the Chinese partner but was playing for time. When he discovered that the assets were insufficient for a listing, he came up with an ingenious solution. He transferred four million dollars' worth of land out of our joint venture back to the Chinese company, thereby neatly solving the assets requirement and netting a huge gain. Chen had been caught red-handed in a case that involved a huge amount of money. I thought that the Government would now have no option but to intervene on our behalf.

However, requests for a meeting with the Government still came to nothing. I became more and more confused and frustrated. Every official we talked to made the same excuse: they had important meetings and they were too busy to get involved. So I was almost relieved when at last we received a request from the Factory Workers Union for a meeting. I guessed that Chen might be using the Union as a cover for serious negotiations. Avoiding direct contact might be a way of saving face. Li Wei was sceptical, but I thought that whatever happened at the meeting it would be a good opportunity for us to get information.

The Union officials came to the little meeting-room in the hotel just behind reception. They opened by saying that they were very upset that they hadn't been consulted about the change in management. I said that I was sorry if I had offended them, but that it was really the job of the Chinese partner to keep them updated. I thought to myself that it was probably an opening ruse to put me at a disadvantage. It was a standard tactic to start a meeting by trying to capture the high moral ground prior to making a concession.

The discussions continued in a rather directionless fashion for about half an hour when I noticed suddenly – and uneasily – that there were now about thirteen people on the other side of the table whereas at the start there had only been six. One of the newcomers became quite aggressive and kept interrupting in a harsh croaky voice that what we had done was '*fei fa, wei fa; fei fa, wei fa*' – 'illegal and invalid; illegal and invalid.' He was being deliberately provocative so I responded aggressively in English and when it was translated there was a storm of protest from the other side, with the workers standing up and shouting over the table and shaking their fists in my face. By this time several more workers had squeezed into the room so I got up to leave, only to find that my exit was blocked. I could see through the door that there were about another sixty workers in the reception hall, milling around and in a state of some anticipation. My heart sank as I realized that I had so innocently fallen into a trap.

We were held for about nine hours in the tiny room. It had space for a meeting of maybe ten people; the only window had bars across it. At one point there were more than forty screaming workers pressed into the tiny space. One of the original six had been trying to get me to sign a piece of paper that overturned the board resolution. I glanced at the paper. It read, in badly typed English:

> The 29 October event, an illegal activity under Foreign partner's elaborate plot, which snatched the Chinese partner's management right under the contract by way of swindle and compulsion, disrupted the normal operating system, and the Foreign partner should take the whole responsibility

I didn't get any further. I was amazed that he seemed to think that I might actually sign it. My instinct was to tell him to shove it up his nose, but surrounded by workers baying for blood I opted for the less heroic option of stubborn silence. The worker who was pressing me to sign the document was scruffily dressed and smoked heavily.

He wore a blue cap pulled over his forehead. He seemed unusually confident and when someone shouted from the back of the scrum that, under Chinese Law, the Chinese side should appoint the Chairman of any joint venture, he responded immediately that the recent Chinese Company Law had changed the regulations. I realized that this 'worker' was no worker at all. He was a local lawyer in factory uniform that the Chinese partner had drafted in to try to get me to revoke Chen's dismissal with a letter that would stick.

Throughout the nine hours of shouting and fist-shaking, I didn't have much time to think. My nerves were ragged and my head was aching, but I was only seriously rattled once when a couple of workers came in, their faces red. They had obviously been drinking heavily and stood in the doorway, swaying gently. Even the Union leader seemed worried at that point and I just prayed that no one would do anything stupid and that there were no knives about. I clung to the hopes that most of the workers were just play-acting and curious about the foreigner.

As the time rolled on, I became sure that Chen had drafted them in to put pressure on me. But there was no way that I was going to sign the document so we just sat there. I could see that, with one or two exceptions, the workers weren't bad people. Towards the end of the afternoon they started to get bored, so I started chatting with one of the workers during a lull in the protests. He responded amicably enough until he remembered where he was and snapped back into mock aggression.

Li Wei was masterful. He just talked the workers out: talked and talked and talked, in the same circuitous rambling fashion, never getting to the point and exhausting them on the way. In the end, they got bored with it and by early evening they were hungry. They started to drift off.

I finally got out in the early evening and realized suddenly how exhausted I was. It had been a very unpleasant experience. As I walked up the stairs back to my room, I glanced through a door into one of the many private dining rooms in the hotel. Seated at the head of the table, face sweating and reddened with alcohol, stuffing local freshwater crabs into his mouth, was Mayor Shang. The man who'd promised to sort out the mess had been carousing upstairs with his cronies while his foreign investors were held hostage in a room below.

After seeing Mayor Shang upstairs in the hotel, I had almost given up hope of getting any help from the Government but two days later Li Wei came in with the news that the Party Secretary of Jingzhou, Liu Heji, was having dinner in a private room in the hotel. I put on a suit and went downstairs. We sat outside the Secretary's room and waited. Shortly afterwards Secretary Liu's office manager came out. I was obviously causing embarrassment inside so he asked what I wanted. 'Five minutes with the Party Secretary' was my reply and after a brief disappearance the office manager came back with the message that Secretary Liu would meet us after dinner.

Liu Heji was the Prefectural Party Secretary. It was a position of considerable power within the Chinese hierarchy and several rungs higher than Secretary Wu in Ningguo, which was just a small municipality. Jingzhou Prefecture, which included the towns of Jingzhou and Shashi plus the surrounding counties, had a population approaching ten million. Secretary Liu, unusually, had been in his position for at least five years, which was ample time for him to have consolidated his position in the area. Although it was usual for officials to be rotated regularly from place to place, somehow Secretary Liu had managed to stay put.

He was a small, neat man who initially gave little away in his words or expressions. I remember being surprised that he was wearing a tweed jacket more appropriate for an English country squire than for a Chinese Party Secretary. We met in the little meeting-room where I had so recently been trapped by the workers. It was a short discussion. I used the deliberately vague language of Chinese officials. Li Wei had suggested that I should embed the key sentence concerning the stolen land in among other remarks and use the ambiguous expression *zichan guanli queshi you wenti*: 'the asset management indeed has problems.'

I could gauge from his expression that Secretary Liu knew exactly what I meant. He replied, equally vaguely, *shi chu you yin*: 'when something happens there is a reason' and told me to wait for a week. It was a classic exchange with a Chinese official. They go to great lengths to avoid any directness that might lead to confrontation and use an extreme form of vagueness, pregnant with hidden meaning. Secretary Liu's remark said everything and nothing all at the same time.

He ended the meeting and told me that he would instruct the Government to find out what had been going on.

Exhausted, bored and rapidly gaining weight after weeks of sitting around in Jingzhou, we returned to Beijing. I thought we should give Secretary Liu some time to clarify the facts and come up with a solution to the land but these illusions where broken when a couple of days later Li Wei came into my office and told me that three court officials had arrived from Jingzhou. They were looking for me. I called Lawyer

Xie and he told me that I should meet with them but that I should not sign anything. He would come over immediately.

The court officials were stiff and formal and I tried to relax the atmosphere with small talk. The leader of the group, a woman, wore a green uniform with huge gold epaulettes and a large peaked hat with badges that looked decidedly military. She got straight down to business. They told me that our joint venture in Hubei was owed a large amount of money by our Beijing office and that it had sued us. They had come up to Beijing to seize our assets as security and they had already frozen our bank accounts. I couldn't understand what had happened. The court officials seemed to be telling me that we had sued ourselves and frozen our own assets. How could the joint venture sue its controlling partner? I looked at the writs and slowly the picture came into focus.

The joint venture did business with a company whose name, when translated into Chinese, was similar to ours. That company did owe the joint venture some money so Chen had found our bank details in Beijing and filed a claim in the Jingzhou Intermediary People's Court freezing all our assets in China. This was madness: any claim to the Court had to be chopped by the company seal. Hou had handed all the chops over to Wang Ping at the Machinery Bureau and when I compared the chop on the court papers to the original on file we saw that it was a different chop. In China, using a false chop is a criminal offence.

I could see that the fight was beginning to paralyse the whole of our operation, so we put a call through to the General.

The Chinese press, like that of any other country, wields enormous power. Mao regularly used it to attack his opponents within the Government as well as outside. The Government still controls the newspapers but it has cautiously allowed wider reporting in certain areas particularly in exposing corruption or wrong doing by mid-level officials. The press has almost been used as an informal police force by the Central Government in its campaigns to root out corruption. But it a dangerous weapon for the journalists concerned; if they attacked an official and failed to bring him down, the journalist would be finished.

The General came in to see us. He told us that in China there are two parallel systems in the media. One system, which gives the filtered version and concentrates mostly on good news, is for public consumption. The clearer picture of the Chinese reality is reserved for *nei can*. This *nei bu can kao* – 'internal reference material' – is a summary of the unvarnished truth to be read in private by the top leaders of the country. All the major newspapers produce a weekly pamphlet for circulation to the State Council and the ministries in Beijing. Local officials do not like their names appearing in *nei bu can kao* in connection with anything scandalous.

'This,' said the General, 'is the weapon you must choose.' Making a sudden gesture, as if to swipe something off my head, and using a reference to the formal clothing worn by Tang dynasty ministers, he said, 'That Old Secretary, he'll soon back down if you try to knock off his official's hat!!'

We put together a booklet describing our story in simple terms. The General said that we had one chance only so we had to be absolutely clear. The Chinese partner would exploit any hint of complication in order to confuse the issue. Over the next fortnight, we embarked on a campaign of saturation bombing. Every day, for two weeks, we sent faxes to thirty or forty officials in the Provincial Government.

Then Pat arranged a dinner with several journalists in Beijing and gave them our story. It was one of those times when his skills for explaining complicated stories were put to the test; I knew it went well because the journalists had already heard of Mayor Shang. He had been involved in a case where some investors from Macau had lost a lot of money in Jingzhou and a lengthy and messy dispute had finally ended up on television. They were non-committal but I was encouraged when they said that the Central Government had recently started one of the periodic campaigns to track down cases of corruption involving government officials. We finished the dinner and they left with smiles but no promises.

Three journalists from the *Economic Daily* and the *Guangming Daily* arrived in Jingzhou the following week. Whereas we had been kicking our heels in Jingzhou for six weeks, they managed to arrange a meeting with the Government within an hour of arriving and spent the afternoon with Mayor Shang and Chen Haijing. Chen appeared from the shadows for the first time, apparently having staged a miraculous recovery. He gave lots of complicated explanations, but no one was taken in.

That evening Secretary Liu invited the journalists to a dinner. When I heard the news, I knew that the fight was drawing to a close. His personal attendance at a dinner meant that the Government was seriously rattled. The General had been right. Liu was worried about losing his official's hat.

On Christmas Day at about three o'clock in the afternoon I received a call from Chen Haijing. He had arrived in Beijing and he wanted to meet. I tried to explain that immediately after lunch on Christmas Day wasn't an ideal time for a business meeting, so Ai Jian went to see him instead. He told us that they'd like to settle the dispute and wanted to know when Pat would be back in Beijing.

Two weeks later, Secretary Liu himself came to Beijing in the cold. He sat irritably across the table as Chen and I went through all the tedious details. It was a long haul, but eventually the land went back in, Chen agreed to resign from managing the joint venture and we sent a new finance manager to Shashi who had to sign every cheque.

Several weeks later we went down to Jingzhou to tour the factory. The trip was uneventful and operations were back to normal. I noticed one of the workers who had been in the stormy meeting with the Union, on his lathe in the little workshop. I waved at him and he returned a wide smile. It was business as usual.

In the early evening, we shook hands with the new managers and drove out of the factory. The car left the city, passing under the gateways and over the moats, winding its way through the knot of hooting trucks and ringing bicycles. As it sped along the highway through the marshes, the sun set behind us. I looked at Li Wei and said, 'Do you really think that Chen was ill, or do you think the whole thing was staged to try and push us out?'

I couldn't see his expression as he turned his face to gaze out of the window. He thought for a moment and then said,

'*Ey-aah, jiutouniao, jiutouniao!* Nine-headed birds, nine-headed birds!'

I didn't know what he meant.

'Don't you know the expression? Up in the sky, there are nine-headed birds, but down on the earth there are people from Hubei!'

The saying rhymes in Chinese and has a resonance to it. It went round and round in my head. I've never found anyone who could really explain what it meant. But for me, the nine-headed bird is a potent image of something strange and unknowable, with all the wildness, cunning and unpredictability that I had found in those marshlands in central China.

Eleven

一髮千鈞

The Bottle Finally Bursts:
Nineteen Thousand Catties Hanging by a Single Hair

Han Dynasty literary idiom; 202 BC–AD 220:
a hundredweight hanging by a single thread
or a moment of imminent peril.

The fight with Shi up in the hills had revealed a powerful and explosive character. He was a man whom I couldn't help but admire but the skirmishes with Chen had left a very different impression. After four years in a joint venture, Shi had felt that we were hopelessly bogged down in problems at our other businesses that were not of his making. It seemed to him that we had lost the ability to deliver on our promise; the chance to build the leading components company in China. Shi was stuck; other entrepreneurs all around him were raising capital on the newly opened stock markets, but Shi had already sold a majority of his shares to us so that route was closed. Shi felt that we'd changed our deal, so he came straight out and told us that he wanted to change his. This brings into sharp focus a core difference between Chinese and Western business: for a Westerner, a contract is a contract, but in China it is a snapshot of a set of arrangements that happened to exist at one time. When he tried to change the terms, Shi's mistake was that he underestimated our determination to fight. He hadn't realized that we had no option: there was nowhere else for us to go.

Shi had been upfront but Chen just helped himself to our assets. Shi had stood his ground and fought for what he had built but Chen fled into the sidelines and manipulated events from the safety of his hospital bed. Shi had built something from nothing. Chen just climbed the bureaucrat's ladder. In that sense, Shi's fight was more honest.

In the next battle, the final rout with its headlong tumble into chaos, we were repulsed and forced into a tactical withdrawal. The final showdown took place in China's capital where we had invested heavily in three state-owned breweries.

Shortly after we bought up three breweries in Beijing, just as the sounds of celebration started to die away I received a note from Xu. It was in poor English but seemed to be asking for 'understanding that he had made some urgent payments while Chairman Pat was out of the country.'

Xu was the Factory Director of the Five Star Brewery that we had just acquired. I didn't take much notice at first, but asked someone to get me a cash balance from the joint venture. I was told that there were only a few million left in the accounts. It couldn't be true. We had wired over sixty million dollars into the account in early February so I asked again. The answer was the same so I called the brewery. Xu was not there, but his finance manager told me that a number of large payments had gone through the account

252

and that there was now only five million left. About fifty-eight million had been transferred out over the previous three days. I was speechless. How could that have happened? The signature cards lodged at the bank required signatures from our side before payments could be made. It couldn't be true. As I tried to understand what had happened, Pat called in from the States. After I had gone through it with him and explained that fifty-eight million appeared to be missing, there was a long pause and then: 'We gotta find that fucking money or it'll be time-out from the investors!'

The beer market in the early 1990s produced a great deal of froth. Multinational brewers piled into China, mesmerized by the prospect of a billion thirsty beer drinkers. The market was already the second largest in the world and the signs were that it was about to explode.

I knew that China had a long tradition of distilling spirits from grain and sorghum and I had been well trained by Mayor Huang in the art of weathering raucous banquets where the initial formality quickly collapsed under a deluge of *baijiu*. In imperial times these banquets, with their elaborate drinking rituals designed to push the guests to the point of mental disintegration, were reserved for the rich and cultured.

Drunkenness was almost considered a virtue. It was said that the best poetry and calligraphy came from artists in a state of deep inebriation. The story inevitably came up at banquets of Li Bai, a Tang dynasty poet who wrote a thousand years ago:

How many great men are forgotten through the ages?
Great drinkers are better known than sober sages . . .
I only want to drink and never wake up.

His wish was shortly fulfilled when he drowned in a pond. Blind drunk, he toppled in during a conversation with the moon's reflection. His accident was invariably billed as the ultimate sacrifice in pursuit of art rather than as an idiotic thing to have done. Despite these ancient alcoholic traditions, beer for the masses is a recent development.

The Germans were the first to introduce beer into China at the turn of the last century when they built a brewery at Tsingtao on the Shandong coast. First tastes of the new drink confirmed the local suspicion that the foreigners were incomprehensibly barbarian: beer was bitter, sent clouds of stinging gas up the back of the nose, and bloated up the stomach painfully before reaching the head. But gradually it became more popular. The Russians followed shortly afterwards and in 1915 set up a brewery in Beijing called Five Star. They built a strangely-shaped oast house with turrets, Gothic arches and a kiln for drying and storing hops. An image of the building was still used as the trademark of the beer produced in Beijing the last time I looked.

Over the following decades beer gradually became more popular. Hops were brought in from Xinjiang in the far west of China and the local barley malt was adapted for brewing. More and more locals acquired the habit, but even in the 1970s beer was a luxury. As the Chinese economy opened up during the 1980s beer gradually became popular and hundreds of small breweries sprang up all over China. A brewery was a status symbol for the local Party Secretary. It not only provided employment but also implied subtly that the water was pure and that there was enough money around to indulge in modest luxuries. By the beginning of the 1990s there were over eight hundred breweries all over

China churning out beer of dubious quality, mostly on a tiny scale that was hopelessly inefficient. But these problems were hidden and, on the surface, the market appeared to be huge. Government statistics showed explosive growth; China overtook Germany as the second-largest consumer of beer, guzzling nearly ten million tons every year. With the economy booming and wages rising, young Chinese flocked to the bars, pockets full of cash, in search of a good time and beer consumption went through the roof.

The big multinationals that came to China had one significant disadvantage. Famous brand names such as Budweiser, Carlsberg and Heineken meant nothing in China. They might as well have tried to launch Chinese brand names such as King Benefit, Cloudy Lake, Clock Tower or Dragon-and-Elephant in the States. The real prize for a brewer serious about the Chinese market was to capture a famous local brand.

Despite the huge number of breweries there were really only a handful of nationally recognized brands in China: Tsingtao in Shandong, Snowflake up in the north-east of the country and the two Beijing breweries, Beijing Beer and Five Star. After Liberation, Premier Zhou Enlai had encouraged Tsingtao to be China's national export brand so it became well known outside China. He chose Five Star as the premium domestic brand and from then on it always appeared on the banquet tables in the Great Hall of the People.

Five Star grew into the largest beer brand in China by licensing its trademarks to local breweries all over the country. In return for a royalty based on the amount of beer produced, Five Star agreed that these breweries could sell beer under the Five Star name and use its labels and the famous blue logo with the five white stars. For the consumer it was all Five Star beer and often they didn't know that it had not been produced in Beijing. By 1993, Five Star had forty-eight licensee breweries all over the country churning out more than a million tons of beer a year. It was the ultimate prize for a foreign investor in this exploding market but something that appeared hopelessly out of reach. However, we had set our sights high and in early 1994 we got a lucky break.

In January of that year, Jenny Jiang walked into my office and demanded a job. There was a lot to do and I couldn't think of any reasonable objection off the top of my head so she started there and then. She had just graduated from Fu Dan University in Shanghai and had an unusually dominant character. Tall and sinuous, she had an athletic appearance and a brisk manner that told you she would brook no nonsense. She became my assistant dealing with the breweries and we worked together for five years.

During the Spring Festival in 1994, Jenny was invited to a dinner where she met a mid-level official in the Beijing Government. He had been intrigued to hear about Pat's investment strategy and asked her whether someone might like to visit the Government. I grabbed the chance to go.

The Municipal Government of Beijing presides over its citizens from behind high, nondescript walls along a leafy lane called Justice Street just east of Tiananmen Square. Inside the compound are groups of buildings that look like colonial houses, with shutters over the windows. There are walkways and roundabouts and neatly planted fir trees and the first impression is one of businesslike efficiency. But after a while I sensed an air of soporific exhaustion, more like something you might expect in a career bureaucrat's retirement home.

As we sat inside on a huge dusty sofa waiting for our hosts, I took in the surroundings. The room reminded me of that first trip to the Land Bureau in Shanghai all those years ago with the boys in pinstripes from New York. It looked as though it had last been decorated in the 1930s. It was lifeless and exuded a strange heaviness. There was a smell of dust and old furniture polish. The dark-painted wood, thick maroon carpet and the clock slowly ticking in the corner made me want to tear open the suffocating brown curtains and grimy windows and let in the light and air.

When the officials finally arrived, I saw from the name cards that they were unusually senior for an appearance at a first meeting. I went through my normal introductions and the assistants scribbled in their little brown notebooks. The meeting was uneventful but the next day Jenny received another call. A tinny voice at the end of the line said that. 'It all went so well that we want you to come back. Today, if possible.' I was puzzled but made no comment. The next meeting was the same as the first except that the officials attending had real power. Layers of secretaries and assistants normally protected the directors of the Investment Bureau and the Planning Commission and they rarely appeared in person. They listened politely, without commenting, and asked me to come back the next day.

Pat arrived back from one of his trips to the States that evening and attended the next meeting. We were shown into a huge meeting-room where Lu Yuchang, Deputy Mayor of Beijing was waiting with a dozen bureau chiefs. Each bureau was responsible for an industry sector and we soon found out that the one responsible for the breweries in Beijing was the First Light Industry Bureau. In a matter of minutes, Deputy Mayor Lu instructed the Bureau Chief to arrange a visit to Five Star. It was a bizarre stroke of luck;

an introduction from the Government would surely get attention at the brewery.

Two days later another call came, inviting us to a fourth meeting. We arrived at the gates of the compound and were shown into the same fusty room. As we walked in there was an audible hum and a huge array of lights was switched on. The Mayor himself walked from the shadows and shook Pat by the hand. A battery of cameramen and sound recordists stood at the back of the room as Pat sat next to the Mayor and exchanged platitudes. Moments later, the lights went off. Blinking and confused, we were whisked over the road in a line of black limousines to the Beijing Hotel for dinner with the Deputy Mayor.

This weird sequence of events, culminating in the televised meeting with the Mayor, a member of China's Politburo, had taken about ten days. It would normally take months of patient lobbying to see a deputy director and a meeting with the Mayor would be unobtainable for an outsider. The real motive behind these events was only clear in retrospect. It came out a few weeks later that the State Council had been worried by the slow progress of trade talks with the United States. The Mayor just wanted to be seen on television with an American investor. As always in China, it was a matter of politics and the officials withdrew afterwards as suddenly and silently as they had appeared. But we had our prize: the introduction to Five Star.

As we drove back late from the dinner, I was thinking about the officials that we had met. I didn't like them. Their remarks were so predictable that it betrayed an inner reserve that was spooky. I couldn't decode their hollow flattery and elaborate words but I felt a heaviness and exhaustion about them. It was as if a vast weight had crushed out all the joy in their lives. It made me uneasy.

I said that I thought I could hear the echoes of the gunfire in Tiananmen Square resonating in those fusty corridors with their high ceilings and antimacassars but Pat was scornfully dismissive.

'If you can't deal with that level of people in China, you shouldn't be here,' he said.

We grabbed our chance with both hands and went straight to the man who ran Five Star. Xu Lushan had been born in the early 1950s. His name, meaning 'Lu Mountain', referred to a southern resort town where the Communist Party had held a famous conference. He was a scruffy man, unshaven and wearing a shabby grey suit. Years earlier, he had been the factory director of a famous *baijiu* factory in Beijing, *er guo tou* or the top of the second wok, but he had moved over to Five Star in the mid-1980s. He always looked a bit sweaty and his collars were brown around the edges. Balding and with fleshy lips and large watery eyes, he seemed distracted and difficult to pin down. But slowly, through the hot summer, we made progress.

The Five Star Beer Company had three breweries. The original site founded in 1915 lay to the west of Beijing City. Factory Number One was located at 63 South Handkerchief Junction, next to the south-western railway station. It was a lively area with bustling shops and restaurants.

Somehow the brewery seemed to have taken over the whole street with its smells and its bottles and its crates stacked up high against the walls. Much of the beer in Beijing was delivered on flat-backed tricycles and the tricycle men sat around in the clogged alleyways, chatting and playing Chinese checkers, waiting for their next assignments. The restaurants were popular and were always packed at lunchtimes because the beer was so fresh. The door of the brewery led straight into the street and it was always open, so customers used to come in and order beer from reception. In the entrance hall there was a huge black and white picture of Zhou Enlai. It showed him at a state banquet, toasting the Hungarian Prime Minister with a glass of Five Star.

The brewery itself was chaotic. The oast house stood in the middle of a large courtyard, surrounded by ancient brick buildings that had seen better days. Neglected storehouses were piled high with old wooden barrels. Outside there was an ancient dray and great heaps of broken pallets. Pipes leaked everywhere and the smell of bitter hops and sickly malt mixed with the sour tang of spilt beer. Old Russian bottling lines squirted beer under pressure into lines of jostling bottles. The crash of the bottles in constant motion was deafening. But despite this dilapidated appearance, the brewery seemed functional and the beer tasted good, so with a little new investment we thought that it could be restored to its former glory.

Brewery Number Two was much more impessive. It was located on the northern outskirts of Beijing City and had only been completed in the late 1980s. The cost of construction had spiralled as the building work had taken much longer than expected. Five Star had huge loans from the local banks and they wanted to pay them off, so Xu was interested in doing a joint venture to bring in new capital. There had also been some soft loans from the Danish and Belgian governments but he didn't seem particularly interested in discussing those.

The equipment at Brewery Number Two was all imported and it shone. Vast metal brewing kettles held several tons of beer wort at a time and you could walk up and down staircases surrounding the tanks. A network of gleaming pipes and filters led to the colossal steel fermenter tanks. These were in a separate building and were each about forty feet high. There were thirty-two of them. There was a malthouse and the canning lines could fill hundreds of cans every minute.

The facility was vast and even had its own dedicated railway spur for the delivery of bulk raw materials. The noise and the steam and the smells; the constant activity with cans roaring through the fillers and the shouts of sweating bare-chested workers as they loaded crates onto the queue of trucks gave an air of excitement to the place. It was in contrast to the more sedate pace at Number One.

I never went to Brewery Number Three. It was much smaller and I had been told that the brewing kettles looked like something out of a Frankenstein movie. The quality of the beer was terrible; this brewery would clearly have to be closed but the land was valuable so it was included in the discussions.

During our talks with Xu Lushan, we discovered that there was another brewery nearby. It was called Three Ring and produced Five Star beer under licence. It was located in the hills north-east of Beijing next to the huge reservoirs that serve the city. We visited the brewery and met the man who ran it, Fang Jingyu. Tightly wound, this shaven-headed man ruled his brewery with a rod of iron. It was obvious that, unless we could bring him inside the tent, Mr Fang would prove a strong competitor for the plodding Xu at Five Star so we agreed that if we did a joint venture with Five Star we would also invest in Three Ring.

We beat fourteen other suitors when we signed the deal with Five Star and Three Ring. We had trounced many famous names and, in the autumn of that year, amid great celebration, the contracts were signed, making us the majority partner in four large breweries in China's capital.

A foreign investment in such a famous old brand as Five Star was a sensitive issue and because of the size of the investment it was beyond the approval limits even of the Beijing Municipal Government. Without the chops from the state ministries the contract was not effective. Over the coming months, the Government investment bureaux in charge of approving the contract raised endless questions and difficulties. We began to despair of ever receiving approval – and then someone suggested asking Ambassador Carla Hills for help.

Carla Hills was the United States Trade Representative from 1988 to 1992 and served in the US Cabinet. On leaving office, she became a highly effective international consultant with particular expertise on China. During the trade talks between China and the US, she had negotiated face to face with Madame Wu Yi, the only female politician of Cabinet rank in China. Wu Yi was in charge of foreign investment.

Carla arrived very late on a freezing evening in early January. I met her at the airport and despite the fact that she was no longer in office she was given the most courteous VIP treatment. On the way into town, she grilled me about the Five Star deal. She was in Beijing only for a few days and visited the two key ministries involved in the approval, the Ministry of Foreign Trade and the State Planning Commission. The officials had tried to fob her off, each promising to approve the deal once the other ministry had signed off, but she outmanoeuvred them at a banquet in the Diaoyutai State Guesthouse. Spotting the top officials at both ministries, she asked them to step into a side room. Brought face to face, they could no longer blame each other, so they had to agree to approve the contracts. Carla left the next day, leaving behind a very satisfied client.

The contracts were approved several days later and the cash injected. It was one of the largest equity investments ever made in Beijing's industry and to mark the event there was a huge celebration in the Great Hall of the People on Tiananmen Square. This vast Stalinist palace with its cavernous banqueting halls, located on the western flank of the square, can swallow thousands of people at a time. Our banquet, a modest affair, was attended by only a few hundred.

Deputy Mayor Lu Yuchang reappeared to host the reception. In his speech he said, 'The issue facing every business in China is not whether they should or should not absorb foreign investment, but which foreign partner they should chose. Pat came to me and he said that he would invest millions of dollars in Beijing. Many people say that, but he did it.' Fixing his gaze on the bureau chiefs' table and gesturing towards Pat for added effect, he slipped into English and repeated slowly in his thick accent. 'This is an honourable man. This is an honourable man.' There was absolute silence. It was extraordinary for a Chinese politician to endorse a foreigner so directly.

It took a week to unravel the story of our missing fifty-eight million. We knew that our Chinese partner at Five Star had huge loans from one of the state banks, loans that had been used to build Brewery Number Two. The loans were overdue and the bank officials were worried that they could face a huge bad debt. When they saw such a large balance of cash arrive in the joint venture bank account, the temptation had been too much. They called in Xu and persuaded him to take back the signature card for the account, replace it with one requiring Xu's signature alone and pay off the loans. Xu, always the malleable one, had agreed, but he was now very nervous about our reaction.

Xu came to see us with guilt written all over his face, sweating more than usual and gulping loudly as he struggled through some weak explanations about penalty interest charges. But it was more or less a fait accompli. The final business licence could not be issued until both sides had put in their assets and without that it was difficult to go to Court. Anyway, that route would take years and there was a business to run.

Next Xu admitted that he was having trouble transferring the Chinese assets into the joint venture. There was a dispute over a large piece of land at the Third Brewery and this had created a huge shortfall in the Chinese partner's contribution. Wherever we looked more problems emerged. Xu confessed that the land at the other two breweries was problematic too. The problem could be fixed but he needed to pay a large Land Transfer Fee to the Government and the Chinese partner had no money.

It started to dawn on me that we were sliding helplessly into a huge quagmire. After Carla had persuaded the ministries to approve the investment, Xu had somehow taken in the wrong set of documents. The mid-level officials had been given instructions to approve the contracts from the top and had never bothered to review them. Completely circumventing normal procedures, Xu got the red chops in two days – but the documents approved were early drafts and contained some horrible inconsistencies. The idea of going to court to force the Chinese partner to put in their assets on the strength of those contracts was a non-starter.

Calls to the Beijing Government for help were met with a numbing silence. Weeks after the praise and flattery the lines went dead. It was a familiar pattern of meetings and elaborate toasts at banquets, followed by a disappearance after the cash had arrived. It left a bitter taste. Our only course now was to deal with the intermediate level, Xu's direct boss.

Madame Wu Hongbo, Chief Engineer of the First Light Industry Bureau of the People's Municipal Government of Beijing, stalked into the meeting-room with a scowl and threw her handbag on the table. She had been given the task of sorting out the mess but clearly had the greatest distaste for the job. Hunkering down on the other side of the table, she announced that she would first interview the management and deal with me later.

'I have here,' she said, eyeing the wretched Xu suspiciously through old-fashioned thick-framed glasses, 'three schedules with the results of each of the big Beijing breweries for the first quarter.'

Pausing momentarily for Xu to grasp the awful truth that she had armed herself with facts, she raised her voice and, poking the air with her index-finger, lashed him with statistics.

'Why did Five Star use thirty-five *renminbi* of electricity per tonne of beer when the others used only twenty?' she said. Without waiting for an answer she surged on.

'And what were we doing about this fourteen per cent beer-loss? Don't give me that old excuse about broken filters, you should have fixed that months ago.

'Why are sales discounts so high when we can never collect the cash?'

I listened, somewhat aghast, to the scolding, as I realized

that it might be my turn next. After an hour or so of pummelling, the management team withdrew.

Plucking a small notebook from the depths of her handbag, Madame Wu asked me what I proposed to do to sort out the mess. I told her that I really thought that it was the Chinese partner's problem.

'We came up with the cash,' I said, 'and investors just want to know when the deal will close. The Mayor seems to think that we are trustworthy and wants to sort it out,' I added.

Brushing aside this transparent bluff, she responded sharply that our investors were nothing to do with her and that if we really wanted to solve the problem we could have some workers' old dormitories instead of the land at Brewery Number Three. I said that there was no way we'd take them. 'Those useless assets would be a huge burden for the joint venture and anyway we've been through all that with Xu.'

'Well, how about a kindergarten, then?' she said. 'There's one next to Brewery Number Two.'

'A kindergarten? What possible use is that in a brewery?!'

Then Madame Wu offered part of a nearby water treatment plant. 'It might be valuable if you drain away the pond.'

A huge row developed and we got nowhere. Using a strange analogy she said, 'You agreed to buy some teacups, and it was up to you to check whether they were cracked or not.' I said that was fine, but if the teacups weren't there in the first place she should come up with some cash.

She retorted, 'Oh, no, I never use money meant for vinegar to buy soy sauce, so there's no cash for that sort of thing!'

And so round and round we went. After two hours

there was deadlock and we glowered at each other over the table.

Short, stout, rather flat-footed and, from my point of view, entirely invulnerable to reason, Madame Wu had trained as an engineer and worked her way up to the position of factory director. She had taken on a loss-making food-processing business and hauled it round into profit by pure force of personality prior to her promotion to the Bureau. One of five children, she had been born in Shanghai but had moved to Beijing as a young girl in the 1960s. She came from tough stock and her mother was still fit and healthy well into her late nineties. She was clearly competent at her job, but she had a ranting style of debating that instantly raised hackles and made me think that she was more intent on exacting catastrophic loss of face from her opponent than on reaching any reasoned compromise.

After a while I became less convinced that she had any real motivation to solve the problems. It seemed as if she deliberately picked on minor issues and teased them into huge rows by using provocative language or dismissive gestures. I had realized that she only did it to distract attention when she was on shaky ground but she was so infuriating that it normally worked. On the occasions when I managed to control my temper, she would adopt the alternative tactic of working herself up into a rage, closing the little notebook on the table and leaning back in her chair. With folded arms and defiance in her face, she'd shout '*bu tan le!*' – 'No more discussions!' The meetings were a nightmare for the assistants trying to keep notes because we regularly shouted at each other simultaneously in different languages. It got so bad that Jenny once completely lost her temper with *me*, took me into my office and yelled that I never listened to anything Madame Wu said. It rather shocked me into listening.

Despite almost weekly meetings it took an exhausting eighteen months of shouting, rows and door-slamming to sort out the mess. Throughout, Madame Wu deliberately reinforced her image as a Chinese Boadicea, wrapped in the national flag and fearlessly defending the nation's honour against the wealthy foreigners. It went down famously with her superiors at the Bureau. She was proud of the image and once told me shamelessly that she 'used to be a soft young girl from Shanghai, but what you see now is a battleaxe from Beijing!' But, in addition to her innately turbulent nature, I knew that she felt justified in dealing with us roughly because of the way the joint venture had been set up. We had approached the Beijing Government, rather than the Bureau, and had used Carla's connections to get the contract approved. All the normal procedures had been ignored and the first thing that the First Light Industry Bureau knew of the deal was when it had been chopped by the Ministry. They were livid for having been kept in the dark and probably relished a certain poetic justice in the way things had turned out. Carla had done a superb job in manoeuvring the ministers, but it had been an object lesson in how not to use *guanxi* in China.

The mess was only resolved when I had legal papers drawn up to sue the Chinese partner and threw the bundle on to Madame Wu's desk. We'd been on the brink of agreement for months so I told her that I'd lodge the suit and go to the newspapers if she didn't come up with something by the end of the week. I knew that we had a deal because she didn't immediately tell me to go to hell.

It was a patched-up compromise but deep down I was pleased with it: we got stronger management rights, a bigger shareholding and extended the period of the joint venture from thirty to fifty years. We had to take on some of the useless dormitories, which increased the burden on the joint venture, but they were sold a few years later to the employees.

The only thing that Madame Wu and I had ever agreed on was that Xu Lushan had to go. She called him into the Bureau after our first meeting and axed him. I never saw him again. Meanwhile, the business had deteriorated rapidly. The Three Ring Brewery, our other factory in the north-eastern suburbs, was still producing Five Star beer under licence and selling it in Beijing. This meant that we had the absurd situation where we were competing against ourselves. The licence agreement between Five Star and Three Ring consisted of one page of extremely vague Chinese with two beautiful red seals at the bottom. Neither party really understood what it meant. Five Star insisted that Three Ring should stop using the Five Star labels whereas Three Ring insisted that they should continue. The dispute became highly acrimonious after Madame Wu called Mr Fang a 'peasant hooligan' and I had the thankless task of trying to resolve the row. Prices fell and a new competitor from the eastern suburbs started to eat into our markets. We had little time to pick a new general manager to replace the hapless Xu and the pressure was mounting.

After a few weeks, Madame Wu presented her candidate. He was the Party Secretary of a piano factory. I rolled my eyes and asked 'What next?' but I suppose that I shouldn't have been surprised. Pat went down to meet him and spent a whole day at the piano factory. Lin Huichen had originally been the manager of a sewing-machine business and had made a success of it. He moved to the piano factory and hired a German engineer to take the product upmarket. With the one-child policy, many affluent Chinese couples bought pianos for their 'Little Emperors' and the market was booming. Lin's factory was one of the few state-owned Beijing businesses that made money. I had initially thought that it was a ridiculous idea, but Pat came back impressed and told me to meet Lin.

I met him at the brewery and was rather annoyed to see Madame Wu there as well. I had asked to meet Lin alone but she beamed from ear to ear with an almost maternal pride as she introduced him. He was a handsome man in his early forties with clear skin and an honest open face. He took me through his work history, which sounded fairly routine, but when it was my turn to ask questions Madame Wu repeatedly interrupted or corrected Lin's answers. The only time she was silent was when I asked him why, after his success at the piano factory, he wanted to become the General Manager of Five Star. I was hoping for some response that might indicate his drive and determination to turn around a former state-owned business and restore the famous Five Star brand to its former glory, but he just said flatly, 'Because Madame Wu told me to.' I glanced sideways at Madame Wu but she sat absolutely immobile, purring quietly and looking intently at the curtains. The interview dragged on a little and I queried Lin's lack of brewing experience. He said, 'You aren't employing me to make beer, you are employing me to make other people make and sell good beer. I can't play the piano but at least I can drink beer.' By this stage there wasn't much alternative, so he was duly appointed by the Board as the second General Manager of Five Star.

Lin started out with great enthusiasm and with a belief that he could turn the business around. The following year, 1997, showed great progress, with sales advancing and losses cut to near break-even. Lin was an engaging character and his cheery manner did wonders for morale. The sales force was motivated by a new bonus plan and the atmosphere at the factory changed for the better. There was even progress on sorting out the dispute with Three Ring and we encouraged them to seek new markets. Fang and his sales team at Three Ring put enormous effort into exploring fresh possibilities. They came out with a new brand that was designed gradually to replace their dependence on Five Star and they made numerous sales trips all over China. They captured nearly half the market in a town called Chengde just over the Hebei border and decided to make more ambitious forays further afield. One of these early trips was to Outer Mongolia.

In the summer, Fang, the General Manager of Three Ring, together with his sales manager, Yang Ping, had somehow arranged a meeting with one of the members of the Mongolian Parliament who they hoped would introduce them to distributors. Sensing that it would be an interesting trip, Jenny had tagged along. She came back highly upset. Her normal equilibrium had been severely knocked and it took me several days to persuade her to tell me what had happened.

Apparently, they had all set off on the overnight train journey and arrived in Ulan Bator, the Mongolian capital, on the following day. The main meeting was several days later so there was time for sightseeing. Fang had hired a translator since Mongolian and Mandarin are mutually unintelligible languages. On the second day the translator took them on a 'picnic' out in the grasslands. After several hours' drive out into the grasslands in a couple of battered Jeeps, Jenny discovered that a 'picnic' meant a few hunks of roasted mutton washed down with several bottles of vodka. She was the only girl on the trip and she didn't drink so it was only natural that she felt uncomfortable in the remote site on a hillside miles from anywhere. Moreover, there were a number of ragged-looking wild dogs roaming about. Jenny had been frightened of dogs since she was a child and this added to her discomfort.

Fang and the translator drank heavily and soon got into an argument. Yang Ping passed out and Jenny spent quarter of an hour trying to get him back into one of the Jeeps. Then she tried to calm the argument, which was still raging, but Fang and the translator were too drunk to listen to her. They were standing on opposite sides of a low table with their red faces pressed up against each other, screaming at the top of their lungs. By this time, Jenny was truly frightened and she made her way back to the Jeep.

Suddenly the translator took a step back and in an instant pulled out a knife, rushed at Fang and with one movement sliced Fang's ear clean off, just above the earhole. Everyone was too frightened or drunk to react as the translator ran to one of the Jeeps and drove off. The shock of the wounding put Fang almost into a trance, and there was a lot of blood. Jenny eventually managed to get them back to the city but it had been a horrifying experience. To crown it all, one of the other salesmen who had not been on the picnic had severely criticized Jenny for not trying to find Fang's ear. She was absolutely livid and yelled at them that it had been eaten by one of the wild dogs. Then she packed her bags and came back to Beijing.

I would have found the whole story a little far-fetched if I hadn't known the participants. But the proof came out at the next board meeting. Fang was completely bald so there was no way to hide the injury. He attended the meeting with a badly shaped plastic ear stuck to the side of his head. The remains of his ear were eventually reconstructed rather imperfectly by surgery and I heard that Fang was a little more careful with drink after the experience. Madame Wu said gleefully, 'What did you expect?' when she heard the news.

Jenny still won't talk to him.

Lin's first full year showed a marked improvement in the business results, partly because of an unusually hot summer. We knew he wasn't perfect but he seemed to be pulling the business in the right direction. But as 1998 rolled on, it was clear that this upturn had only been a temporary reversal of our fortunes. A strong new competitor had emerged in the market. The Yanjing Brewery had been founded by a local entrepreneur and as Beijing's only Chinese-owned independent brewery, it had received many favourable government incentives. It grew rapidly and became a ferocious rival. Without a level playing field, Five Star found it harder and harder to compete and was slowly pushed out of the city centre towards the suburbs where prices were lower and distribution costs higher.

Under this intensifying pressure, Five Star quickly defeated Lin and his cheery optimism gave way to a morose exhaustion. Five Star employed eighteen hundred people existing in a state of almost total isolation from the markets outside. The main building had offices arranged like monastery cells off long passages coated to waist height with dark green gloss paint. It was the absolute image of a

Victorian lunatic asylum. This layout only added to the managers' sense of psychological isolation, while on the factory floor there were three times too many workers so there was never enough for them to do. They sat around in offices with the doors closed, drinking tea and reading newspapers. Laying them off in those days was impractical; there was still no social security system in China.

The indolence was infectious – what was the point in working hard if colleagues could sit around all day for the same salary? Boredom was a major problem so middle managers engaged in constant infighting. This incessant feuding led to the formation of tight cliques so that dismissing incompetent staff or even moving employees between departments would involve the most exhausting and draining battles. Extended families worked at the brewery and these blood bonds made promotion on merit virtually impossible. Many Chinese people share the same family names, such as Chang, Chen, Wang or Li, so it was well-nigh hopeless for an outsider to try and work out the true relationships.

There were absolutely no business systems or rules. Nothing was ever written down in a systematic or ordered way and quality control was a shambles. In the summer, it hit rock bottom and a popular local saying seemed to sum it all up in four rhyming characters: 五星不行 'wu xing bu xing' 'Five Star's no good!'

I went to Brewery Number Two many times and watched the bottling line during the busy summer months. Towards the end of the process, just before the caps are forced on, the bottles pass in front of a brightly lit white board so that the operators can see through the glass and gauge the level of beer inside. Occasionally a bottle will have been slightly misplaced on the automatic fillers and end up only half full.

It is the operator's job to grab these bottles as they pass in front of the white board and pull them out of the production line.

I watched the operators gossiping and making half-hearted grabs for the occasional bottle but generally watching the containers go past, sometimes even less than half full. Whenever I went over to yell at them the operators looked at me as though I was a madman. They had grown so used to lax management that they just didn't bother any more and, together with a thousand other ills, it was having a terrible effect in the market place. There was a similar deterioration at some of the licensee factories that were producing Five Star in other parts of China, so I ordered a survey. I wasn't encouraged by the result. When the report arrived, I saw that the licensee breweries had been divided into four categories. The second category was called 'Breweries reconstructed from fertilizer plants.'

Late that summer, I was given several samples of our beer that had been recovered from the Beijing market. One bottle had leaves in the bottom, several contained only an inch of beer, and another was full but contained a large ball of adhesive tape. We could never figure out how it ever got in there. I had a case of cans that were perfect – except that they were empty.

The worst instance of incompetence was a bottle that had not been washed properly during the cleaning process. Most breweries in China used bottles many times, collecting the empties from the market. Five Star recycled old bottles by putting them through a machine where they were scrubbed and cleaned before being refilled and labelled. In this case, the original label had not been washed off and was still stuck next to the new Five Star label. It was dirty brown, frayed and wrinkled and read *Soy Sauce*.

(Years later I met a manager from the Fosters joint venture in Tianjin who had experienced similar problems. He was once shown a bottle that must have been used for pickling garlic and had been found in the market. The bottle had been returned to the brewery for recycling in the normal way, put through the whole production process, filled with Fosters lager, neatly labelled, capped, and sent back out into the market packed with garlic bulbs! A dazed customer had returned it to a supermarket.)

On top of the quality issue, we had a very confused image in the market. As Yanjing, the upstart brewery in the eastern suburbs, pushed us out, instead of fighting back by reinforcing the brand image Lin kept changing the labels and bringing out new brands. Some of these only lasted for a few months and we ended up with countless different labels, names and colours for the same product. There was Five Star, Nine Star, Five Star Lite, Five Star 10 degree, 11 degree, 12 degree, Fresh Beer, Cherry Beer, Clear Beer, All Malt, Export Beer and finally Green Beer. Draught beer was available in kegs, which were marketed as '15 litre buckets'. The labels within each category were inconsistent and the famous Five Star logo appeared in variant forms in red or blue or gold – or a combination of these. The actual beer inside this profusion of different packaging was all exactly the same. Lin was convinced that his new packaging would help revive the brand but we felt the opposite. I tried to illustrate the point by asking him which companies he felt had strong brand images and when he picked Coca-Cola I asked him how often he had seen blue Coca-Cola cans. He just replied, 'Ah, yes, but beer is different!'

So I would press on and say, 'Well, how about green Budweiser or orange Carlsberg?'

'Yes, but they are foreign brands.'

'Well, OK, how about purple Tsingtao labels? Tsingtao's always green, right?'

'Yes, but Tsingtao is in Shandong.' And so on until I was exhausted of further examples.

Finally I came across 'Red Beer'. In contrast to the other types, this was actually a different beer from the normal lager product. It was a deep rich red colour and Lin told me about a 'special situation in Tianjin', a town some seventy miles south-east of Beijing, where consumers were apparently clamouring for dark-coloured beer. I found out months later that, in fact, a fire had broken out at the malthouse in one of the hoppers and a big batch of grain had been badly singed. Rather than discard it, the workers were told to pick out the badly burnt bits and use the rest. Whilst the colour of 'Red Beer' probably attracted a bit of attention, it had a distinct taste of charcoal.

At the launch of the new red brand, Lin held a party for distributors in the Brewery Number Two. Halfway through the celebrations the stocks ran out and he hastily sent a truck down to Brewery Number One, only narrowly avoiding becoming the first person literally to fail to organize a piss-up in a brewery.

With volumes falling dangerously and losses mounting, there was little choice but to cut costs. But the Chinese side were terrified of upsetting the workforce and resorted to endless prevarication and delay. Board meetings got worse and worse. At one there was a huge row after we insisted again on using uniform colouring on our labels and Madame Wu told me that I was 'talking in dog farts!' The ensuing fight was only brought under control when Lin, who was often caught between the two of us, promised to stop using red labels and bottle tops and focus only on the traditional blue colour for the Five Star logo. I confirmed the agreement several times ('Blue! You'll only use blue!') and Madame Wu stalked off, muttering under her breath.

Two days later I went to the brewery for a meeting with Lin. It was a Saturday morning and dreadfully hot, and my temper had been frayed by the traffic on the way over. The constant hooting and barging had scuffed my nerves. My mood darkened as I stepped over a large turd on the doorstep of the brewery. I was fuming and I asked myself how the hell any customers put up with Five Star as I stomped round into the yard at the back of the office building. On impulse I stuck my head into the bottling-line workshop and, sure enough, row upon row of bottles were crashing through the fillers. Blood throbbed in my temples as I saw the red labels and bottle tops churning through the machines. It was my defining moment of despair after the agreement with Lin just two days earlier only to use blue. I called Pat from some derelict office on the ground floor and screamed down the crackling wire, 'This guy's gotta go!'

During the following few months, as I searched for a replacement to Lin, I suddenly received a fax out of the blue. It came from a man called Ren. The fax claimed that he had run several breweries and that the Five Star brand needed revamping. I certainly agreed with that. It concluded with the question: 'Why don't you try me?' We arranged for him to come to Beijing for an interview and he told me the following story.

Originally from Shanghai, Ren had moved to Hong Kong as a boy and had later been educated in the United States. Fluent in English, Mandarin and Cantonese, he had returned to China in 1984 and had ended up running a brewery in Hongzhou, a small seaside town on the mainland just up the coast from Hong Kong. In 1992, he persuaded Carlsberg to grant the brewery a licence. Carlsberg was one of the few foreign brands available in hotels all over China. After a few years, Carlsberg decided to expand up in Shanghai and Ren went to set up the new project. When it was completed, he was offered a desk job in Hong Kong. He declined and found a job running an edible-oils business in Jiangxi. But his heart was still in the beer business and he wanted to get back into it.

Ren looked like the perfect candidate: a Chinese with experience of international business, of turning around a loss-making brewery and establishing a new brand in China and who had a desire to come back to the beer business. The issue fast became one of how to remove Lin and replace him with Ren. To do that, we needed Madame Wu's agreement and I knew we'd never get that. I saw no alternative other than to present her with a fait accompli so I drove over to the brewery.

I found Lin sitting dejectedly on the huge plastic sofa in his office. He guessed what was coming and took it cheerfully enough. The meeting lasted less than ten minutes. I explained that we had found someone with experience of turning round a loss-making brewery and before I got into the details he interrupted to say, *'ni xiang rang wo zou de hua, wo mei yi jian'* – 'If what you are saying is that you want me to go, I have no objection.' I set up a meeting with Madame Wu for the next day.

I steeled myself for the showdown. I took a suitcase full of defective bottles and cans of Five Star that we had found in the market place in case Madame Wu needed any further convincing. It started off calmly enough, but we were soon back to the old form. She said that if we tried to manage the breweries it would be *yi ta hu tu* – 'a whole mass of confusion'. I pressed on. After another twenty minutes I was getting nowhere so I pulled out the suitcase. I took out a case of cans that we had found and placed them in a row on the table.

'Madame Wu,' I said, 'look at these.'

'They're fine,' she snapped.

I opened the first one. Not a sound. Then the second. Not the slightest hiss. They were all completely flat. At the third, she said, 'All right, all right, but if you lot were in control it'd be even worse!'

'Madame Wu,' I said, 'it cannot get worse. It is not possible. We are already at rock bottom. We are sending out flat beer that tastes like rotten vinegar packaged in beer bottles with filthy old labels that say "Soy Sauce". There hasn't been "a whole mass of confusion" like this since the collapse of the Qing Dynasty. At least that was presided over by an Empress Dowager with six-inch finger-nails who was carried around in a yellow sedan chair!'

Madame Wu raised her finger and opened her mouth. But then she shut it abruptly. After a few moments of glowering at me, she said, '*Xing le! Ni lai guan ba!*' – 'Fine, you run it then!' She agreed to meet with Ren.

Ren's manner was smooth and assured and, as I had expected, it rubbed Madame Wu up the wrong way. But with Lin's agreement to go she had little choice. Ren was appointed as General Manager of the joint venture by unanimous resolution of the Board. Madame Wu extracted a concession: she became Chairman of the Board.

With Ren's appointment as General Manager, a picture of complete and seemingly irretrievable chaos was brought into sharp focus. It seemed that Lin himself had enjoyed little control over daily events. He had been new to Five Star and many of the people he had managed had strong relationships with his superiors at the Bureau. They could safely ignore his instructions without fearing any serious consequences. The truth was that Lin had never been able to assert control. In this respect he had my sympathy. It was virtually impossible to control a state-run business from within the system. What was needed was a complete outsider.

Ren realized immediately that drastic action was needed so he spent his first month recruiting new people, revamping the offices to build a sense of pride in the workplace and designing business systems. The first few months went well and he collected about five million from overdue accounts. But there were things that Ren knew he had to do which would enrage the Chinese partner.

When he tightened controls over cash payments there were squeals of protest from all parts of the business. He had discovered that Factory Number Two had a substantial cash balance under their own control outside of the records of the central accounts department: a 'little gold warehouse' as it was known in Chinese. The main accounts department knew about it (and several others) but didn't seem to mind that all over the factory there were cash balances outside their control. A thorough audit of the payments out of the 'little gold warehouse' showed that they were all related to the business and appeared perfectly reasonable. It was purely a matter of convenience; the employees just wanted to decide how to run their part of the business independently. So, although there was no evidence that the money was being used wrongly, it nevertheless made the business hopelessly unresponsive to central management.

Ren tightened employee regulations with new rules speci-fying misdemeanours that would result in dismissal. No one had ever been fired from Five Star so the new rules came as a shock. Most of them were recognizable in a Western con-text: dismissal for theft of company property, suspension for persistent lateness and so on, but some had been tailored to deal with the specific problems at Five Star. These included a ban on making insurance claims on behalf of the company and then keeping the proceeds; organizing gambling syndicates in the office; growing vegetables for personal use on the factory sites. Finally there was a new rule calling for dismissal for 'fighting with customers'. Apparently there had been cases where point-of-sale girls promoting Five Star in supermarkets around Beijing had set upon customers who complained about the quality.

I could believe it. Over the years I had seen several instances of customers being insulted by shop assistants, most notably in the Beijing Friendship Store where, during an altercation with a customer over ice cream, a shop assistant threw a tub of it at the customer. Breaking free from the other shop assistants restraining her, she ran after the retreating customer and attempted to give him an enormous kick up the backside before being dragged off behind the scenes by her colleagues. Now it seemed that Five Star's customers faced a situation where if they drank the beer they could end up with a mouthful of leaves and risk being assaulted if they complained about it.

Meanwhile, Pat was hell-bent on an export scheme to push Five Star in the States and had been spending months negotiating with a drinks distributor. There was a contrary argument that, since we had such difficulties in selling our beer in the Beijing suburbs, concentrating on the home market might do us more good. But he persisted and signed an agreement with the distributor. Pat made a big splash about the deal and appeared in a double-page spread in *Forbes Magazine* standing on Tiananmen Square near the Gateway of Heavenly Peace. For some reason the article was entitled 'Mao's Brew'. It took months to get the first shipment out of the factory and when it arrived in the States the distributor found that most of the bottle tops were rusty and that some of the labels were on upside down. We never sold a cent and, about three months later, the distributor went bust so that was the end of that.

Back in Beijing, Ren was becoming more and more unpopular and I knew that Madame Wu was getting nettled. But there didn't seem to be any alternative so I encouraged him to plough on. The denouement in Ren's attempts to restore discipline came when he finally tackled the accounts department. They were much too cosy, having worked together for years, and I had always been nervous about their habit of providing elaborately confusing answers to the simplest questions. When Ren issued a notice reassigning thirteen accounts clerks to other parts of the factory it provoked a rebellion and they barricaded themselves into the offices, refusing to come out. Aware that the factory was by now a tinderbox, Madame Wu arrived at the brewery. Fearing that the situation might escalate now that Boadicea herself had arrived on the battlefield I went over as well.

As I turned down the corridor towards Ren's office I could hear her raised voice – I could have heard it a hundred yards away. Ren was obviously getting a severe larruping. As I walked in, she leant back in her chair and folded her arms, bristling with righteous fury. 'I told you it'd be a complete mess if you lot got control,' she said triumphantly, 'and now we've got a right stir-fry of pubic hairs and garlic!'

Ren had arranged for Madame Wu to meet with the staff

and I offered to go and support her. Surprisingly, she thought that would be a good idea.

I left several hours later, impressed with the way that Madame Wu had handled the situation. The accountants were in a state of high emotion, alternating between hysterical rage and sobbing, complaining bitterly about Ren's unfairness to them after their lifetimes' devotion to the factory. She was calm but firm and extraordinarily patient as she listened to their complaints. I realized that she was using the standard tactic of 'talking them out' just as Li Wei had done with the Union workers in Jingzhou; but I feared that this could be a marathon session. At her request, I left after a couple of hours in the late afternoon but heard later that the accounts staff had finally agreed to the reassignment after Madame Wu stayed until three in the morning listening to their outpourings of woe.

Over the coming months my role changed. Madame Wu and Ren became more and more disputatious and I became the buffer, adopting Lin's role of former days. The state of the business, with depleted cash, beleaguered markets and low morale, had provoked a real crisis that drew us together. Initially I really couldn't handle her but after a while I grew to enjoy how impossible she was. She was a class-act when angry and deep down, beneath the turbulent surface, I knew that she wanted Five Star to succeed even if she didn't agree with our methods. Unfortunately, there were strong undercurrents in the relationship between Ren and Madame Wu. They were both from Shanghai and were of a similar age, but Ren had left for Hong Kong and an American education. His salary was astronomically high in comparison to her bureaucrat's wage but he seemed to regard any of the petty perks that are the sole consolation for a Chinese offical as a type of corruption. He detested the fawning and flattery that, as senior official, Madame Wu received from her other factory managers. Madame Wu in turn resented Ren's high-handed style of management and felt that his capitalistic training had crushed out any real feeling for the ordinary workers. They were never able to get on.

The defining moment in Five Star's crisis arrived early in Ren's tenure as General Manager. Every year in China, exploding beer bottles seriously injure scores of people, even killing one or two who bleed to death before help can arrive. The glass used in the bottles is of poor quality and thin patches in the bottles' walls become weak after they are thrown about in rough crates. Moreover, the bottles are reused many times and blasted with steam during the cleaning process. In the freezing Chinese winters, these extremes of temperature can produce minute but dangerous cracks. So in early 1999 the Government decided to act and introduced new regulations requiring breweries to use 'B-bottles'. These new bottles were much stronger, made of robust glass and with a minimum thickness specified for the walls. They were also much more expensive. Nevertheless, the government directive was clear and notices were circulated specifying heavy fines if the regulations were not observed.

Ren invested heavily in new B-bottles. I asked him how he would be able to collect the B-bottles back from customers rather than being fobbed off with old, obsolete stock but he said he could address that with deposits from customers.

The new regulations were a disaster for Five Star. Except for a handful of foreign-invested breweries, every other brewery in China – including Yanjing, which had the Beijing Government as a big shareholder – refused point-blank to implement the new regulations and continued using the old bottles. The authorities made a half-hearted attempt to enforce the rules by raising fines but the breweries refused to pay since everyone else was also breaking the rules.

Faced with the prospect of trying to fine the entire domestic beer industry, the Government retreated and business went back to normal. Customers demanded back their deposits and our precious B-bottles disappeared into a sea of broken glass. Within a few weeks, we had lost over 90 per cent of the new bottle stock and, together with it, the cash investment that we had made. Market share continued downwards and with loans already standing at several hundreds of millions of *renminbi* the banks withdrew any further support. Morale at the factory was at rock bottom and key managers were leaving. By this time, it was obvious that Five Star's condition was terminal and, faced with this unpleasant reality, the Board decided to dispose of the business.

I was given the job of selling it.

After the euphoria of the earlier years, an ugly mood had settled over the beer industry. The newspapers dubbed it 'the biggest bar-room brawl in history.' More than a billion dollars had poured into the Chinese brewing industry in the three years to 1996 and the capacity at the high end of the market far outstripped demand. Foreign brewers realized that they had hopelessly over-invested but when they tried to tap into the medium-level market where demand was stronger they faced vicious price wars.

Hundreds of the smaller inefficient local breweries across China were virtually bankrupt but local governments, anxious about unemployment, kept bailing them out. These dying breweries churned out beer at or below cost and dragged down pricing in the whole market. It was quite impossible for any foreign brewer to make money at any level since local protectionism, creaking distribution systems and conservative consumer buying habits meant that foreign brands failed to achieve any credible market share. The cold winds of reality about the Chinese beer market started to blow through boardrooms all over the world and, one by one, the foreign brewers fled, scrambling out of China with the same haste that they had shown in getting in.

Fosters bailed out first at a fraction of their original cost, followed closely by Bass. Carlsberg and Asahi followed suit, selling their businesses to local brewers. Becks got embroiled in a trade-mark dispute and the others were caught with no exit and facing years of operating losses. In this environment, the prospects for selling Five Star were bleak indeed. Nevertheless, I found introductions to the top managers of most of the multinational brewers in China to see if any of them might take on Five Star, but not one of them returned my phone calls. The only alternative was to look for buyers inside China.

The two top brewers in China were Tsingtao and Yanjing. They each produced about a million tons of beer a year and were locked in a bitter struggle for the number one slot, using different statistics to show that they were the largest. Both companies had gone public on Chinese stock exchanges so they had plenty of cash and started making cautious plans to buy up breweries in other parts of China. Tsingtao bought a brewery in the western city of Xi'an and another on the banks of the Yangtse at Yangzhou. Yanjing ventured further south with an acquisition in Hengyang. But these were all timid first investments in Chinese-owned businesses and neither had attempted to purchase a large brewery from a foreigner. However, there weren't many options, so I arranged a visit to Tsingtao.

The Tsingtao Brewery was the first PRC company ever to raise capital on Hong Kong's stock market when, in 1993, it netted an equivalent of sixty-five million bucks. Shortly afterwards it came out that Tsingtao's management had taken the cash and, instead of investing it in the brewery as they had promised, had lent it to their friends – who happened to be property developers. Investors were outraged but there was little that they could do as the management retreated to Tsingtao and ignored the furore. However, the Central Government was embarrassed by the scandal and eventually the Tsingtao Municipal Government kicked out the old management team.

The episode had a lasting effect on the town. On the northern side of a little peninsula that juts out into the sea, across from the old town of Tsingtao with its quaint German architecture, stands a vast new city centre. A cluster of glass skyscrapers has sprung up on the farmland and, across a well-appointed plaza with fountains and palm trees, the palatial offices of the Local Government, crowned with the red emblem of the People's Republic of China, stare magisterially out to sea.

The man who was brought in by the Government to restore the Tsingtao Brewery's tattered reputation was called Peng Zuoyi. I went to Tsingtao in the early autumn and spent an hour with him. Short, pugnacious, able and down to earth, Peng reminded me of Old Shi down in Ningshan. He had the same easy manner and charisma, combined with a quick mind and the inclination to make decisions. Above all he gave the impression that he was on top of his business and that he was enjoying it immensely.

I was cautious at the first meeting but my hopes leapt inside me when he said that he had thought of contacting us but that he 'knew that we wouldn't be interested in selling a majority of Five Star'. Thinking inwardly that he'd be welcome to the lot, I hinted that there might be some flexibility. He took the lead and the discussions progressed over the coming weeks, quickly moving on to substantive negotiations.

Meanwhile, through the autumn, Five Star lurched from one crisis to the next. After the banks withdrew support, cash quickly ran out and payment of wages became delayed. Inevitably, the desperate state of the business became clear to Tsingtao and they suspended negotiations. Madame Wu and I agreed that whatever happened we had to keep the business going; if it collapsed, Tsingtao would just wait on the sidelines until we were so desparate that we'd sell at any price. A war of nerves began.

A few weeks later the first blow fell in the form of a writ from one of Five Star's main suppliers who were suing for payment of overdue accounts. It was from the Tsingtao Can Company, which seemed more than a coincidence to me. The news quickly spread and several other suppliers decided to get in on the act. I was in New York at the time and just before I stood up in front of the Board to run through the progress with Tsingtao I was handed a piece of paper. It said that Ren had resigned, the joint venture's assets had been frozen by Court Orders, production had stopped, the Chinese partner had withdrawn the rights to use the Five Star trade mark, the banks had called their loans and the Beijing Environmental Bureau had issued an order to close down Factory Number One.

As soon as I got back to China I went to see Madame Wu. Faced with such a dire situation, and with Ren now gone, the quarrels swiftly became a thing of the past. We had to restart the business so we focused on the few remaining customers who were paying their bills and the handful of suppliers who would still give us credit. For four months we ducked and weaved, hopping around suppliers and bailiffs as they pursued us from bank to bank. Whenever we were tipped off that a new freezing order might have been issued we rushed to the bank, took the remaining cash and hid it in a new account out of the reaches of the Court officials. The Court then went back to issue a new search order and, if they found any new accounts, they'd come out with another freezing order, so we'd hurry off to the bank and move the cash on. Payment of wages got later and later, but that was nothing unusual for China and the workforce remained stable.

For four months we lived on a knife-edge expecting collapse at any moment, but for the first time we were the beneficiaries of the chaotic legal system: the Court orders proved too impractical to implement. We managed to restart the fermenters and Tsingtao realized that the business would not collapse. By May we were back at the negotiating table.

Two months later the contracts were ready and Tsingtao invited two hundred journalists to a signing ceremony in Beijing. The ordeal was still not over and Tsingtao's lawyer demanded several late concessions. We refused point-blank and the journalists were kept waiting for two and a half hours as we haggled in a back room. Finally, Peng and I signed the deal. The relief was intense. We had retrieved more than twenty million dollars from the wreckage. Our Board was amazed by the price but I was just happy that it was all over. The arguments with Madame Wu had finally come to an end. The *Financial*

Times summed it up when it reported the event. Asked how I felt about the whole Five Star experience, I had been lost for words.

'Not thrilled,' was all I could manage.

Twelve

鐵樹開花，雄雞生卵，
七十二年搖籃繩斷

The Iron Tree Blossoms,
The Cockerel Lays Eggs and the Rope on a
Seventy-two-year-old Cradle Suddenly Snaps

> *From the writings of a Song Dynasty monk:*
> *'Something extraordinary and difficult*
> *to bring about may unexpectedly occur.'*
> *c. Eleventh Century* AD

The three struggles with Old Shi, Chen Haijing and Madame Wu all came to a resolution at about the same time. These main battles had been rumbling along during the same period together with smaller skirmishes elsewhere. In the end, during those three years, we replaced fifteen out of the original seventeen Chinese factory directors; almost a clean sweep. Sometimes we had to do it more than once when our first choice didn't work out. And each fight was different: some took a couple of meetings with a bit of straight talking, but not many were so clear-cut. Most needed months, maybe a year, of laborious, convoluted negotiations which often came to nothing; then, and only then, if patience failed us completely, would we resort to the pitched battles.

Booting out the factory directors affected the company's results almost immediately. In our worst year, when the battles were at their height, we reported losses of about forty million; a few years on, and the company was making profits of nearly twenty million and it was churning out cash. Of course, the turnaround was helped by some other factors: we were lucky with the market and Michael eventually figured out a system of proper incentives for the new Chinese managers. But if we hadn't hurled out the original Chinese factory directors, it would all have come to nothing. Even with the turnaround, according to Wall Street's equations the whole endeavour had failed dismally; the hole we had made for ourselves in the earlier years was too deep and the investors lost a lot of money. But on a human level it had been the ultimate turnaround in China, one that ultimately saved thousands of jobs. Somehow it had happened. Our iron tree finally blossomed.

The turnaround was better news for the investors but for me, sadly, it was a paradox. There were no more battles to fight; no more deals to win; no more sieges to plan. I realized that I had worked myself out of a job.

As I started thinking about what to do next, I knew that we were anything but an isolated case in the combat zone of Chinese investment; the whole business landscape was littered with the wrecks of failed joint ventures. Ten years after we had first raised the money hardly anyone did joint ventures any more. Even Pat had learnt a little humility; he developed a habit of describing China as 'the Vietnam War of American business.' Most of the big multinationals set up their own wholly owned companies unless the Government threw up restrictions. All but the most innocent of new-comers had concluded that joint ventures were just too hard to be worth it. And of the billions already invested, much of it was languishing in dysfunctional joint ventures entangled in all those familiar circuitous cross purposes where no one was in control.

The experience at Five Star had shown that, with careful handling, considerable value could still be extracted from the most dire of situations in China. Five Star had been utterly bankrupt by any customary standards of business: wages were four months late, the bank had called in the loans and we had been pursued from bank to bank by Court officials with freezing orders for months on end. When I called around to talk to the multinational brewing companies to see if they might be interested in Five Star, I knew in my heart that buying the business would make no sense for them. So I hadn't been surprised that no one had returned my phone calls.

And yet Tsingtao had paid more than twenty million dollars for a share in the breweries, offshore and in hard currency. It made no sense in a conventional business context – but it was worth it for Tsingtao. They had raised plenty of capital on the stock exchanges in Hong Kong and Shenzhen so cash was no problem. Moreover, local inves-tors still seemed so keen on buying up shares that Tsingtao's stock was trading high and their shareholders appeared relatively unconcerned with short-term profits. Paradoxi-cally, that meant that Tsingtao's management could take the long-term view and try to buy up market share in China.

Acquiring the Five Star breweries enabled Tsingtao to establish a strong foothold in a major market in China without the pressure for short-term returns. They were building market share to the stage where they could reach economies of scale and, as Pat had said years earlier at that dinner with the Mayor of Changchun, 'take out the opposition.' It was an irony that he had been right that Chinese industries would inevitably consolidate along lines that would seem familiar to a student of American history. It was just that the consolidators were Chinese and not from Wall Street.

The same process of industrial consolidation was happening in the components industry. One spark-plug factory in Hunan, which I had visited eight years earlier, had grown from a small company about the same size as our business in Jingzhou into a large multiproduct group that was bigger than all of our seventeen businesses put together, just in the space of eight years. It had managed to get money from the stock exchange and buy up several larger companies that were exporting components to America. At one stage it expressed an interest in buying some of our businesses. Although it might have got money back to the investors, Pat would have none of it. Selling out to more flexible and quick-footed Chinese was something that wasn't in the original plan; it was something that simply could not be accommodated within his view of the world. But with plenty of well-funded Chinese companies out looking for businesses to buy, and the huge stock of dysfunctional joint ventures like Five Star all across the country, I felt that there might be an opportunity to put the two together and recover value. So I parted company with Pat and went out to look for opportunities to extract value from difficult situations.

As China moved into the new millennium, it became obvious that the minor mishap with a few hundred billion dollars of foreign investment during the 1990s was dwarfed by the problems of China's domestic banking system, which is a cock-up of truly astronomical proportions.

Buried under a mountain of non-performing loans or 'NPLs' left behind by the state planners, the banks were struggling with bad debts that some economists estimate to be the equivalent of seven hundred billion dollars. But even there, in those most dire of situations, which the financiers rather coyly called 'distressed', I became convinced that some value could be recovered, that some of the 'distressed' businesses could somehow be resuscitated and given some hope. So I ended up wading into the new morass of the Chinese NPL market to see what I could find.

It was only after I left the company and emerged blinking into the sunlight that I realized how completely out of touch I had become. I was so preoccupied with the battles that I had failed to see what had been going on all around me. I quickly realized that where one iron tree had blossomed for us it was as if a whole forest had burst into flower along the Chinese coast. Everything had changed in those ten short years; there had been a seismic shift in the economy. China began to generate its own cash from the stock exchanges in Shanghai and Shenzhen.

As huge amounts of cash had trickled slowly down to street level the lives of hundreds of millions of ordinary Chinese had improved unrecognisably and, probably irreversibly. Everything had changed in the coastal cities: the appearance and dress of the people living there, their access to information, transport, food and decent living accommodation, their choice in education and health care. Many families began to send their children overseas to university while back in China the cityscapes had changed so much that I felt like a complete stranger in the country that I had made my home.

When I went down to Shanghai after a three-year gap, I

didn't recognize the place. I told the taxi driver to keep driving around on the huge elevated roads that sweep across the city so that I could gape at the vast towers and skyscrapers dominating the skyline; I felt like a child staring out of a car window at the Christmas illuminations. Occasionally I could pick out the odd familiar building squashed in between the towers, but not often.

I thought back to the time years earlier, in the late 1980s, when I had first gone over to Pudong on the eastern bank of the river in Shanghai. Pudong lies opposite the Bund, the line of imposing colonial buildings where I had visited the Land Bureau with the pinstriped bankers from New York. Back then, before it was chosen as China's main development zone in the early 1990s, I had enjoyed a walk in the country. I remember seeing the occasional water buffalo squelching around in the mud and an ancient temple where women with perfect white hair and faded blue cotton jackets hobbled across the stone flags to push joss sticks into the huge piles of ash in the three-legged bronze incense burners. Ten years later, the fields had disappeared for ever but the temple had been preserved and made into a museum. It stood just opposite the Shanghai Stock Exchange. The crush of skyscrapers towered eighty storeys above the temple roofs, the towers of steel and glass overwhelming the stooping curves of the old temple eves and the cracked glaze on the tiles; no one burns incense there any more.

Further on, the roads through the industrial parks behind the city stretch for miles towards the horizon, past huge car-assembly plants, software institutes and microchip foundries. Shanghai had been swept up in the same mad dash for growth that had gripped Shenzhen and Zhuhai in the days after Deng's Southern Tour. But whereas the Pearl Delta down in the south has a population of maybe a hundred million, the Yangtse River Delta, which spills through the sprawling waterways and oyster beds into the sea near Shanghai, is home to nearly three hundred million people. The river connects the financial centre to the huge population of the inland provinces: Sichuan alone has a hundred million people, Jiangxi eighty, Hubei another ninety, and so it goes on, each province bigger than a European nation.

The inexorable industrialization of the Chinese countryside creeps further inland, crawling along the river's banks, seeping into the mountain villages in its never-ending search for labour. There is an inevitability about China's march onwards; those stamping feet have their own relentless rhythm – in a few years the Yangtse basin will be the largest manufacturing base in the world. It's only a matter of time, and the changes churned up in its wake will affect the whole world. At its centre, in ten years the Shanghai Stock Exchange had grown from nothing into one of the largest in Asia; for a well-run Chinese company, raising a hundred million has become almost routine. The Chinese economy has reached a self-sustaining momentum and it seems as if the explosion that Pat predicted all those years earlier at dinner with the Mayor of Changchun has finally happened. The foreigners helped light the fuse but much of it has been powered by the Chinese themselves.

It seemed for a while that this new economic growth might spark a second foreign investment wave, a decade after the first; billions were lost by foreign investors, but they still kept coming. I had been forced to dismantle entirely my assumptions about China and relearn all the basics, but many investors still appeared supremely confident that China would eventually view the world their way, that it would eventually 'see reason' and begin to conform to the familiar business school model. But as China continues to press ahead with opening up to the world at a speed that can be astounding, my hunch is that it will always retain an intense sense of its own place in world history. It remains more complex, more aware of its unique 'Chineseness' and in tune with its own past and much less conformist than can be imagined by visitors like Charlene Barshevsky, the US Trade Representative. When China signed the World Telecoms Agreement, she said, 'This is a triumph for the American way.' We'll see.

As I thought about Old Shi, Chen Haijing and Madame Wu with a clearer perspective once the battles were over, those three characters, for me, gave a picture of China in transition. Old Shi, the risk-taker, the entrepreneur always running out of time, had escaped from the system. To me, he represented the type of Chinese who took all those experiences of turmoil and wild reversals under Mao and Deng and learnt to survive by keeping ahead of the game. Completely unbound by convention or regulation, he remained an irrepressible showman with the short-termism, adaptability and speed needed to run rings around his opposition. Unsurprisingly, his business is thriving down in the valley and he recently set up a new factory in Shanghai. He started to get export orders from America and every so often he calls me in Beijing and we have lunch.

Chen Haijing has his foot in both camps; he has traces of Shi's business flair but for some reason he hasn't made the break. Stuck in some middle ground, halfway between official and entrepreneur, he has been forced into a constant compromise, endlessly balancing interests within his business and the local government. He represents the entrepreneur within the system, the man struggling with the basic incompatibility between China's economic and political systems, the mismatch between Shi's raw Victorian capitalism and the largely unreconstructed and poorly paid Communist bureaucracy that still controls the country. In retrospect, it was not surprising that our difficulties in Jingzhou involved land; problems concerning land are common throughout China. It is a highly valuable asset that is still controlled by officials who earn a miserable wage. It is hardly surprising that there have been so many problems with officials misallocating land in return for favours.

And Madame Wu. For me, she represents the changelessness of China. She is the Qianlong Emperor who will argue for months about the *kow-tow*, accept the tribute gifts and then continue serenely on her path, undeflected by the foreigners who have come before her. In the end, she had survived without needing to compromise. In fact, she came out on top. She had started off with a Beijing brewery with millions of dollars of bank debt but ended up with the loans paid off by American investors and a new partner, Tsingtao, which was the strongest beer company in China. I had to admire her for that. And some understanding had sprung up between us. We're still in touch and every Mid-Autumn Festival she sends me mooncakes, little round pastries stuffed with red bean-paste. It makes me laugh. I'm sure I told her that I can't stand mooncakes.

Pat is still there, running his components business. The plan to consolidate the industry has been quietly jettisoned, but he is still on the trail for new capital. Last time I heard, he was raising more money in the States to invest in the export business. In the earlier years, some of his rivals used to mutter that raising so much money and getting into difficulties after investing so quickly had ruined the private equity market in China. But that always sounded like sour grapes to me. Out of all the China funds set up in the early 1990s, his was the only one to survive. And you know, I still admire him; China didn't work out according to his financier's equations but at least he had the guts to try.

China had been modernized in a way that I wouldn't have believed possible ten years earlier, and the Government delivered on its promise of stable growth. The lives of millions of ordinary Chinese had been improved beyond recognition as the planners began to fade into the past. But I still knew that the coastal region was the showcase and that the inner provinces remained poor. Whenever I flew west from Beijing, I gazed down over the endless expanse of 'Yellow Earth', the great loess plateau that stretches inland beyond the Taihang Mountains at the western fringes of Beijing. It was there, in Shanxi Province, that Ai had worked with the peasants. I tried to imagine what it would be like down there on the dusty yellow soil, in the landscape of crumbling earth pitted with ravines. On a flight out westwards, a colleague once told me that she had heard how a group of peasants in Shanxi had won a competition and had been invited up to Beijing where their hosts had treated them to a banquet. Some of them had cried when they saw the table: so much food, so much waste when back home there was nothing.

I wanted to know what it might have been like for Ai in the fields; I wanted to get some feel of the land. I'd travelled through Shanxi by car and by train, but that was too insulated. I decided to go by bike. I would go right into the guts of China, unprotected so that I could see what it was really like.

I flew to Xi'an in central China, bought a bike and rode it

back to Beijing alone. It was a journey of nearly a thousand miles through some of the poorest parts of China. The first few days were uneventful as the roads wound through rolling countryside and picturesque villages with neat cave dwellings carved out of the hillsides and vines and gourds growing around the doorways. But on the third day the landscape changed.

Over the course of the morning the countryside became rockier and steeper. The road became narrower and more congested as I climbed up through a valley. I suddenly noticed a couple of coal mines over on the other side. I knew that up in Datong where Chang Longwei had spent all those years in a gearbox factory there was a big coal-mining region, but that was several hundred miles to the north. It hadn't occurred to me that I would need to go through a coal-mining area so far south, but I pressed on.

By midday the entire landscape was black. The valley narrowed down to a few hundred yards across and the craggy sides towered over me. I realized that I was in a 'third front' area where Mao had hidden all the military facilities in the 1960s. Huge factories were tucked up in side valleys under great clouds of yellow smog. The smell of sulphur hung in the air.

I'd never seen such pollution: the soil was black, the air was thick with diesel fumes and factory smoke. The rivers had run completely dry, their beds a mass of smashed rock and thorn bushes. Every few miles I saw slag heaps and the towers with the wheels on top that lowered down the miners in their cages. Even from a distance these coal mines looked badly managed and much too small to be economically viable. Local village committees ran them, but they had no access to cash or resources to put in proper safety measures.

Everywhere was black and the whole valley was filthy: the rocks were black, the soil was black, clothes and faces were black, and there were no trees. Coal dust was in my eyes and in my lungs, its smell was in my nose and the taste was in my mouth. By the time that I struggled to the head of the valley, I was filthy and exhausted. I stopped for a rest.

As I sat by the roadside to catch my breath, I looked up and my heart sank. A few hundred yards ahead the road disappeared into a tunnel. I hadn't thought of that particular hazard so I took out my maps. Avoiding it would involve a thirty-mile detour. I just didn't have the strength for that; I'd done nearly eighty miles and had to travel another forty to the next big town and it was already early afternoon.

I looked into the darkness, past the hulking trucks and through the thick fumes, and I could make out the vague shape of the tunnel's exit at the far end in a yellowy light. So I plunged in. But halfway through I was in pitch darkness. Trapped next to a wall I couldn't see, with huge trucks rumbling past next to me, I was choked with filthy diesel fumes and deafened by the air horns blasting in my ears. Suddenly I ran into something sticky on the road's surface and I felt my wheels twitch sideways. Eventually I got out, with my nerve almost broken, black from head to foot. That was the only time in China when I remember being really frightened.

As I came out of the tunnel and into the sunlight, I saw that an oncoming truck speeding towards me was shedding its load. The driver hadn't noticed and carried on as huge thick logs ten feet long bounced along the road towards me like matchsticks. I managed to avoid them but the near miss completely shattered my nerve. I threw myself on the ground and lay in the dirt and rubbish at the side of the road, my chest pounding.

I often think of that valley in Shanxi. Every day, mine workers go through that tunnel. Every day, they breathe the polluted air and the diesel fumes and scrape the coal dust from their eyes. There's nowhere else to go; no other employment. Many have to serve a life sentence in those horrible mines. When I got back to Beijing, I saw in the papers that fifty-two miners had been killed in an underground explosion the day after I had been there.

The vast majority of rural Chinese, like those miners in Shanxi, are still yoked to the land, mired down in the daily struggle, stuck out on the yellow earth. Their lives are also improving, but slowly, too slowly. And the others, the ones who have just emerged from that five-thousand-year tunnel to face the oncoming logs, the people with their mobiles in the smart restaurants along the coast, they know that they're just one step ahead. That's why they fight so hard for what they've got. To understand that context – the ancient country with its archaic but beautiful writing system, its burden of five thousand years of history where for hundreds of millions of ordinary people the iron tree might finally blossom – to understand all that is to see the Chinese for what they are. Then the Shis and the Chens, the Changs, the Ais and the Lis become people just fighting for a better life. The illusion is broken and our differences melt away.

If by writing this book I can make the Chinese people seem more human, less mysterious or threatening, just flawed and beautiful like us, then the troubles of the past ten years will all have been worthwhile.

Author's Note

We live in a monopolar world but this state can't last for ever. Unless, by some bizarre turn of events, the people of Europe opt for real political union the key global power balance in the next hundred years will probably be between the United States and China.

The Americans and the Chinese have a lot more in common than they think. Acutely aware of their current disadvantage, many Chinese have consciously gone out to educate themselves about America. Their conclusions tend to be balanced and favourable. But, so far, not so many Americans have shown an interest in China or made much effort to understand it. As the effects of the steady migration of jobs and manufacturing across the Pacific to China start to hurt in Middle America, a slow realization is dawning that Washington is going to have to deal with Beijing increasingly as an equal over the coming decades. I hope there might be a short cut in the process of misunderstanding, conflict and reconciliation that I have described here. If these two great peoples can develop a relationship underpinned by their similarities and where differences are respected and enjoyed, that would be a source of great hope for everyone.

*　　*　　*

My thanks go to Jenny Lawrence, who ploughed through early drafts with a sharpened pencil and an enthusiasm that was quite unwarranted by the contents. I wish that her other students would realize how lucky they were. James Kynge was a constant source of ideas and encouragement and is as close to a real live *zhongguo tong* as any of us can get. Jasper Becker, Rowan Pease, Ian Maskell, Susan Watt and Paul Cartwright all helped with changing a mass of jumbled papers into something resembling a book. Jung Chang had the kindness to remember a student from a decade earlier when she introduced me to Toby Eady. As she said years ago, he is the best agent that anyone could have. Nick Robinson and Gary Chapman were brilliant with their new ideas and images and I am grateful to them for providing me with a much clearer direction. I also want to thank Ludwig Meier for giving me a break early on, Catherine Pugnat for her great kindness in France and Lizzie Hicks for suggesting a trip up to China in the first place.

As always, my love and gratitude go to my mother who set us out on our own paths to happiness. And, of course, those same feelings go to Lorraine. She was there throughout all the ups and downs. Despite the odd moments of exasperation, she unfailingly filled the lives of four marvellous children with love and hope and never lost her nerve.

Tim Clissold
Beijing 2003,
立冬